TEACH YOURSELF BOOKS

ESPERANTO

NTC Publishing Group

TEACH YOURSELF BOOKS

ESPERANTO

John Cresswell and John Hartley

Revised
with additional material
by
J. H. Sullivan, BA, FIL

Long-renowned as *the* authoritative source for self-guided learning – with more than 30 million copies sold worldwide – the *Teach Yourself* series includes over 200 titles in the fields of languages, crafts, hobbies, sports, and other leisure activities.

This edition was first published in 1992 by NTC Publishing Group, 4255 West Touhy Avenue, Lincolnwood (Chicago), Illinois 60646 – 1975 U.S.A. Originally published by Hodder and Stoughton Ltd.

Revised by J. H. Sullivan.

Library of Congress Catalog Card Number: 92-80873

Printed in England by Clays Ltd, St Ives plc.

Contents

Preface to the third edition

In revising this book and bringing it up to date, I have found it necessary to make a number of significant alterations. I have also increased the vocabulary and made it two-way, and added a series of dialogues. However, this is basically the book written by my late friends John Cresswell and John Hartley, and I have retained their system of 'newspaper article' texts, altering them only insofar as they had become out of date. Since this system did not, however, lend itself to dialogue, I have, in a separate dialogue section of each unit, followed the family introduced in Unit 1 as they experience some aspects of esperantist life.

I should like to express my thanks to all who have helped with suggestions and information, and especially to Henriette and Pierre Fort for help with the sections on the Château Grésillon, to Pierre Babin for permission to reproduce the illustration of the Château, and to Maria Becker-Meisberger for permission to reproduce the recipe in Unit 9 (first published in the Esperanto-language magazine *Monato*). Finally, my thanks go to Shirley Baldwin (editor), Allan Nutton and Stephen Thompson for valuable suggestions and advice, and to my wife Barbara for much help and constant encouragement.

J. H. Sullivan

Esperanto-Asocio de Britujo (EAB)
140 Holland Park Avenue, London W11 4UF

EAB is the central organising body for Esperanto activity in the UK. Members receive two bi-monthly magazines, one in Esperanto and one in English, and from the Esperanto Centre at the above address the following services are offered:

Bookshop A wide range of books in and on the International Language is available, as well as stationery and other publicity material. Book tokens are sold and exchanged.

Correspondence Courses Beginner's, Intermediate, Intensive and other correspondence courses are administered from the Centre.

Examinations EAB conducts its own examinations, all but one of which can be taken by post.

Subscription Service The Centre also acts as subscription agents for all the major Esperanto journals.

Junularo Esperantista Brita JEB is EAB's youth section; anybody under 26 can become a member and anybody over 26 can become a Patron Member.

Universala Esperanto-Asocio The Centre accepts and forwards payments for UEA membership and subscriptions; also for the World Congress of Esperanto and the International Youth Congress of TEJO (UEA's youth section).

Specialist Groups These exist for a large number of professions and interests – details are in the Association's handbook.

Advice The Centre also provides information, material and advice on publicity, organising groups and meetings, planning local Esperanto activities and so on.

Local Representatives EAB has representatives throughout the country.

For further information on any of the above, and for an enrolment form, please send an SAE to the Esperanto Centre at the above address.

The **Esperanto Teachers Association** is a group of teachers and advisers who are themselves Esperanto speakers, and whose aim is to help those who share their opinion that the teaching of Esperanto in schools will be of benefit to the pupils. This association, too, can be contacted through the Esperanto Centre.

● ● ●

Introduction

Esperanto is the auxiliary language created by the Polish oculist, Dr L. L. Zamenhof (1859–1917), and first published in 1887. Some people think of Zamenhof as a dreamy Utopian who imagined that if a neutral second language were introduced, all wars would cease and the world would become a Garden of Eden. In fact, his contention was that we must *first* find some solution to the 'language problem'. Not until we have settled this comparatively minor matter can we begin to understand each other across the frontiers and then to discuss the grave social and economic problems which face us. Esperanto is intended as a simple second language for all people, so that each of us may have it within his or her power to speak to, and to understand, those in other countries throughout the world. It is in no way opposed to the national languages; on the contrary, it creates in those who learn it an interest in communication, and this very often leads to their learning one or more of the national languages.

Characteristics of Esperanto

Most languages may be divided into three parts:

1 Vocabulary (i.e. the mass of words which make up the language).
2 Spelling and pronunciation.
3 Grammar and syntax, or word order.

In each of these three departments, Esperanto shows enormous simplification when compared with any national language.

The *spelling and pronunciation* are absolutely phonetic, and there are only five vowel sounds (most national languages have twenty or more). Each letter has one sound only, and any sound is always rendered by one and the same letter.

The *grammar and syntax* are so ingeniously devised that in place of the usual maze of rules, occupying a sizeable volume, which most other languages present, we have only sixteen short rules, which may be written comfortably on a sheet of notepaper. They are reproduced in the Appendix.

The *vocabulary* gave Zamenhof many sleepless nights, until he hit upon the idea of carrying the principle of *affixes* through to its logical conclusion. The result was that an Esperanto dictionary is only one-tenth the size of that of a national language. In national languages, regularisation is only partial, and often illogical, whereas in Esperanto it is complete. For example: in English we often form the feminine of a noun by adding *-ess*: host/hostess, lion/lioness. Often, but by no means always. We do not say bull/bulless or hero/heroess. In Esperanto, the feminine ending may be added to *any* noun; and so throughout the language – there is no exception to any rule and no limit to its applicability.

As for the words themselves, Zamenhof did not invent them arbitrarily, but took them from the most important languages of Western civilisation, mainly from Latin, which is the origin of so many modern languages. Some words look exactly as they do in English, for example **birdo** (*a bird*), **rivero** (*a river*). In others, the connection is less obvious, but often nevertheless there is a connection, if we look a little further. For example, **mano** (*hand*) does not resemble the English; but we have the same root in 'manual' ('pertaining to a hand'), 'manufacture', 'manipulate', 'manuscript', etc. – because **mano** comes from the Latin **manus**, which has likewise given rise to these English words. We shall draw the student's attention to some of these etymological connections, especially in the first few lessons, whenever it seems likely to help in memorising.

How to learn

If you know something about grammar and grammatical terms, so much the better; but if not, it does not matter. We are not assuming any knowledge of grammar. A few basic concepts are all that is required, and these we shall explain as clearly as we can.

However eagerly you learn at first, you are sure to find at the end of a few days that you have forgotten some of it. Do not be at all upset about this! Every day we accept a thousand and one new facts, and promptly forget them again. If we retained everything in our minds we should go mad in a week. So, to forget is a natural process; to remember is unnatural and requires effort. You may find that out of ten new words learnt, only two or three are retained in the memory. The others you will forget, and will have to re-learn. When you learn them for the second time, they will come much more easily to you, and this time you will probably remember nearly all of them. A small minority, however,may elude you again, and will have to be learnt for a third time. The moral of this is that *constant repetition* is necessary. You cannot learn a language as you would read a novel, by merely going straight through from the first word to the last. You must continually re-read each section and as it were *over-learn* it, until you have thoroughly assimilated it.

It must be heavily emphasised that *language consists of sounds*. We are becoming so accustomed to silent reading and writing that we are apt to lose sight of this fact. Language must have existed for at least 20 000 years, but only for the last 4000 has there been any sort of written record. Writing, therefore, is an invention of yesterday, comparatively speaking. It bears the same relation to language itself as a page printed with staff-lines and black dots does to the sound of music. Even when we read silently, we are unconsciously 'hearing' the words with an inner ear, and literary style is judged by the sound which the words make when spoken, never by the pattern which they may happen to make on paper. Take great pains, therefore, to master the pronunciation. Read the pages on pronunciation very carefully, and on no account skip them to come to 'more important' matters. The section on pronunciation is as important as any in the book, and it would be a pity to neglect it in that (*a*) a good pronunciation of Esperanto is quite easy to acquire, and (*b*) it is one of the most beautiful-sounding languages on earth. If this seems a rash claim, consider what *is* the most beautiful language. Tastes differ, of course, but if a vote were taken, perhaps Italian might be the winner: and the general sound of Esperanto very closely resembles that of Italian.

It follows, also, that you should try to *speak* Esperanto as much as possible, right from the start. If you can make contact with an experienced esperantist, he will be delighted to help you. But if you have no one else to speak to, you should speak, aloud, to yourself. Put a question and answer it. Imagine that you have at your side a four-year-old child who never stops asking 'What? . . . Why? . . . Where? . . . Who? . . .' Ask yourself these questions and answer them. The answer will often contain precisely the same words as the question ('Is Esperanto a beautiful language?' 'Yes, Esperanto is a beautiful language', etc.), but say them again, nevertheless. This repetition is part of your training and gives an encouraging feeling of fluency. The important thing is to use Esperanto itself as much as possible. No doubt you will need to use some English at first, but regard it as a crutch to be dispensed with whenever possible, and finally to be discarded altogether. The only way to learn to swim is to go into the water and try. Books may tell you many interesting things *about* swimming, but however much you read them, you will never become a swimmer if you never actually enter the water. Similarly, the only way to learn how to speak Esperanto is by *speaking* Esperanto. Not until you can think in Esperanto without any English in your mind can you be said to know the language. This is not a superhuman achievement – merely a question of practice. More detailed notes on this will be found after the first four units.

A trained linguist will probably acquire a reasonable command of Esperanto after no more than a dozen hours of study. Those who are not specially trained will need rather longer, perhaps up to a hundred hours. For them it is necessary to study it in *small but frequent doses.* If you study for only ten minutes, carefully and deliberately, you will almost certainly remember most of it, and so make small but definite progress. Whereas if you sit for two solid hours 'swotting' Esperanto, your time will probably have been wasted. Not only will you not have advanced, but you may have so bemused yourself as to have forgotten most of what you knew when you started. So train yourself to short periods of intensive study in which you really do learn something; and when you feel that you have learnt something, train yourself to stop! This requires considerable self-discipline, for the tendency is to go on, and as you go on, so your mind becomes vaguer. An hour a day for four or five weeks should give you an excellent foundation; and divide the hour into two half-hour or – better still for most people – four quarter-hour periods. But it must be *every* day; if you miss a day or two, you will lose ground badly.

Layout of this book

Each unit contains:

1 Explanations in English of certain points of grammar, with examples.
2 A short text or texts, which include the same grammatical points.
3 A dialogue, usually embodying the grammar introduced in the unit, and also revising points from previous units.
4 Various exercises – some of which occur between the grammatical explanations, to break up the solid learning and allow you to practise immediately what you have learnt. You should work through all exercises thoroughly, checking your answers (after you have finished) in the key at the end of the book.
5 A vocabulary list, containing all the words used in the unit.

After the introductory section on spelling and pronunciation there are fifteen units, of which the first four are designed to provide a working foundation of essential grammar and vocabulary. Having mastered these four only, you are already in a position to use Esperanto in all four ways (reading, writing, listening and speaking), and you should do so as much as you can. The more you use the language, the sooner you will become proficient in it. More detailed notes on practice will be given after Unit 4.

Above all, enjoy your studies! Treat each unit as a mental challenge and get the same satisfaction from conquering it as you would from solving a crossword or other puzzle. Do not be too anxious about all the details at first, but concentrate on getting the general meaning.

Pronunciation

(*Note*: This section looks complicated, because it takes a lot of space to explain in writing what could be explained verbally in a few minutes. Read it carefully once, proceed with Unit 1, then re-read it.)

1 English spelling and pronunciation are highly irregular; one letter may have several different sounds, and one sound may be represented by several different letters. There are also many silent letters, which are written but not pronounced (e.g. the *ugh* in 'though'). The accentuation of words varies unpredictably, and may fall on any syllable (e.g. ph**o**tograph, phot**o**graphy, photogr**a**phic).

There are none of these irregularities in Esperanto.

1 Spelling and pronunciation are phonetic – as a word is spelt, so it is pronounced, and vice versa.
2 The sounds are all sharply differentiated, with none of such subtle differences as English bed/bad/bard/bawd.
3 The accent always falls on the last syllable but one. Each vowel counts as a syllable – i.e., there are as many syllables as there are vowels, so that in **familio** the final **i** and **o** are counted separately, and the pronunciation is **fa-mi-*li*-o**. Words therefore often have an accentuation different from that of similar words in English. For example, **rivero**, **kosmopolita**, **Ameriko** are accented: **ri-*ve*-ro**, **kos-mo-po-*li*-ta**, **a-me-*ri*-ko**.
4 There are no silent letters; every letter is pronounced, exactly in the order written. For example, **pale**, **knabo**, **piede** are sounded: **p*ah*-leh**, **k-n*ah*-bo**, **pee-*eh*-deh**. Take care about this! There is an inevitable tendency to pronounce a word in the English way, especially when it looks exactly like an English word.

2 The Esperanto alphabet contains twenty-eight letters: five vowels and twenty-three consonants. The consonants give little trouble; it is the five vowels which need to be practised. They are **a**, **e**, **i**, **o** and **u**, and correspond to the same symbols in the International Phonetic Alphabet. Using examples from English, their sounds are as follows:

a as in 'father': **tablo (t*ah*-bloh)**; **kato (k*ah*-toh)**.

e as in 'there': **afero (a-f*eh*r-roh)**; **per (p*eh*rr)**; **teo (t*eh*-oh)**.
i as in 'machine': **filmo (f*ee*l-moh)**; **birdo (b*ee*rr-doh)**.
o as in 'November': **mikrofono (mee-kroh-f*oh*-noh)**.
u as in 'moose': **pure (p*oo*-rreh)**; **suno (s*oo*-noh)**.

(*Note*: The **h** in the imitated pronunciation **ah**, **eh**, **oh** is not pronounced; it is merely intended to indicate the correct sound of the vowel.)

Important notes
1 Do not make the vowels too long! There is a tendency to say '**maaahno**' instead of just '**mah-no**'. Some people in southern England even say '**Esperaaarnto**'. These vowels are at most only 'half-long'.
2 The vowels are all 'pure', i.e. single, sounds. This applies especially to **e** and **o**. In English, **e** has a **-y-** sound creeping after it, and **o** a **-w-** sound. Resist this in Esperanto; it is horrible to hear **mono** pronounced as '**mouw-nouw**', or **petas** as '**payy-tas**'.
3 Words must not be glided into one another. **Ne estas** should be spoken with a slight, but definite, pause between the words. Similarly, **la alia (la a-l*ee*-ah)**; at all costs do not slip an **r** in here! **(lahralia)**.

Negative advice is not generally to be recommended, but a little here should be helpful in forestalling unconscious error. Note, then, that:

(*a*) **a** is never pronounced as in English 'pale' or 'false'. Both of these words exist in Esperanto (meaning 'palely', 'falsely'), but they are pronounced **p*ah*-leh, f*ah*l-sseh**.
(*b*) **e** is never as in 'here', nor as the obscure sound in 'the': **pere** = **p*eh*-rr*eh***; **lernas** = **l*eh*rr-nass**; **generalo** = **g*eh*-n*eh*-rrah-lo**.
(*c*) **i** is never as in 'mile': **fine** = **f*ee*-neh**.
(*d*) **u** is never as in southern English 'cut', nor as in 'mute': **pure** = **p*oo*-rreh**; **luksa** = **l*oo*k-sah**.

3 The consonants are as follows:

b, c, ĉ, d, f, g, ĝ, h, ĥ, j, ĵ, k, l, m, n, p, r, s, ŝ, t, ŭ, v, z.

In reciting the alphabet, or in spelling out a word, we add **o** to each of these, i.e.: **bo**, **tso**, **cho**, **do**, etc.

The consonants are pronounced as in English, except for the following:

c is as **ts**: **cent** = **tsent**; **gracia** = **gra-tsee-ah**.
ĉ is as English **ch**, as in 'church':**ĉeko** = **cheh-ko**.
g is always as in 'got', never as in 'gem'.

ĝ is always as in 'gem', never as in 'got'. **Ĝermana** = **jehrr-mah-na**; **ĝardeno** = **jarr-deh-no**.

ĥ is the guttural heard in Scots 'loch'. You need not worry about it, as there are barely half a dozen common words which contain it. (**Ĥoro** *a choir*; ***eĥo*** *an echo*).

j corresponds roughly to English **y**: **Julio** = **yoo-lee-o**.

ĵ is the sound **zh**, as in 'pleasure': **ĵaluza** = **zha-loo-za**. Distinguish carefully between this sound and **ĝ**.

r should be well trilled. All Scots and Welsh people can do this; but the English find it more difficult. The English tend to pronounce **kato** (*cat*) and **karto** (*card*) alike, except that they lengthen the **a** in **karto**. In fact, there should be no difference between the '**a**'s but in **karto** the **r** should be trilled: **kahrr-to**.

s is always as in 'gas', never like **z**. So **optimismo** = **op-tee-mee-ssmoh**; **pesilo** = **peh-ssee-loh**.

ŝ is as English **sh**: **ŝipo** *a ship*.

ŭ corresponds roughly to English **w**. It occurs always with a vowel. **Aŭ** is equivalent to **ah+oo**; said quickly, this becomes **ow** as in 'cow'. So **Aŭstralio** = **ow-strah-lee-oh**. Similarly, **eŭ** is equivalent to **eh + oo**, a sound which occurs in 'f**air**way' (but do not sound the **r**). So **neŭtrala** = **neh-oo-trah-la** (the **oo** being as short as you can make it!) **Aŭ** is a common sound, **eŭ** is rare; and any other use of **ŭ** is so extremely rare as to be negligible.

Four diphthongs are formed with **j**:

aj=as **y** in 'cry'
ej=as **ei** in 'vein'
oj=as **oy** in 'boy',
uj= as **oo+y** in 'too young'.

Notes

(*a*) There are normally no double consonants, but they sometimes occur accidentally in compound words. For example, **mallonga** is formed from **mal + longa, sennacia** from **sen + nacia**. Such double consonants must be pronounced double, i.e., lingered over. The same thing occurs in English; for example 'pa*lel*y', 'mea*nn*ess', 'se*t-t*o'.
(*b*) Notice that Esperanto has no **q**, **w**, **x**, or **y**. Words containing these, which are adopted into Esperanto, have their spelling modified. 'Quality' becomes **kvalito**; 'extra' becomes **ekstra**; 'weather' becomes **vetero**.

In general, you should obtain a very fair pronunciation by following the instructions given above. There is no real substitute for *listening* to the language, however, and a supplementary cassette has been specially recorded to accompany this course. The cassette will aid your pronunciation as well as your fluency and understanding of spoken Esperanto, and is available from bookshops or, in case of difficulty, from the publisher.

If you can also enlist the help of an accomplished esperantist, so much the better.

For details of other recorded material in Esperanto, write to the British Esperanto Association at the address given on page 187.

Some radio stations make regular broadcasts in Esperanto, and current details can also be obtained from the Association. You will not understand the words at first, but at least you will hear the language and get an idea of the effect to be aimed at.

Failing these aids, Zamenhof himself recommended the Italian language as a model –listening to spoken Italian will help you to acquire the sounds, especially the *vowel* sounds, and the general intonation of Esperanto.

Numbers

Practise the pronunciation by learning the numbers:

1	unu (oo-noo)	6	ses
2	du (doo)	7	sep
3	tri (tree)	8	ok
4	kvar	9	naŭ (now)
5	kvin	10	dek
100	cent (tsent)	1000	mil (meel)

From these twelve numbers, all the others below 1 000 000 are formed by simple juxtaposition. 'Eleven' is 'ten and one'; we don't bother to say 'and', but say simply 'ten one'.

11 dek unu (*two words*)
12 dek du
13 dek tri ... *and so on until* 19 dek naŭ
20 dudek (*one word*)
21 dudek unu ... *and so on until* 29 dudek naŭ
30 tridek; 31 tridek unu; 32 tridek du; *etc.*
40 kvardek; 50 kvindek; 60 sesdek; 70 sepdek;
80 okdek; 90 naŭdek; 99 naŭdek naŭ; 100 cent
101 cent unu; 102 cent du; 112 cent dek du; 120 cent dudek
200 ducent *(one word)*; 234 ducent tridek kvar
1234 mil ducent tridek kvar; 2345 dumil tricent kvardek kvin.

Practise these by working out any number, great or small, with which you come in contact. If you play any scoring game, say each figure to yourself as you keep the score. You should quickly become proficient.

EXERCISES

1 What is the number of your house; your friends' and relatives' houses; your work-place; the bus you catch; your phone; your friends' phones (1212 = **mil ducent dek du**; 999 = **naŭcent naŭdek naŭ**); your car or bicycle?

2 Transcribe the following dates into Esperanto words: 1066 (Battle of Hastings); 1789 (French Revolution); 1815 (Battle of Waterloo); 1666 (Great Fire of London); 1588 (Spanish Armada); 1415 (Battle of Agincourt); 1564 (birth of Shakespeare); 1887 (Esperanto published); 1905 (first World Congress of Esperanto); 1969 (first steps on the moon); 1953 (conquest of Everest); 2061 (return of Halley's comet).

1 Familio kaj domo

Nouns

1 The words used to name things – living or inanimate – are called nouns. In Esperanto, all nouns in the singular end in **-o**:

patr**o** *a father*	tabl**o** *a table*
best**o** *an animal*	mebl**o** *a piece of furniture*
fil**o** *a son*	vir**o** *a man*
dom**o** *a house*	pom**o** *an apple*
hund**o** *a dog*	pup**o** *a doll*

The singular noun can be shown in English by putting 'a' or 'an' before it, although it is often omitted. As all nouns end in **-o** in Esperanto, there is no need for a separate word for 'a' or 'an'. Therefore **patro** = *a father* or just *father*; **tablo** = *a table* or just *table*; and similarly with all other nouns.

2 Nouns in the plural add **j** to the **o**:

patr**oj** *fathers*	tabl**oj** *tables*
best**oj** *animals*	mebl**oj** *pieces of furniture*
fil**oj** *sons*	vir**oj** *men*
dom**oj** *houses*	pom**oj** *apples*
hund**oj** *dogs*	pup**oj** *dolls*

(Remember: **oj** is sounded **oy** as in 'boy'.)

3 ***La*** (*the*)
La is used with nouns both in the singular and plural without change:

la patr**o** *the father*	la patr**oj** *the fathers*
la fil**o** *the son*	la fil**oj** *the sons*

4 ***Kaj*** (*and*)
Kaj is pronounced like the *ky* in 'sky'.

patro **kaj** filo *father* and *son*
viro **kaj** hundo *a man* and *a dog*

Verbs – the present tense

5 The words used to name an action or state are called verbs. When we wish to show that the action is taking place at the present time, or the present state of something (i.e. the present tense), the verb ends in **-as**:

Tablo est**as** meblo.
A table is a piece of furniture.

Hundoj est**as** bestoj.
Dogs are animals.

La patro star**as**.
The father stands, or *is standing*.

La filoj sid**as**.
The sons sit, or *are sitting*.

La viroj leg**as**.
The men read, or *are reading*.

Note: Do *not* put **estas** before another verb.

6 *Continuous tense* Although there is a form in Esperanto similar to the English 'am —ing', it is little used, and the ending **-as** is generally used to translate both the simple and continuous tenses:

Mi legas *I read* and *I am reading*
Li staras *He stands* and *He is standing*
Ni sidas *We sit* and *We are sitting*

In translating from Esperanto into English, either of the English forms is used, according to the context.

Pronouns

7 ***Kiu*** (*who, which*) **and *tiu*** (*that, that one*)
As *who* = *which person*, **kiu** (pronounced *kee-oo*) is used to translate both *who* and *which*; **tiu** (pronounced *tee-oo*) is likewise used of persons and things known by name:

Kiu estas la patro? *Who is the father?*	**Tiu** estas la patro. *That one is the father.*
Kiu legas? *Who reads?*	**Tiu** legas. *That one reads.*
Kiu domo estas tiu? *Which house is that?*	**Tiu** estas la domo. *That is the house.*

Kiu besto estas hundo?	**Tiu** besto estas hundo.
Which animal is a dog?	*That animal is a dog.*

When either of these two words refers to plural nouns, **-j** is added to it:

Kiu estas la viro?	**Tiu** estas la viro.
Who is the man?	*That is the man.*
* **Kiuj** estas la viroj?	**Tiuj** estas la viroj.
Who are the men?	*Those are the men.*
Kiuj domoj estas tiuj?	**Tiuj** estas la domoj.
Which houses are those?	*Those are the houses.*

Note that **kiuj** is translated by *who* or *which*, like **kiu**, but that **tiuj** is translated by *those*.

PRAKTIKO (Practice) 1.1 Translate into English:

La patro kaj la filo. Tablo estas meblo. La patro estas viro. La filo estas knabo. La du filoj estas knaboj. La patro kaj la filo staras. Tiu viro estas la patro. Tiu meblo estas tablo. Tiuj tri bestoj estas hundoj. Tiu viro staras. La filo sidas kaj legas. Kiuj estas tiuj viroj? Kiu viro sidas kaj legas? Kiuj viroj sidas kaj legas?

PRAKTIKO 1.2 Translate into Esperanto:

The father and the son. The fathers and the sons. The father is a man. The man stands. The man is standing (*Think!* –See notes **5** and **6**.) The father and the son are sitting. The father is sitting and reading. Dogs are animals. Those four animals are dogs. Which man is the father? Which boys are the sons? Who is reading? That man is reading. A table is a piece of furniture. Tables are pieces of furniture.

Prefixes and suffixes

8 In Esperanto, as in English and other languages, affixes are widely used to build up many words from a single root. However, as mentioned in the Introduction, in Esperanto the prefixes and suffixes are used much more regularly than those of other languages, and can be added to any root with which they make sense. Thus a large vocabulary can be obtained from comparatively few roots, and indeed, this is one of the distinctive features of Esperanto.

* pron. ***kee*-oo-i**

9 *ge-*

The prefix **ge-** is used to denote people of both sexes taken together:

patro *father*	**ge**patroj *parents*
frato *brother*	**ge**fratoj *brother(s) and sister(s)*
filo *son*	**ge**filoj *son(s) and daughter(s)*
knabo *boy*	**ge**knaboj *boy(s) and girl(s)*

***Ge*sinjoroj** is used both for *Ladies and gentlemen* and *Mr and Mrs*; ***Ge*sinjoroj Lang** *Mr and Mrs Lang.*

10 *-in-*

The suffix **-in-** gives the feminine of any word to which it is attached. Note that the suffix goes between the root (e.g. **patr-**) and the grammatical ending **-o**:

patro *father*	patr**ino** *mother*
frato *brother*	frat**ino** *sister*
filo *son*	fil**ino** *daughter*
viro *man*	vir**ino** *woman*
knabo *boy*	knab**ino** *girl*
sinjoro *gentleman, Mr*	sinjor**ino** *lady, Mrs*

11 *-ej-*

The suffix **-ej-** is used to denote the *place* specially used for the action or object indicated by the root:

lernas *learn*	lern**ejo** *school*
kuiras *cook*	kuir**ejo** *kitchen*
preĝas *pray*	preĝ**ejo** *church*
kafo *coffee*	kaf**ejo** *(café)*
hundo *dog*	hund**ejo** *kennel*
aŭtomobilo *car*	aŭtomobil**ejo** *garage*

Texts

Treat the following, and all texts in the book, as an enjoyable exercise in comprehension. Work out the meaning with the help of the vocabulary at the end of the unit, but try to keep your mind running in Esperanto, rather than translate into English. Don't be afraid to go over it several times.

La familio

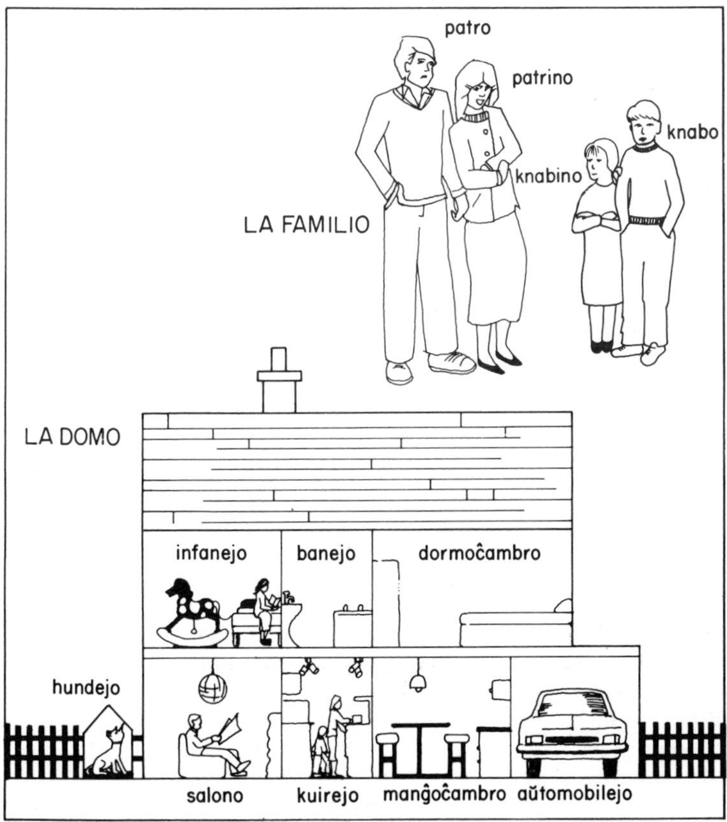

La familio Lang* konsistas el kvar personoj: sinjoro Lang, sinjorino Lang kaj la du infanoj, Andreo kaj Maria. Andreo estas knabo kaj Maria estas knabino. Sinjoro Lang estas la patro de la infanoj. Sinjorino Lang estas la patrino. Gesinjoroj Lang estas la gepatroj; Andreo kaj Maria estas la geknaboj. Andreo estas la filo, Maria estas la filino. Andreo kaj Maria estas la gefiloj. Andreo estas la frato de Maria. Ili estas gefratoj.

* *Not* 'La Lang familio'.

La domo

Jen la domo de la familio Lang. En la domo estas ses (*six*) ĉambroj: manĝoĉambro, salono, kuirejo, infanĉambro (aŭ infanejo), banĉambro (aŭ banejo), kaj dormoĉambro. En la manĝoĉambro la familio manĝas. En la dormoĉambro gesinjoroj Lang dormas. En la infanejo la infanoj ludas dum la tago kaj dormas dum la nokto. En la salono sinjoro Lang legas. En la kuirejo sinjorino Lang kuiras kun Andreo. Ekster la domo estas hundejo por la hundo kaj aŭtomobilejo por la aŭtomobilo de la familio.

PRAKTIKO 1.3 Translate into English:

La patro estas sinjoro Lang, kaj la patrino estas sinjorino Lang. Andreo kaj Maria estas la infanoj. Andreo kaj Maria estas la gefiloj de gesinjoroj Lang. Kiu estas sinjoro Lang? Kiu estas sinjorino Lang? Kiu estas Andreo? Kiu estas Maria? Jen la domo de la familio Lang. En kiu ĉambro la familio manĝas? En kiu ĉambro gesinjoroj Lang dormas? En kiu ĉambro la infanoj ludas? En kiu ĉambro la infanoj dormas? En kiu ĉambro sinjoro Lang legas? En kiu ĉambro sinjorino Lang kaj Andreo kuiras? La hundo estas en la hundejo, kaj la aŭtomobilo estas en la aŭtomobilejo.

PRAKTIKO 1.4 Translate into Esperanto:

Who is Mr Lang? Who is Mrs Lang? Who are the children? Which is the house of Mr and Mrs Lang? Which is the dining-room? Which is the kitchen? Which is the bedroom? Which is the children's room? Which is the bathroom? Which is the lounge? In which room do the children play? In which room do the children sleep? In which room is Mr Lang reading?

Note: En kiu ĉambro la familio manĝas? *In which room* does *the family eat?* En kiu ĉambro la infanoj ludas? *In which room* do *the children play?* In such sentences, the words 'do' and 'does' (which do not add anything to the meaning) are not translated in Esperanto.

Dialogo

Kie estas . . .?

Sinjoro Lang (*calls*) Maria! Maria! Kie vi estas?
Maria Mi estas en la infanejo, Paĉjo.
Sinjoro Lang Kion vi faras?
Maria Mi legas.
Sinjoro Lang Kie estas via frato?

Maria Li estas en la kuirejo.
Sinjoro Lang Kion li faras?
Maria Li kuiras kun Panjo. Kie vi estas, Paĉjo?
Sinjoro Lang Mi estas en la salono. Mi legas.

Note: Esperanto speakers whose names have an Esperanto form frequently (though not always) use these when speaking or writing to each other. These Esperanto names are used for the characters in the dialogues.

Demandoj (*Questions*)

1 Kie estas Maria?
2 Kion ŝi faras?
3 Kie estas Andreo?
4 Kiuj kuiras?
5 Kie ili kuiras?

Vortlisto (Vocabulary)

(Words introduced in the grammar notes and examples during units will not normally be included in the unit vocabularies, but are all in the general vocabularies at the end of the book.)

aŭ *or*
banas *bathes;* **banejo** *baths, bathroom*
ĉambro *room* (cf. *chamber*)
de *of, from*
domo *house* (cf. *domestic*)
dormas *sleeps* (cf. *dormitory*)
dum *during, while*
ekster *outside* (cf. *external*)
en *in*
familio *family*
filo *son* (cf. *filial*)
frato *brother* (cf. *fraternal*)
fumas *smokes*
infano *child;* **infanejo** *children's room, nursery*
jen *here is! behold!*
kato *cat*
kie *where*
knabo *boy*
legas *reads* (cf. *legible*)
li *he, him*
ludas *plays*
manĝas *eats* (cf. *manger*)
mi *I, me*
nokto *night* (cf. *nocturnal*)
nun *now*
Paĉjo *Dad, Daddy* (pron. **patch-yo**)
Panjo *Mummy* (pron. **pan-yo**)
patro *father* (cf. *paternal*)
persono *person* (pron. **pair-*soh*-no**)
por *for*
salono *lounge, sitting-room*
ŝi *she, her*
tago *day*

Esprimoj *(Expressions)*:
Kion vi faras? *What are you doing?*
Kion ŝi faras? *What is she doing?*
konsistas el *consists of*

2 La ĉambro

Adjectives

1 The words used to describe people and objects (nouns) are called adjectives. In Esperanto, adjectives take the ending **-a**:

bon**a** hundo	*a good dog*	bel**a** domo	*a beautiful house*
jun**a** viro	*a young man*	nov**a** tablo	*a new table*

2 Unlike English, the adjective must agree with the noun it qualifies, in that if the noun is plural, **-j** must also be added to the adjective:

bon**aj** hundo**j**	*good dogs*	bel**aj** domo**j**	*beautiful houses*
jun**aj** viro**j**	*young men*	nov**aj** tablo**j**	*new tables*

3 The adjective may be placed *after* the noun with no change in meaning: **bon**a **hundo** and **hundo bon**a both mean *a good dog*; **jun**aj **viro**j and **viro**j **jun**aj both mean *young men*.

However, in the majority of cases the adjective comes first, as in English.

4 As in English, the adjective is placed after **estas** (*am*, *is*, *are*) when we wish to say something descriptive about the noun:

La hundo **estas** bon**a**.	*The dog* is *good.*
La viroj **estas** jun**aj**.	*The men* are *young.*

Personal pronouns

5 The words used in place of nouns are called *pronouns* (pro = instead of), and those pronouns used for persons are called personal pronouns:

mi	*I*	**vi**	*you*	**li**	*he*
ni	*we*	**ŝi**	*she*	**ili**	*they*
		ĝi	*it*		

6 The verbs in Esperanto are perfectly regular, and the following may be taken as models for *all* verbs:

mi estas	*I am*	**vi estas**	*you are*
li estas	*he is*	**ni estas**	*we are*
ŝi estas	*she is*	**ili estas**	*they are*
	ĝi estas *it is*		

mi legas	*I read*	**vi legas**	*you read*
li legas	*he reads*	**ni legas**	*we read*
ŝi legas	*she reads*	**ili legas**	*they read*
	ĝi legas *it reads*		

7 As with all question words, when **kiu** is used with a personal pronoun (**mi**, **vi**, **li**, etc.), unlike English, the pronoun is usually put in second place:

Kiu **mi** estas? *Who am* I?	Kiu **vi** estas? *Who are* you?
Kiu **li** estas? *Who is* he?	Kiuj **ili** estas? *Who are* they?

Asking a question

8 *Ĉu*

In English, a great many *questions* of the type that can be answered by a simple 'yes' or 'no' are formed by putting 'do' or 'does' in front of the *statement*, as follows:

Statement		*Question*
I stand	becomes	*Do* I stand?
You sit	,,	*Do* you sit?
The man reads	,,	*Does* the man read?

This 'do' or 'does', which has no real meaning here, is similar to the Esperanto **ĉu** (pronounced like *chu* in *Chu Chin Chow*):

Mi staras	becomes	*Ĉu* **mi staras?**
Vi sidas	,,	*Ĉu* **vi sidas?**
La viro legas	,,	*Ĉu* **la viro legas?**

However, in English when we use part of the verb 'to be' (am, is, are, etc. – in Esperanto: **estas**), instead of using 'do' or 'does' we merely interchange the position of 'am', 'is', 'are', etc., and the noun or pronoun, as follows:

I am beautiful	becomes	*Am I* beautiful?
He is standing	,,	*Is he* standing?
She is sitting	,,	*Is she* sitting?
The son is reading	,,	*Is the son* reading?

No exception is made in Esperanto, and **ĉu** is used even for this type of question:

Mi estas bela	becomes	***Ĉu* mi estas bela?**
Li staras	,,	***Ĉu* li staras?**
Ŝi sidas	,,	***Ĉu* ŝi sidas?**
La filo legas	,,	***Ĉu* la filo legas?**

Note 1 No interchange of position takes place in Esperanto. For 'Am I beautiful?' do *not* say: **Estas mi bela?** but always use **ĉu**, as above.
2 As there is only one form in Esperanto for this type of question, **Ĉu vi sidas?** can be translated by either *Do you sit?* or *Are you sitting?* according to the context.

Negative sentences

9 *Jes* and *ne*
jes (pron. *yes*) means *yes*;
ne (pron. *ne* as in 'net') means *no, not.*

When **ne** is used in the sense of 'not', it is usually placed *before* the verb:

Mi **ne** estas la viro.
I am not the man.

Mi **ne** parolas.
I am not speaking.

Mi **ne** fumas.
I am not smoking; I do not smoke.

With most English verbs, the word 'do' or 'does' is added to a negative sentence, but these are not translated in Esperanto:

Mi parolas. *I speak.*	Mi **ne** parolas. *I* do not *speak.*
Li legas. *He reads.*	Li **ne** legas. *He* does not *read.*

PRAKTIKO 2.1 Translate these questions into English:

Ĉu Maria estas la filino de gesinjoroj Lang? Ĉu Andreo estas la filino de gesinjoroj Lang? Ĉu sinjorino Lang estas la patro? Ĉu Andreo estas knabo? Ĉu Maria estas hundo? Ĉu la familio manĝas en la kuirejo? Ĉu gesinjoroj Lang dormas en la dormoĉambro? Ĉu la hundo dormas en la dormoĉambro? Ĉu sinjoro Lang legas en la banĉambro? Ĉu la infanoj ludas en la infanejo?

PRAKTIKO 2.2 Translate into Esperanto:

Is Mr Lang the father? Who is the mother? Is Andrew a boy? Is he the son of Mr and Mrs Lang? Does the family eat in the dining-room? Mr Lang is not the mother. Mary does not sleep in the kennel. The boy-and-girl (*one word*) do not sleep in the bedroom, they sleep in the children's room. Is the dog in the garage? No, it is not in the garage, it is in the kennel. The brother-and-sister learn in school. They play in the children's room and outside the house.

PRAKTIKO 2.3 Answer, in Esperanto, the questions in exercise **2.1**. Begin each answer with **Jes** or **Ne**, and write as full a sentence as you can for each, e.g. **Ĉu sinjoro Lang estas la filo de Andreo? Ne, li ne estas la filo de Andreo, li estas la patro de Andreo**.

Correlatives

10 In English, there are a number of words which are mutually related, as follows:

Where – there – somewhere – nowhere – everywhere.
Who – that (one) – someone – no one – everyone.
What – that (thing) – something, nothing – everything.
When – then – some time – never – always.

and so on.

As you can see, there is also some relationship in the formation of these words, but as there are so many exceptions and variations in English, they are not usually set out in a table. In Esperanto, however, the pattern is perfectly regular, as may be seen from the full table in the Appendix, pp. 188–9. For example, in English all the question words (where, who, which, when, etc.) begin with 'wh-', with the exception of 'how'. In Esperanto *all* nine question words start with **k-**.

You have already met two of these correlatives (**kiu** and **tiu**), and now you will meet four more. The rest will follow as you work through this book. Some of these correlatives are used more than others, and some very seldom. For this reason, it is not recommended that the beginner should try to learn all these words at once from the table, which is given only for reference. The most important will be given a few at a time.

11 *Kio* (*what*) and *tio* (*that, that thing*)

There are two words for 'that'. **Tiu** correlates with **kiu** and is used for people and things particularised by name. **Tio** (pron. *tee-o*) correlates with **kio** (pron. *kee-o*), and these are used as pronouns for things which are unknown until named:

Kio estas tio? *What is that?*	Tio estas tablo. *That (thing) is a table.*
Kio estas la patro? *What is the father?*	La patro estas viro. *The father is a man.*

12 *Kia* (*what kind of*) and *tia* (*that kind of, such*)

Kia (pron. *kee-a*) asks after the quality or nature of a thing or person. **Tia** correlates with it, and is often translated by *such*:

Kia besto estas hundo? What kind of *animal is a dog?*	**Tia** hundo estas danĝera. Such *a dog is dangerous.*
Kia ŝi estas? What *is she* like?	Ŝi ne estas **tia** virino. *She is not* that kind of *woman.*

Kia is often used in exclamations, meaning '*What a . . .!*'

Kia viro! *What a man!*	Kia bela bildo! *What a beautiful picture!*

13 *mal-*

The prefix **mal-** is one of the most useful, and perhaps most greatly used, in Esperanto. It gives the exact opposite of the word to which it is attached:

bela	*beautiful*	**mal**bela	*ugly*
bona	*good*	**mal**bona	*bad*
juna	*young*	**mal**juna	*old*
nova	*new*	**mal**nova	*old*

Note: As you see, 'old' can be translated in two ways; it can be the opposite of both 'new' and 'young'. Usually **maljuna** is used for living beings (**maljuna viro** *an old man*) and **malnova** for objects (**malnova domo** *an old house*). However, **malnova amiko** isn't always **maljuna amiko** (and vice versa!)

antaŭ	*before, in front of*	**mal**antaŭ	*behind*
granda	*big, large*	**mal**granda	*small, little*
larĝa	*wide*	**mal**larĝa	*narrow*
pura	*clean*	**mal**pura	*dirty*

Possessive phrases

14 You may have noticed that a phrase containing the word **de** can sometimes be translated in two ways, for example:

la domo de la familio Lang
the house of the Lang family
or *the Lang family's house*

The English possessive form in ' 's' does not exist in Esperanto, so, for 'Mary's brother', we have to say 'the brother of Mary'. Similarly:

the father's cupboard	*Mary's toys*
la ŝranko de la patro	la ludiloj de Maria

Text

La ĉambro

Jen ĉambro en la domo de la familio Lang. Ĝi estas moderna kaj komforta, kaj ekster la domo estas bela ĝardeno. La mebloj estas novaj, kaj sur la muro pendas bela bildo.

En la ĉambro sidas sinjoro Lang kaj la filino Maria. Ili ne laboras. Sinjoro Lang sidas en komforta seĝo antaŭ la fajro, kaj legas. Maria sidas ĉe la tablo. Sur la tablo, antaŭ ŝi, estas du ludiloj. La aŭtomobilo estas nova kaj pura, sed la pupo estas malnova kaj malpura. La patro diras al ŝi: 'Ĉu vi estas kontenta pri la nova aŭtomobilo, Maria?' Kaj ŝi respondas al li: 'Jes, Paĉjo, mi estas tre kontenta!'

Malantaŭ kaj super Maria estas du ŝrankoj. Unu ŝranko, kiu estas granda kaj larĝa, staras sur la planko. Ĝi estas la libroŝranko de la patro. La alia ŝranko, kiu pendas sur la muro, estas malgranda kaj mallarĝa.* Ĝi estas por la ludiloj de Maria.

* *Note*: There are no real double letters in Esperanto. When the same letters occur together, each one must be sounded: **mal-larĝa**.

PRAKTIKO 2.4 Translate into English:

Jen la domo. Jen la ĉambro. La ĉambro estas moderna kaj komforta. Ĉu la ĉambro estas moderna kaj komforta? Ĉu la mebloj estas novaj? Sinjoro Lang kaj Maria sidas en la ĉambro. Ĉu ili laboras? Kiu sidas en komforta seĝo? Kiu legas? Kiu sidas ĉe la tablo? Ĉu du ludiloj staras antaŭ ŝi? Ĉu la ludiloj estas novaj aŭ malnovaj? Ĉu ili estas puraj aŭ malpuraj? Ĉu Maria estas kontenta? Ĉu vi estas kontenta? Ĉu la ŝrankoj staras antaŭ Maria aŭ malantaŭ ŝi? Ĉu ili estas grandaj aŭ malgrandaj? Kiu ŝranko estas granda? Kiu ŝranko estas malgranda? Ĉu la ŝranko estas larĝa aŭ mallarĝa? Ĉu la ĝardeno estas bela aŭ malbela?

PRAKTIKO 2.5 Translate into Esperanto:

Which is the house? Which is the room? Is the room modern? Is it comfortable? Is the furniture new or old? Is the chair comfortable? Who is sitting in the chair? Who is working? Who is reading? Who is sitting at the table? Is she pleased? Are you pleased? One toy is new, and one is old. One toy is clean, and one is dirty. Which toy is clean? Is the garden beautiful? Is it big or little? Is it wide or narrow? Behind Mary are two cupboards. One cupboard is big, and the other is small. One cupboard is wide, and the other is narrow.

PRAKTIKO 2.6 Answer these questions in Esperanto. (Remember that the answer to a **Ĉu** question must begin with **Jes** or **Ne**.)

Antaŭ kio sidas sinjoro Lang? Kie sidas Maria? Kio estas antaŭ ŝi sur la tablo? Kio estas en la kameno? Ĉu sinjoro Lang sidas sur la tablo? Ĉu la granda ŝranko estas por libroj? Ĉu ĝi estas larĝa? Ĉu ĝi pendas sur la muro? Kia ŝranko pendas sur la muro? Por kio ĝi estas? Ĉu la ĝardeno estas antaŭ la kameno? Ĉu la ludiloj estas sur la planko? Ĉu ili estas novaj? Kia estas la brakseĝo? Ĉu la libroŝranko estas granda? Kio pendas super Maria?

Dialogo

Kafo kun amikino

A neighbour, Mrs Brown, calls in to chat and have coffee with Mr and Mrs Lang.

Sinjorino Lang	Jen la kafo, Elena. Ĉu vi soifas?
Sinjorino Brown	Dankon. Jes, mi tre soifas.
Sinjorino Lang	Ĉu tiu seĝo estas komforta?
Sinjorino Brown	Tre komforta, dankon, Klara.
Sinjorino Lang	Ĉu la kafo estas bona?
Sinjorino Brown	Jes, ĝi estas tre bona. La infanoj estas en la lernejo, mi supozas?
Sinjoro Lang	Jes. Maria estas tre kontenta nun, ĉar ŝi iras al nova lernejo.
Sinjorino Brown	(*looks out of the window*) Kia bela tago! Kaj kia bela ĝardeno! Vi bone laboras en ĝi, sinjoro Lang.
Sinjorino Lang	Jes, kaj mi laboras en ĝi.
Sinjoro Lang	*Ni* laboras en ĝi. Ni estas kontentaj pri ĝi.

Sinjorino Brown Ho, mi ne estas kontenta! Mi laboras en la ĝardeno, sed Johano ne laboras en ĝi. Li sidas en la domo kaj legas dum mi estas en la ĝardeno!

Demandoj
(Remember to answer using complete sentences, for practice.)

1 Ĉu la seĝo de sinjorino Brown estas komforta?
2 Ĉu la kafo estas bona?
3 Ĉu la infanoj estas en la ĝardeno?
4 Kiu estas kontenta pri tio?
5 Kia estas la tago?
6 Kiuj laboras en la ĝardeno?
7 Ĉu ili estas kontentaj pri ĝi?
8 Ĉu sinjorino Brown estas kontenta?
9 Ĉu sinjoro Brown laboras en la ĝardeno?
10 Kion li faras?

---

al *to*
alia *other* (cf. *alias*)
antaŭ *before, in front of*
bela *beautiful, fine*
bildo *picture*
bona *good*; **bone** *well*
brakseĝo *armchair* (**brako** *arm*)
Ĉe *at*
ĉu *whether (introduces a question)*
dankon! *thank you!*
diras *says*
fajro *fire*
fenestro *window*
granda *big, large*
ĝardeno *garden*
iras *goes*
jes *yes*
komforta *comfortable*
kontenta *pleased, satisfied, content*
laboras *works*
larĝa *wide**
lernas *learns*; **lernejo** *school*
libro *book* (cf. *library*)
ludilo *toy*
moderna *modern*
muro *wall* (cf. *mural*)
ne *no, not*
pendas *hangs* (cf. *pendant*)
planko *floor*
pri *about, concerning*
pupo *doll* (cf. *puppet*)
pura *clean*
respondas *answers, replies*
sed *but*
seĝo *chair*
super *above, over*
supozas *suppose*
sur *on*
ŝranko *cupboard*
tre *very; very much*

Esprimo:
Ĉu vi soifas? (so-*ee*-fass) *Are you thirsty?*

---

* *Note:* **larĝa** does not mean *large*.

3 La urbo

Adverbs

1 The words which show the how, why, when, and where of the verb, i.e., those which describe the manner, etc. of the action (or state), are called *adverbs*. The majority of adverbs are derived from adjectives and in Esperanto end in **-e**:

bel**a**	*beautiful*	bel**e**	*beautifully*
rapid**a**	*quick*	rapid**e**	*quickly*
fort**a**	*strong*	fort**e**	*strongly*

Note: In English, most adverbs – *but not all* – end in '-ly'.

Subject and object

2 In the sentences used up to now, we have shown what someone or something does or is:

La patro sidas en la manĝoĉambro.
The father sits in the dining-room.
La patro estas sinjoro Lang.
The father is Mr Lang.

This someone or something is called the *subject*. In both the above sentences, **patro** is the subject.

However, in many cases we are concerned not only with what the subject does, but what it does *to* someone or something. For example, when we *read* we must read *something*; when we *love* we must love *someone* or *something*; when we *eat* or *drink* we must eat or drink *something*. This someone or something, then, is called the *object*, and when it is named in Esperanto, we add **-n** to distinguish it from the subject:

Subject		*Object*
la viro	amas	la virino**n**
the man	*loves*	*the woman*

We know who *loves* – **la viro** – because the noun ends in **-o**, and we know who is *loved* – **la virinon** – because of the added **-n**. Consequently, it doesn't matter if we reverse the sentence (**la virinon amas la viro**), the meaning is still the same – **la virinon** is still the object (i.e., the one who is *loved*), although it comes first in the sentence. This inversion is not unusual in Esperanto, for the **-n** clearly shows which is the object. (You can think of **la virinon amas la viro** as meaning *the woman is loved by the man.*) An adjective used with the object also takes **-n** in agreement.

The object can, of course, also be a pronoun, for example:

La viro amas ŝi**n**. *The man loves her.*

and it can be plural, for example:

Maria amas la pup**ojn**. *Mary loves the dolls.*
Ŝi amas ili**n**. *She loves them.*

More correlatives

3 *Kie* (*where*) **and *tie*** (*there, in that place*)
Kie (pron. *kee-e*) and **tie** (pron. *tee-e*) are used as follows:

Kie vi loĝas? *Where do you live?*	Mi loĝas tie. *I live there.*
Kie li estas? *Where is he?*	Li estas tie. *He is there.*

4 *Kiel* (*how*) **and *tiel*** (*in that way, so*)
Kiel (pron. *kee-el*) and **tiel** (pron. *tee-el*) are used as follows:

Kiel vi fartas? *How do you do (fare)?*	Ili ludas tiel. *They play like this (thus).*
Kiel li laboras? *How does he work?*	Ĝi veturas tiel rapide. *It travels so quickly.*

In comparing two ideas, **kiel** is translated by *like*:

Ĝi ne estas urbego, kiel Londono.
It is not a city like London.
Li ne ludas, kiel vi.
He does not play like you.

The combination **tiel . . . kiel . . .** is translated by *as . . . as . . .*

Aŭtomobilo ne estas **tiel** granda **kiel** aŭtobuso.
A car is not as *big* as *a bus.*
Aŭtomobilo ne veturas **tiel** rapide **kiel** trajno.
A car does not travel as *quickly* as *a train.*

PRAKTIKO 3.1 Translate into English:

Kie estas la ludiloj de Maria? Ili estas sur la tablo antaŭ ŝi. Kion faras la patro? Li sidas kaj legas libron. Kian libron li legas? Li legas bonan libron. Li sidas komforte kaj legas rapide. Maria estas tre kontenta ĉar ŝi iras al la lernejo. Ŝi iras rapide. Sed Andreo ne estas kontenta. Li iras malrapide al la lernejo. Maria amas la lernejon, sed Andreo malamas ĝin.

PRAKTIKO 3.2 Match the answers to these questions:

1	Ĉu la brakseĝo estas komforta?	(*a*)	Li legas rapide.
2	Kie estas la ludiloj de Maria?	(*b*)	Li legas libron.
3	Ĉu Maria estas kontenta?	(*c*)	Ĝi estas granda.
4	Kio estas sur la tablo?	(*d*)	Ne, ĝi ne estas granda.
5	Kion legas sinjoro Lang?	(*e*)	Jes, ĝi estas urbego.
6	Kie estas la ŝranko de Maria?	(*f*)	Ili estas sur la tablo.
7	Ĉu la ŝranko de Maria estas granda?	(*g*)	La ludiloj estas sur la tablo.
8	Kiel legas sinjoro Lang?	(*h*)	Ĝi estas sur la muro.
9	Ĉu Londono estas urbego?	(*i*)	Jes, ĝi estas komforta.
10	Kia estas urbego?	(*j*)	Jes, ŝi estas kontenta.

PRAKTIKO 3.3 Answer the following questions:

Ĉu urbego estas malgranda urbo? Kion legas sinjoro Lang? Kie sidas Maria? Kia estas la ŝranko de Maria? Kie pendas la elektra lampo? Ĉu vi loĝas kun gesinjoroj Lang? Ĉu aŭtomobilo estas tiel granda kiel trajno? Ĉu Maria estas maljuna? Kia estas la bildo en la ĉambro? Ĉu la brakseĝo estas malkomforta? Ĉu fajro estas malvarma? Kiu ludilo estas malpura? Kiu amas la patron? Kiun amas la patro? Ĉu la familio Lang konsistas el tri personoj?

Suffixes

5 *-et-*

The suffix **-et-** is used as a diminutive to denote a small size or degree:

domo *house*	dom**et**o *cottage*
varma *warm*	varm**et**a *lukewarm*
malvarma *cold*	malvarm**et**a *cool*
dormas *sleeps*	dorm**et**as *dozes*
ridas *laughs*	rid**et**as *smiles*

6 *-eg-*

This suffix is the opposite of **-et-** and shows a great size or degree:

dom**eg**o *mansion*	varm**eg**a *hot*
dorm**eg**as *sleeps heavily*	rid**eg**as *guffaws*

Note: The suffix **-eg-** is not just another way of saying **granda**; nor is **-et-** the same as **malgranda**: both **-eg-** and **-et-** add to the meaning.

granda viro *big man*	vir**eg**o *giant*
malgranda viro *little man*	vir**et**o *dwarf*

7 *-ul-*

The suffix **-ul-** is used to denote a person characterised by the idea contained in the 'root' of a word:

riĉa *rich*	riĉ**ul**o *rich person*
sana *healthy*	san**ul**o *healthy person*
sporto *sport*	sport**ul**o *sportsman*

Of course, we can add the suffix **-in-** to all of these to indicate the feminine:

sport**ulin**o *sportswoman*

or the prefix **mal-** to indicate the opposite:

malriĉ**ulin**o *poor woman*

Note also **mal-san-ul-ejo** – a place for sick people, i.e. a hospital!

Text

La urbo

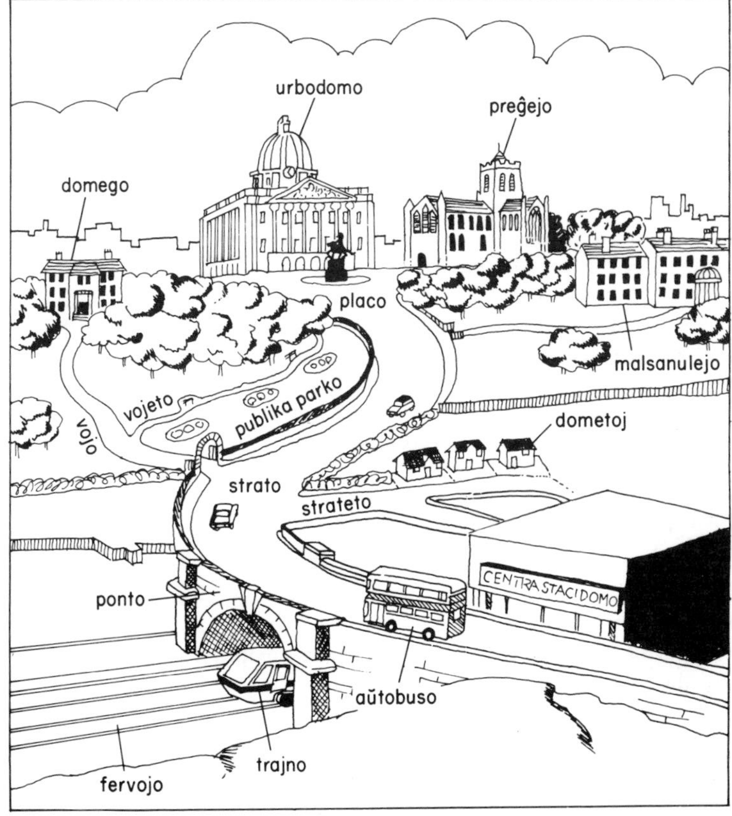

La bildo montras parton de urbo. Ĝi ne estas urbego, kiel Londono; nur malgranda urbo. Ĝi staras alte, sur monteto. La granda strato iras rekte al la centro de la urbo, la ĉefa placo. Ĉirkaŭ la placo, ni vidas la urbodomon, preĝejon kaj multajn arbojn. Kio staras en la mezo de la placo? Statuo.

Ĉe la dekstra flanko de la placo, vi trovas malsanulejon. Kontraŭ la malsanulejo staras granda domo aŭ *domego*. Tiu domo estas nun art-galerio. Ĝi staras en publika parko kaj florĝardeno, kie la gesinjoroj de la urbo promenas kaj ripozas. Tie, ankaŭ, la infanoj ludas. Vojo kaj vojetoj kondukas tra la parko al la domego.

Sur la ĉefstrato, aŭtomobiloj rapide veturas. Kaj kio veturas sur la ponto? Tio estas aŭtobuso. Kiel veturas trajno? Ĝi veturas *rapidege*! Sub la ponto vi vidas parton de trajno; ĉar la urbo havas ankaŭ fervojon. Vi vidas la tegmenton de la fervoja stacidomo malantaŭ la ponto, ĉe la dekstra flanko de la bildo. Flanka strateto, sur kiu vi vidas kelkajn dometojn, kondukas de la ĉefstrato al la stacidomo.

PRAKTIKO 3.4 Translate into English:

La urbo estas malgranda. Ĝi ne estas urbego, kiel Londono. Ĉu la stratoj estas larĝaj aŭ mallarĝaj? En la mezo de la placo staras statuo, kaj malantaŭ tio estas la urbodomo. Sur la placo estas ankaŭ granda preĝejo. Kie estas la artgalerio? Ĝi estas en la publika parko. Kaj kie estas la parko? Ĝi estas maldekstre de la ĉefstrato. Ĉe la alia flanko de la strato estas la malsanulejo. Vojeto kondukas de la ĉefstrato al la malsanulejo. Kie promenas la gesinjoroj de la urbo? Kie ludas la infanoj? La gesinjoroj promenas en la publika parko, kaj la infanoj ludas tie. Sur la ĉefstrato veturas aŭtomobiloj kaj aŭtobusoj. Kiel veturas la aŭtomobilo? Ĝi veturas rapide. Trajnoj ne veturas sur la strato; ili veturas sur la fervojo.

PRAKTIKO 3.5 Translate into Esperanto:

Where do you live? I live in a large city. It is not as large as London. It has two railway stations. Trains run (travel) on the railway, but cars travel on the roads. Have you (got) a car? Yes, I have a small car, but it does not go (travel) very fast. The main streets in the town are wide, but the other streets are narrow. What is the town like? It is modern and clean.

PRAKTIKO 3.6 Here are some answers. Write down the question which has been asked in each case.

1 Ĝi veturas sur la ponto.
2 Domego staras en la parko.
3 Jes, ĝi iras rekte al la ĉefplaco.
4 La gesinjoroj promenas kaj ripozas tie.
5 Ne, trajno ne veturas sur la strato.
6 Ĝi staras sur monteto.
7 Ĝi veturas rapidege!
8 Statuo staras tie.
9 Mi vidas parton de trajno.
10 Mi vidas ilin sur flanka strateto.

Note 1 **Kie promenas la gesinjoroj?** Where *do* the people walk? **Kie ludas la infanoj?** Where *do* the children play? **Kiel veturas la aŭtomobilo?** How *does* the car travel? In such sentences, the words 'do' and 'does' are not translated in Esperanto.

2 In English we often use the word 'got' after 'have' or 'has', but this is not necessary, and is not translated in Esperanto.

Has it got *a park?* Ĉu ĝi havas parkon?
Has he got *a son?* Ĉu li havas filon?

Dialogo

Promeno en la parko

It is a nice day, and Mrs Lang and her friend Mrs Brown are taking a walk in the town.

Sinjorino Brown Ha! Jen ni en la placo. Ĝi tre plaĉas al mi, kun la granda preĝejo kaj la bela urbodomo.
Sinjorino Lang Jes, ĝi estas tre bela. Ĉu ni promenu en la parko?
Sinjorino Brown Kia bona ideo! La vetero estas tiel bela kaj varma, kaj la ĉielo tiel blua. La publika parko plaĉas al mi.

They go into the park and sit on a bench.

Sinjorino Lang Kiel belaj estas tiuj floroj!
Sinjorino Brown Jes, plaĉas al mi la florĝardeno. Nu! Kiel fartas la familio?
Sinjorino Lang Ho, tre bone, dankon. Kiel fartas via edzo?
Sinjorino Brown Li fartas bone. Li eĉ laboras en la ĝardeno ĉar la vetero estas tiel bona!
Sinjorino Lang Kia surprizo por vi!
Sinjorino Brown Jes, granda surprizo!
Sinjorino Lang Ĉu vi vidas tiujn hundojn?
Sinjorino Brown Kie?
Sinjorino Lang Tie, antaŭ la artgalerio.
Sinjorino Brown Ha, jes, mi vidas ilin nun. Ili ludas sur la vojeto kaj sub la arboj. La parko estas bona ludejo por ili.
Sinjorino Lang Ankaŭ por ni!
Sinjorino Brown Jes, sed ni ne ludas en ĝi; ni sidas kaj ripozas.
(Both together) Kaj tio plaĉas al ni!

Demandoj

1 Kia estas la vetero?
2 Kie sidas la du sinjorinoj?
3 Kiaj estas la floroj?
4 Kiel fartas la familio Lang?
5 Kion faras sinjoro Brown dum la du sinjorinoj sidas en la parko?
6 Al kiu tio estas surprizo?
7 Kiujn bestojn vidas la sinjorinoj? (*Careful!*)
8 Kie la hundoj ludas?
9 Ĉu la sinjorinoj ludas? Kion ili faras?
10 Ĉu tio plaĉas al ili?

---

alta *high* (cf. *altitude*)
ankaŭ *also*
arbo *tree*
arto *art*
blua *blue*
centro *centre*
ĉar *because*
ĉefa *chief, main*; **ĉefstrato** *main street*
ĉielo *sky, heaven*
ĉirkaŭ *round (about)*
dekstra *right (hand)* (cf. *dexterity*); **maldekstra** *left*
eĉ *even*
fero *iron* (cf. *ferric*); **fervojo** *railway*
flanko *side*
floro *flower*
galerio *gallery*
ha! *ah!*
havas *has, have*
ho! *oh!*
ideo *idea*
kelkaj *a few, several*
kondukas *leads, guides*
kontraŭ *opposite*
malsanulejo *hospital* (see note **9**)
mezo *middle*
monto *mountain*; **monteto** *hill*
montras *shows*
multaj *many, a lot of*
nu! *well (then)*
nur *only, merely*
parko *park*
parto *part*
placo *square (in a town)*
ponto *bridge*
preĝas *prays;* **preĝejo** *church*
promenas *goes for a walk, drive, ride, etc.*
publika *public*
rapida *quick*; **rapide** *quickly*
rekta *direct, straight*
ripozas *rests*
stacio *station (radio, etc.)*; **stacidomo** *railway station (building)*
statuo *statue*
strato *street*
sub *under, below* (cf. *subway*)
surprizo *surprise*
tegmento *roof*
trajno *train*
trovas *finds* (cf. *treasure trove*)
urbo *town*; **urbego** *(large) city*; **urbodomo** *town hall*
vetero *weather*
veturas *travels, goes, runs (in or of a vehicle)*
vidas *sees*
vojo *way, road*; **vojeto** *path*

Ĝi tre plaĉas al mi *I like it very much* (lit. *It is very pleasing to me*)
Ĉu ni promenu? *Shall we go for a walk?*
Kiel fartas la familio? *How is (fares) the family?*
Kiel vi fartas? *How are you?*

4 Letero

Prepositions

1 Prepositions are the little words used to join a word or words to the rest of the sentence, and to show the relationship existing between the two parts. Take the following sentence:

La kato sidas	la tablo
The cat sits	*the table*

To join the two parts, and to show where the cat is sitting in relation to the table, we use a *preposition*. We can say:

La kato sidas **sur** (*on*) la tablo.
La kato sidas **sub** (*under*) la tablo.
La kato sidas **apud** (*near*) la tablo.
La kato sidas **antaŭ** (*before, in front of*) la tablo.

The prepositions **sur**, **sub**, **apud** and **antaŭ**, then, denote where the cat is sitting in relation to the table, and they are therefore called *prepositions of place*.

2 There are prepositions to show relationships other than place, of course, such as **al** (*to*), **de** (*of, from*), **kun** (*with*), etc., and one of the most useful is **je**. Its meaning is indefinite, and it is used where the relationship is obscure or cannot be clearly defined by any other preposition:

Li vetas **je** ĉevaloj.
He bets on *horses.*

It is particularly used in a *time* sense:

Mi ne laboris **je** tiu tago.
I did not work on *that day.*

Li venos **je** la tria horo.
He will come at *three o'clock.*
(lit. *at the third hour*)

The indirect object

3 The object shown by **-n** is known in full as the *direct object.* But with verbs like give, send, and similar verbs denoting transfer of something, we not only give, send, etc., *something*, we also give, send, etc., it *to someone.* This *someone* is called the *indirect object:*

Subject	*Verb*	*Direct object*	*Indirect object*
La patro	donas	pupo**n**	**al** ŝi.
The father	*gives*	*a doll*	to *her.*
La amiko	sendas	letero**n**	**al** li.
The friend	*sends*	*a letter*	to *him.*

4 The indirect object may be placed before the direct object. In such cases, 'to' is usually omitted in English, but **al** is always included in Esperanto:

Subject	*Verb*	*Indirect object*	*Direct object*
La patro	donas	**al** ŝi	pupo**n**.
The father	*gives*	*her*	*a doll.*
La amiko	sendas	**al** li	letero**n**.
The friend	*sends*	*him*	*a letter.*

The past tense

5 When we wish to show that the action or state has already happened or existed, the verb ends in **-is**:

Mi skrib**is** al vi hieraŭ.
I wrote to you yesterday.
Li parol**is** al ŝi hieraŭ.
He spoke to her yesterday.
La urbo est**is** plena.
The town was full.

6 We often use compound past tenses formed with 'has', 'have', or with 'was', 'were', but although Esperanto has such compound tenses (which you will learn later) the simple ending **-is** is very often used even for these.

Ĉu vi vid**is** tiun libron?
Have *you* seen *that book?*
Mi leg**is** la libron.
I have read *the book.*
or *I* was reading *the book.*

Sinjoro Lang sid**is** kaj leg**is**.
Mr Lang was sitting *and* reading.

The word **jam** (*already*) may be used to indicate the 'has/have' form, for 'already' is frequently used with this:

Mi **jam** skrib**is** al vi.
I have already written *to you.*
Li **jam** leg**is** la libron.
He has already read *the book.*

7 With most English verbs, the word 'did' is added to a negative or interrogative (question) sentence in the past tense, but this is not translated in Esperanto:

Mi parolis al vi. *I spoke to you.*	Mi **ne** parolis al vi. *I* did not *speak to you.*
Li legis la libron. *He read the book.*	**Ĉu** li legis la libron? Did *he read the book*?

PRAKTIKO 4.1 Translate into English:

La patrino donis du belajn ludilojn al Maria. Amiko sendis al mi leteron. La arbo estis antaŭ la domo. La kato sidis sub la tablo. Ĉu vi vidis ĝin? Ne, mi ne vidis ĝin. Ĉu vi legis tiun libron? Jes, mi jam legis ĝin. Kiu sendis al ŝi la leteron? La domo estis plena hieraŭ.

Translate each of these sentences in three ways: 1 Mi ne parolis al li. 2 Ĉu vi skribis al ŝi? 3 Li veturis en aŭtobuso.

PRAKTIKO 4.2 Translate into Esperanto:

In the house were six large rooms. I saw Andrew in the garden. Did you see him? I have-seen Mary in the children's room. I have already seen her. She was-playing. I did not see Mr Lang yesterday. He was not in the house. Have you seen Mrs Lang? Yes, I saw her yesterday. Where was she? She was-sitting in the park. Did you see that car? It was-travelling very fast. I sent a letter to Mrs Brown. I sent her a letter yesterday. She read it at three o'clock. The small cats were-sitting on the new tables. The dog was-sitting near the window.

PRAKTIKO 4.3 Match the answers to these questions:

1	Ĉu vi vidis Andreon en la infanejo?	(*a*)	Ne, mi legas malrapide.
2	Ĉu vi jam legis tiun libron?	(*b*)	Mi legis tiun libron.
3	Ĉu sinjoro Brown laboris en la ĝardeno?	(*c*)	Jes, li donis al ŝi ludilon.
4	Ĉu la patro donis ludilon al Maria?	(*d*)	Ne, li sidis en la salono.
5	Ĉu sinjoro Lang sidis en la salono?	(*e*)	Mi legis bonan libron.
6	Kie sidis sinjoro Lang?	(*f*)	Li sendis leteron al mi.
7	Kiun libron vi legis?	(*g*)	Jes, li sidis en la salono.
8	Kian libron vi legis?	(*h*)	Li sidis en la salono.
9	Ĉu vi legas rapide?	(*i*)	Ne, sed mi legas ĝin nun.
10	Kion sendis la amiko?	(*j*)	Ne, mi vidis lin en la ĝardeno.

Possessive adjectives

8 The personal pronouns (p. 18) can be made into adjectives by the addition of **-a**, to translate 'my', 'your', 'his', etc.:

mi**a**	*my, mine*	ni**a**	*our, ours*	li**a**	*his*
vi**a**	*your, yours*	ŝi**a**	*her, hers*	ili**a**	*their, theirs*
		ĝi**a**	*its*		

Mia patrino parolis al via patrino.
My mother spoke to your mother.

Lia libro estas dika, kaj ŝia (libro) estas maldika.
His book is thick and hers (her book) is thin.

Nia hundo estas bela, kaj ilia (hundo) estas malbela.
Our dog is beautiful and theirs (their dog) is ugly.

9 In order to differentiate 'my' from 'mine'; 'your' from 'yours', etc., the word **la** may be used with the latter:

Jen via libro.	Jen la via.
Here is your book.	*Here is yours.*

The future tense

10 When we wish to show that the action or state is yet to take place or exist, the verb ends in **-os**:

Mi skrib**os** al vi morgaŭ.
I shall write to you tomorrow.

Li parol**os** al ŝi baldaŭ.
He will speak to her soon.

La urbo est**os** plena.
The town will be full.

It should be noted that English has another common form of the future tense using 'going to', and verbs ending in **-os** can also be translated in this way.

The direct object

11 ***Kiun, kion, kian***

When **kiu**, **kio**, or **kia** is the object of the sentence, **-n** is added. In English, 'who' sometimes becomes 'whom', but 'which' and 'what' do not change. Note also that 'do', 'does' and 'did' are used in English, but are not translated.

		Subject	*Object*
Kiu**n** vi amas? *Whom* do *you love?*	=	Vi amas *You love*	kiu**n**? *whom?*
Kiu**n** li vidis? *Whom* did *he see*	=	Li vidis *He saw*	kiu**n**? *whom?*
Kiuj**n** partoj**n** ĝi montras? *Which parts* does *it show?*	=	ĝi montras *It shows*	kiuj**n** partoj**n**? *which parts?*
Kiu**n** libro**n** li legas? *Which book is he reading?*	=	Li legas *He is reading*	kiu**n** libro**n**? *which book?*
Kio**n** li trovis? *What* did *he find?*	=	Li trovis *He found*	kio**n**? *what?*
Kio**n** vi skribas? *What are you writing?*	=	Vi skribas *You are writing*	kio**n**? *what?*
Kia**n** letero**n** li sendis? *What kind of letter* did *he send*?	=	Li sendis *He sent*	kia**n** letero**n**? *what kind of letter?*
Kiaj**n** interesoj**n** li havas? *What kind of interests has he (got)?*	=	Li havas *He has (got)*	kiaj**n** interesoj**n**? *what kind of interests?*

More grammar points

12 *Kial* (*why, for what reason*) **and *tial*** (*therefore, for that reason*)

Kial (pron. *kee-al*) and **tial** (pron. *tee-al*) are used as follows:

Kial li skribis leteron? *Why did he write a letter?*	Tial mi skribis al li. *Therefore I wrote to him.*
Kial vi estas esperantisto? *Why are you an esperantist?*	Mi estas, tial mi ekzistas. *I am, therefore I exist.*

Warning: Do not confuse **tial** (*for that reason*) and **ĉar** (*because*). *For that reason = therefore* (Sometimes *so*):

Mi ne vidis lin, **tial** mi skribis al li.
I did not see him, so (i.e. therefore) *I wrote to him.*

13 *re-*

The prefix **re-** is used to denote the repetition of an act, and also the return of a person or thing to its former place or condition (like English 're-'):

legas *reads*	**re**legas *re-reads*
donas *gives*	**re**donas *gives back*
iras *goes*	**re**iras *returns (goes back)*
venas *comes*	**re**venas *returns (comes back)*

Note that *return* can be translated by either **reiras** or **revenas**, depending on the sense required.

14 *Ĉi*

Ĉi indicates nearness. Its most usual use is with the **ti-** correlatives, thus:

tie *there*	ĉi tie *here*
tiu *that*	ĉi tiu *this*

Ĉi may be placed either before or after the **ti-** word:

ĉi tie *or* tie ĉi

15 *Scias, konas*

Both these verbs mean 'to know', but **scias** means to know a fact, while **konas** means to be acquainted with (usually a person or place):

Mi **konas** lin, sed mi ne **scias** kie li loĝas.
I know him, but I don't know where he lives.

Teksto (text)

Letero

S-ro* kaj s-ino Lang jam lernis la fundamentojn de Esperanto, kaj s-ro Lang serĉis amikojn en eksterlando. Kial li serĉis? Ĉar tiel li uzos la lingvon. Li ĵus ricevis leteron el Norvegujo. Sur la bildo vi vidas paĝon de la letero. Tie la Norvega amiko skribas pri la familio. Sur la alia flanko de la papero li skribas pri la urbo Voss:

Nia urbeto Voss staras sur la belega fervojo de Bergen al Oslo.

* The standard abbreviations are: **S-ro** *Mr*, **S-ino** *Mrs.* **Ges-roj** *Mr and Mrs*, **F-ino** *Miss.*

Apud la urbo kuŝas la lago Vangsvatn, en la mezo de altaj montoj. Ĝi estas bela centro por turistoj kaj sportuloj. Precipe la junuloj kaj junulinoj vizitas nin. En Norvegujo ekzistas multaj junul-gastejoj. Sed ankaŭ la maljunuloj trovas interesojn ĉi tie. Ili kaptas fiŝojn en la lago, kaj rigardas la multajn historiajn domojn.

Feliĉe, la urbo ne forgesis pri eduko. Ni havas kelkajn bonajn lernejojn, kaj ankaŭ kolegion.

Nu, mi sendas koran saluton kaj bondeziron al vi kaj via familio.

Sincere via,

Edvard

S-ro Lang estas tre kontenta pri la letero kaj la bela poŝtkarto. Li ofte relegas la leteron. Baldaŭ li skribos respondon. Li dankos la Norvegan amikon pro lia letero, kaj reciproke sendos al li informon pri la urbo Newtown. Kaj pri la familio Lang!

PRAKTIKO 4.4 Translate into English:

Mi jam lernis la fundamentojn de Esperanto. Nun mi korespondas kun amiko en eksterlando. Mi ĵus ricevis leteron kaj mi baldaŭ skribos respondon. Tiel mi uzos Esperanton. Norvega amiko, Edvard, skribis leteron al sinjoro Lang. Li skribis pri la urbeto Voss, en kiu li loĝas. Tiu ĉi urbeto staras sur la fervojo de Bergen al Oslo. S-ro Lang estas la edzo de s-ino Klara Lang. Ges-roj Lang estas geedzoj (ge-edzoj). Mi ricevis multajn leterojn kaj poŝtkartojn el eksterlando. Mi havas amikojn en multaj landoj. Mia amiko estas junulo, sed li ne estas sportulo. Ĉu ekzistas multaj junulgastejoj en Norvegujo? Mi ne scias. Kion faras la maljunuloj? Ili kaptas fiŝojn en la lago. Ili ankaŭ rigardas la multajn historiajn domojn. Ĉi tie en mia urbo mi ne kaptas fiŝojn. Ĉu vi scias kial? Ĉar tiu ĉi urbo ne staras apud lago.

PRAKTIKO 4.5 Translate into Esperanto:

Do you correspond with a friend (*feminine*) abroad? Have you received a letter? What did she write? Where does she live? Does she live in Norway? Where did the friend of Mr Lang see the announcement? What did he write? Did he write in Esperanto? Will Mr Lang reply soon? What will he write about? What will he send? What are your chief interests? Are you a sportsman? What are you? Do you often re-read letters? Does Mr Lang often re-read the letter? Do you know Mr Lang? Do you know where he lives? Do you know whether he has received a letter?

PRAKTIKO 4.6 Vera aŭ malvera? (*True or false?*)
Say whether the following sentences are true or false (according to the text):

1 S-ro Lang ricevis nur unu leteron el Norvegujo.
2 Li jam skribis respondon.
3 Edvard loĝas en granda urbo.
4 Li havas tridek unu jarojn.
5 Li loĝas en nova domo.
6 La lago Vangsvatn kuŝas en la mezo de altaj montoj.
7 La urbo Voss havas kelkajn kolegiojn.
8 Precipe la gejunuloj vizitas la urbeton Voss.
9 S-ro Lang ofte relegas la leteron.
10 S-ro Lang loĝas en Newtown.

Dialogo

Amiko el Norvegujo

Mr Lang has invited his pen-friend Edvard Olsen to spend a holiday in Newtown, and meets him at the station.

S-ro Lang Saluton! Ĉu vi estas Edvard?
Edvard Mia kara Rikardo! Fine mi renkontas vin! Tio estas granda plezuro por mi!
Rikardo Ankaŭ por mi! Venu; mia aŭtomobilo staras ekster la stacidomo.
Edvard Dankon, Rikardo.
Rikardo Ĉu vi komforte veturis?
Edvard Tre komforte, dankon.

* * *

Rikardo Nu, jen ni ekster mia domo. Envenu, mi petas! Ha, Klara, jen mia norvega amiko Edvard Olsen.
Klara Vi estas tre bonvena, sinjoro Olsen.
Edvard Ne 'sinjoro', mi petas! Mi estas Edvard.
Klara Tre bone, Edvard. Nun, Rikardo montros al vi vian ĉambron, dum mi finos* la vespermanĝon. Ĝi baldaŭ estos preta.

*Note this use of the future tense, where in English we would use the present, e.g. 'while I *finish* the dinner', etc. But when the verb refers to something in the future, we use that tense in Esperanto.

Edvard Dankon, Klara. Mi vere estas malsata.

Rikardo Venu, Edvard! . . . Jen via dormoĉambro. Mi esperas, ke vi trovos ĝin komforta. Ci tiu ŝranko estas je via dispono, kaj ankaŭ tiuj du tirkestoj. Kaj la banĉambro estas ĉi tie!

Edvard Mi scias, ke mi bone dormos ĉi tie.

Rikardo Nu, venu al la salono kiam vi estos* preta, kaj se la vespermanĝo ne estos* preta, vi sidos komforte dum vi atendos*. Mi helpos Klaran en la kuirejo.

Edvard Dankon, amiko. Mi baldaŭ estos preta.

Rikardo Ĝis poste, do!

Edvard Ĝis poste.

Demandoj

1 Kie s-ro Lang renkontas la norvegan amikon?
2 Kie staras la aŭtomobilo de s-ro Lang?
3 Kiu estas bonvena?
4 Ĉu Edvard komforte veturis?
5 Kion faros s-ino Lang dum Edvard iros al la dormoĉambro?
6 Kiam la vespermanĝo estos preta?
7 Kion s-ro Lang esperas?
8 Ĉu tri tirkestoj estas je la dispono de Edvard?
9 Kion faros Edvard kiam li estos preta?
10 Kion la du amikoj faros se la vespermanĝo ne estos preta?

amiko *friend* (cf. *amicable*)
anonco *announcement*
apartamento *a flat*
apud *beside, near to*
atendas *waits for*
bondeziro *good wish(es)*
bonvena, bonvenon! *welcome*
eduko *education*
edzo *husband*; **edzino** *wife*
eksterlando *'outside-land'*, i.e. *abroad*
ekzistas *exists*
el *out of*
esperas *hopes*
feliĉa *happy, fortunate*
finas *finishes*: **fine** *finally, at last*
fiŝo *fish*
forgesas *forgets*
fotografio *photography*
fundamento *foundation, element (of a subject)*
gasto *guest*; **gastejo** *guest-house, hostel*
helpas *helps*
historio *history*
informo *information*
jaro *year*
je (see note **2**)
ĵus *just (of something immediately past)*: **mi ĵus skribis** *I have just written*
kaptas *catch*
kara *dear*
kato *cat*
ke *that* (conjunction)
kolegio *college*
konas *knows (is acquainted with)*
korespondas *corresponds*
koro *heart*; **kora** *cordial*
koverto *envelope*
kun *with*
kuŝas *lies*
lago *lake*
lando *land, country*
leterportisto *postman* (see **poŝtisto)**
libera *free* (cf. *liberate*)
lingvo *language* (cf. *linguist*)
malsata *hungry* (see **sata)**
muziko *music*
nomo *name*
Norvego *a Norwegian*; **Norvegujo** *Norway*
ofta *frequent*; **ofte** *often*
paĝo *page*
papero *(piece of) paper*
petas *asks*
plezuro *pleasure*
portas *carries*
post *after*; **poste** *afterwards*
poŝto *post, mail* (note spelling, to distinguish it from **post** *after*)
poŝtisto *(any) postal worker*
poŝtkarto *postcard*
poŝtmarko *postage stamp*
precipe *mainly, principally*
preta *ready*
pro *for, because of*
reciproke *reciprocally, in exchange*
renkontas *meets*
revuo *magazine*
ricevas *receives* (note spelling, and pronunciation **reet-*sev*-as)**
rigardas *looks at, watches*
saluto *greeting*; **saluton!** *hello!*
sata *satisfied (of hunger)*; **malsata** *hungry*
* **scias** *knows (a fact)*
sendas *sends*
serĉas *looks for, seeks*

* Some people find the combination **sc** difficult to pronounce, yet it occurs in English, e.g. *best-seller*. To say **Mi ne scias**, pronounce the English words 'Me nest see ass'!

sincera *sincere*
tempo *time*
tirkesto *drawer*
turisto *tourist*; **turismo** *tourism*
uzas *uses*
venas *comes*
vera *true, real*; **vere** *truly, really*
vespero *evening*
vespermanĝo *evening meal*
vizitas *visits*

Esprimoj:
je via dispono *at your disposal*
mi tre ĝojas *I'm very glad*
envenu, mi petas! *come in, please!*
ĝis poste *till later*

Interlude

Having mastered Units 1–4, you are already an esperantist. To a limited degree, no doubt; but if only a limited number of people in each country knew the international language, and if even they knew it only partially, the language problem would be essentially solved. The barriers which have always separated the nations would be breached.

Put your knowledge to practical use immediately, by writing a few postcards to beginners in other lands. Addresses may be found in the current issues of Esperanto magazines. Nothing elaborate! Just a few phrases on a postcard of your town or of some national beauty-spot, to a variety of countries, such as Spain, Finland and Austria. There is no more vivid way to the realisation that Esperanto opens before you not merely one foreign country, but the whole world.

Though your knowledge as yet is small, it is complete in itself, and if you master it, you will be surprised at the variety of ideas which you can express.

How to practise The chief difficulty for the solitary student is, how to acquire fluency. This can be done, however, and with enjoyment, if you tackle it methodically. Practise thoroughly with one set of words before you learn more. You can do this at any time, without books or other equipment. Suppose you are waiting for the bus, and opposite you is a house. You know that word – so say it: **domo**. Already you have given some information to an imaginary foreign listener. Now consider *what sort of a* house it is, i.e., add an adjective: **nova domo (malnova, granda, malgranda, moderna, komforta, bela, malbela, malbelega,** etc.). Having named the object and described it, you need only add a verb to make a complete sentence: **la domo estas bela kaj moderna**.

The next step is a simple but important one: make your little sentence into a question, by adding **ĉu** or one of the **ki-** words, and then answer it: **Ĉu la domo estas bela? Jes, la domo estas bela. Ĉu la domo estas granda? Ne, la domo estas malgranda. Kia domo ĝi estas? Ĝi estas malgranda, moderna domo.**

Questions and answers are easy, since you are merely repeating the same words; but they are important, because it is impossible to carry on even the simplest conversation if you are not thoroughly drilled in asking and answering questions.

A further stage in practice is the addition of a preposition – how does the object stand in relation to other objects? **Kio estas antaŭ la domo? Antaŭ la domo estas tri grandaj arboj. Kio estas malantaŭ la domo? Malantaŭ la domo estas ĝardeno kaj aŭtomobilejo.**

If you proceed in this way, starting with a single word and gradually grouping others round it, you should be able to express a really useful amount of information. Try it with another object – **aŭtomobilo**, for instance, or **libro**. The secret is: keep the phrases short and snappy! If you try to embark upon a long sentence, you will be tongue-tied immediately. Often you will find yourself wanting to say something for which you do not know the word. Occasionally you may look up a word in the dictionary, but in general it is better to limit your horizon deliberately for the time being. Practise thoroughly with such words as you do know before adding to them indiscriminately. *Fluency in one topic* is the first aim, and for this we have chosen the family, home and neighbourhood, as being the most natural. When you can say a good deal about these, easily and quickly, the battle is half won. For then it will be easy to learn a small set of new words about another topic, e.g. the seaside, and extend your fluency to it also. The same principles will apply.

A good help is to write a selection of words on pieces of card. Six nouns, verbs, adjectives and prepositions, plus the words **la** and **kaj**, will do for a start. Take one of each, lay them on the table, and thus make up a sentence: **la hundo estas sur la tablo.** Change any of them, and you will automatically form any number of phrases. Often the meaning will be absurd (**la hundo sidas sur la fajro**), but that is all the better, as long as you recognise what the meaning is. Humour and incongruity add to the interest.

With the aim of emphasising the topicality of Esperanto, and at the same time of adding interest to your studies, the following plan has been adopted for the remainder of this book: imagine that one fine day you pick up your evening paper and find – that it has been completely transformed into Esperanto! Each unit from now on will use as its basis a typical article taken from this imaginary newspaper, for instance the Weather forecast, Television and radio, Home page, Letters to the editor, etc. By this means it is hoped that the reader will feel on familiar ground. The dialogues, however, will continue independently, and will concern chiefly Mr and Mrs Lang's experiences as they progress in Esperanto. By the combination of these two separate means, we hope you will be entertained through a good variety of topics and provided with a useful vocabulary of everyday words.

5 Pri via ferio

Movement: to

1 In order to show movement *towards* the place or position indicated by the preposition, **-n** is added to the noun (in English, 'to' is sometimes added to 'in' and 'on'):

La kato saltas sur la tablo**n**.
The cat jumps on to *the table.*

La muso kuras sub la lito**n**.
The mouse runs under the bed.

La viro iras en la domo**n**.
*The man goes in*to *the house.*

In each of the above examples, the subject starts the action in one place and finishes it in another. Note the difference in meaning between these sentences:

La kato ludis **en** la salon**o**. *The cat was playing in the lounge.*
La kato iris **en** la salon**on**. *The cat went into the lounge.*

Now notice the difference in meaning if we omit the **-n** from the three sentences above:

La kato saltas sur la tablo means that the cat is on the table, and, while there, is jumping.
La muso kuras sub la lito means that the mouse is under the bed, and is running about.
La viro iras en la domo means that the man is in the house, and is going from one part to another.

Note: **-n** is never used after **al** (*to*) and **ĝis** (*up to*), because they do not indicate a position, but themselves show movement to some place.

2 If an *adverb* shows place, movement *to* that place is shown by **-n** on the adverb:

Mi restis hejme. Li iris hejme**n**.
I stayed at home. *He went home.*

In English we sometimes use '-ward(s)':

antaŭe**n**	*forwards*
malantaŭe**n**	*backwards*
supre**n**	*upwards*
malsupre**n**	*downwards*
norde**n**	*northwards*
sude**n**	*southwards*
oriente**n**	*eastwards*
okcidente**n**	*westwards*

3 Note particularly the use of **-n** with **kie** and **tie:**

Kie**n** vi iras?
Where are you going (to)?
Kie**n** li veturis?
Where did he travel to?
Mi iras tie**n**.
I am going there (to that place).
Li veturis tie**n**.
He travelled there (to that place).

Movement: from

4 In order to show movement *from* a place, **de** is put in front of the preposition showing place (**-n** is *not* used). This is similar to the English form, for we often use 'from':

La kato saltis **de sur** la tablo.
The cat jumped off (= from on) *the table.*
Li prenis la jakon **de sur** la hoko.
He took the jacket off *the hook.*
La muso kuris **de sub** la lito.
The mouse ran from under *the bed.*

However, instead of **de en** (*from in* = *out of*), we have a separate preposition with this meaning – **el**:

La viro iris **el** (= **de en**) la domo.
The man went out of (= from in) *the house.*
Li trinkis **el** glaso.
He drank from (= out of) *a glass.*

Changing endings

5 You will have noticed that in Unit 3 (note **1**) we changed adjectives into adverbs by simply changing the ending **-a** to **-e**, and in note **2** of this unit we changed a noun (**hejmo** *a home*) to an adverb (**hejm**e *at home*; **hejm**en *to one's home, homewards*).

Similarly, we can make adjectives from nouns by changing **-o** to **-a**:

muro *a wall*	mur**a** bildo *a wall (mural) picture*
urbo *a town*	urb**a** parko *a municipal park*
intereso *an interest*	interes**a** libro *an interesting book*

In the same way, from **nordo** *(the) north*, we can make **nord**a *northern*, **nord**e *in the north* and **nord**en *to the north, northwards*, and from **supro** *(the) top* we can make **supr**a *top* (adj.), **supr**e *at the top* and **supr**en *towards the top, upwards.*

6 The ending *-u*

For giving direct *commands* from the speaker, the verb ends in **-u**:

Ir**u** al la pordo!	Ne ir**u** en la ĝardenon!
Go to the door!	*Don't go into the garden!*

As in English, the person addressed is not usually named:

Ven**u** rapide! = Vi venu rapide!
Come quickly = You *come quickly!*
Est**u** bona! = Vi estu bona!
Be good! = You *be good!*

It is not possible to give commands to ourselves or directly to a third party, but it is possible to express our *will* (wish, desire), and in English we use the verb 'let' for this: 'Let me do it', 'Let him wait', etc.:

Ni ir**u** al la kinejo.	Ĝi star**u** en la angulo.
Let's go to the cinema.	*Let it stand in the corner.*
Li atend**u**.	Ili ven**u** al ni.
Let him wait.	*Let them come to us.*

It is worth remembering that to say 'Let's (do something)' in Esperanto, we say '**Ni . . . -u**'.

Occasionally, the meaning expressed is a *wish* or *exhortation* (in English we sometimes use 'may'):

La Nova Jaro est**u** feliĉa por vi!
May the New Year be happy for you!

Dio vin ben**u**!
(May) God bless you!

Although we cannot give commands to ourselves or to a third party, we can *ask* for orders for ourselves and others. In English we usually employ 'shall' for this; in Esperanto we use **ĉu** with the above forms:

Ĉu mi far**u** ĝin? *Shall I do it?*	**Ĉu** li atend**u**? *Shall he wait?*
Ĉu mi send**u** ĝin? *Shall I send it?*	Ĉu ili komenc**u**? *Shall they begin?*
Ĉu ni ir**u** al la kinejo? *Shall we go to the cinema?*	**Ĉu** ni danc**u**? *Shall we dance?*

PRAKTIKO 5.1 Traduku anglen (*Translate into English*):

Kien vi iras? Kien iras Andreo? Maria kuras en la manĝoĉambron. Andreo ne ludas en la infanejo. Iru antaŭen, mi petas, ĝis la ponto super la fervojo. Ni iru al la parko. Ni rigardu ĉi tiujn bildojn. Mi nun estas je via dispono; kien ni iru? Ĉu ni iru al la stacidomo? Kiel ni iru? Ni iru aŭtobuse! Tiu kato tre plaĉas al mi. Rigardu ĝin; ĝi ludas antaŭ la domo. Kiu estas la fratino de Andreo? Ĉu vi ne scias, ke Maria estas lia fratino, kaj li estas ŝia frato? Parolu al lia patro pri li, mi petas. Mi ne iras al li; li venu al mi! Kion ni faru? Ne faru tion, mi petas! Mi iras hejmen nun; Ĝis revido!

PRAKTIKO 5.2 Traduku esperanten (*Translate into Esperanto*):

Go to the door, please! Go into the lounge, please! Shall we go to a cinema? Let's read this book! Don't go into the garage! Where is the cat? Where did it go (to)? It went out of the house, into the garden. Go up to the bedroom, please. My sisters went to the cinema, but I stayed at home. The cat came into (entered) the room, and the mouse ran under the bed. This room is at your disposal. Take the doll off the table, please. What shall we do now? Come here! Are you going home now? Goodbye!

PRAKTIKO 5.3 Construct as many meaningful sentences as you can from the table on page 53, first using only columns 3, 4 and 5, and then all six columns.

1	2	3	4	5	6
Ĉu	mi li ili	iru restu kuru dancu	al en el sur	la domo la salono la tablo la domon la salonon la tablon	?

Names of countries

7 In naming countries, the world is divided into two parts – the Old World (Europe and Asia) and the New World (America, Africa and Oceania).

In the Old World, the races are more or less stabilised and give their names to the country, thus **Anglo** *an Englishman,* **Belgo** *a Belgian* and **Franco*** *a Frenchman.* By adding the suffix **-uj-**, we get **Anglujo** *England*; **Belgujo** *Belgium* and **Francujo** *France.* (See note **11**.) The suffix **-in-** will give **Anglino** *an Englishwoman,* **Belgino** *a Belgian woman* and **Francino** *a Frenchwoman.*

Although the names of countries are written with a capital letter as in English, the names of the inhabitants are often written with a small letter, and the adjectives derived from them usually take a small letter: **angla** *English,* **belga** *Belgian,* **franca** *French.*

In just a few cases, the name of the country ends in **-lando**, so **-ujo-** is not added and the name of the inhabitant is formed by the addition of the suffix **-an-**.

Thus:

Irlando *Ireland* — Irlandano/anino *an Irishman/woman*
Islando *Iceland* — Islandano *an Icelander*
Nederlando *Holland* — Nederlandano *a Dutchman*

The ending **-lando** may also be used instead of **-ujo**, but in this case, the root is still the name of the inhabitant:

Dano *a Dane* — Danlando *Denmark*
Polo *a Pole* — Pollando *Poland*
Sviso *a Swiss* — Svislando *Switzerland*

***Franco** (pron. *Frant-so*). Always remember **c** sounds as *ts.*

8 Here is a useful list:

Inhabitant	*Adjective*	*Country*
Anglo/Anglino* *an Englishman/woman*	angla	Anglujo
Aŭstro *an Austrian*	aŭstra	Aŭstrujo
Brito *a Briton*	brita	Britujo
Germano *a German*	germana	Germanujo
Greko *a Greek*	greka	Grekujo
Hispano *a Spaniard*	hispana	Hispanujo
Italo *an Italian*	itala	Italujo
Kimro *a Welshman*	kimra	Kimrujo
Norvego *a Norwegian*	norvega	Norvegujo
Svedo *a Swede*	sveda	Svedujo
Dano *a Dane*	dana	Danlando
Polo *a Pole*	pola	Pollando
Skoto *a Scot*	skota	Skotlando
Sviso *a Swiss*	svisa	Svislando
Irlandano *an Irishman*	irlanda	Irlando
Islandano *an Icelander*	islanda	Islando
Nederlandano *a Dutchman*	nederlanda	Nederlando

Note that some esperantists use **-io** in place of **-ujo: Anglio, Francio, Germanio**, etc. Whilst this is particularly acceptable for countries where the races are many (**Bulgario, Ĉeĥoslovakio, Hungario, Rumanio, Jugoslavio** – the English name often ends in '-ia') nevertheless the beginner is advised to use **-ujo** until he is competent to judge for himself.

9 In the New World, the races are generally greatly mixed through immigration, so the inhabitant takes his or her nationality from the country by the addition of the suffix **-an-** (see note **12**).

Alĝerio *Algeria*	Alĝeriano/ianino *an Algerian* (m *and* f)
Aŭstralio *Australia*	Aŭstraliano *an Australian*
Brazilo *Brazil*	Brazilano *a Brazilian*
Kanado *Canada*	Kanadano *a Canadian*
Novzelando *New Zealand*	Novzelandano *a New Zealander*
Tunizio *Tunisia*	Tuniziano *a Tunisian*

* Remember that to make these inhabitants feminine, you change **-o** to **-ino**.

An 'odd one out' is **Usono** (*the United States*) which has apparently developed from the Esperanto names of the letters U.S.N. (United States of North America). **Ameriko** is the name of the continent of America.

Names of cities

10 Some of the more important, larger cities have names in Esperanto form:

Parizo, Vieno, Kopenhago, Glasgovo, Manĉestro, etc.

Others just take the ending **-o**:

Londono, Berlino, Madrido, Romo, etc.

Names of smaller towns – especially if they are difficult to Esperantise – usually remain unchanged:

Cannes, Versailles, Bournemouth, Weston-super-Mare, etc.

Suffixes

11 ***-uj-***
In addition to indicating the name of a country, the suffix **-uj-** is used to denote a *container* for a number or quantity of the articles named by the 'root':

mono *money*	mon**uj**o *purse*
inko *ink*	ink**uj**o *inkpot*
teo *tea*	te**uj**o *tea-caddy*
karbo *coal*	karb**uj**o *coal-scuttle*

12 ***-an-***
The suffix **-an-** is used to denote a *member*, inhabitant, or partisan:

grupo *group*	grup**an**o *group member*
vilaĝo *village*	vilaĝ**an**o *villager*
Parizo *Paris*	Pariz**an**o *Parisian*
Kristo *Christ*	Krist**an**o *Christian*
Londono *London*	London**an**o *Londoner*
Manĉestro *Manchester*	Manĉestr**an**o *Mancunian*
Glasgovo *Glasgow*	Glasgov**an**o *Glaswegian*
Berno *Berne*	Bern**an**o *Bernese*

As in note **9**, the feminine ending is **-anino**.

Teksto

PRI VIA FERIO EN SVISLANDO

Ĉu vi decidis pri via ferio? Se ne, pensu pri Svislando! Ĝi estas ideala feria lando. Ni scias ke ĝi prezentas tre diversajn allogojn. La Alpoj formas belegan naturspektaklon. La aero estas eksterordinare pura – tiel purega, ke malsanuloj venas el tuta Eŭropo al Svislando. La granda komforto kaj bonega kuirarto de la svisaj hoteloj estas mondfamaj. Konstante okazas interesaj popolfestoj, kun belegaj kostumoj; ankaŭ ekspozicioj, muzikfestoj, sportfestoj, lagofestoj, florfestoj, k.s.[1] Vere, turismo estas la ĉefa industrio de Svislando! Ni menciu ankaŭ la luksajn butikojn, koncertejojn kaj teatrojn, kaj la gravajn universitatojn, muzeojn kaj bibliotekojn.

Kiel mi iru al Svislando?

Veturu per aŭtomobilo, biciklo, aŭtobuso aŭ fervojo. Nur ne per ŝipo! La maro mankas al Svislando; sed anstataŭ la maro, ĝi havas la belajn lagojn. Se via ferio ne estas longa, uzu aviadilon! Fluglinioj kondukas rekte de Londono, Manĉestro, Glasgovo kaj aliaj urboj al Berno aŭ Ĝenevo. Vi veturas trans Svislandon ankaŭ al aliaj landoj – orienten[2] en Aŭstrujon, suden en Italujon kaj Jugoslavujon, norden en Germanujon, kaj okcidenten en sudan Francujon.

[1] **k.s.: kaj similaj** *and the like.*
[2] *towards the east.*

Kio estas la nacia lingvo de Svislando?

Ĉu vi scias, ke en Svislando vi trovos *kvar* oficialajn lingvojn? La Bernanoj parolas la germanan lingvon; kiam ni iras en okcidentan Svislandon, ni aŭdas nur la francan; kaj la sudaj Svisoj parolas italalingve. Sed en la montaj regionoj de orienta Svislando ekzistas ankaŭ la *romanĉa* lingvo. Kvankam nur 40,000 homoj parolas ĝin, ĝi tamen estas oficiala ŝtata lingvo, egala al la tri aliaj. Jen la komenco de poemo en romanĉa lingvo; vi vidos, ke ĝi similas la italan lingvon, kaj estas ne malsimila al Esperanto:

Chara lingua de la mamma,
tu sonor rumantsch ladin,
o co t'am eu sainza fin!

(Traduko:
Kara lingvo de la patrino,
vi belsona ladina[3] romanĉa
ho! kiel mi amas vin sen fino!)

En tiu lingvo ekzistas libroj, gazetoj kaj kalendaroj; kaj infanoj en la lernejo ricevas instruon per romanĉa lingvo. Sed eĉ de tia lingveto ekzistas kvar diversaj dialektoj!

Vi vidas, ke Svislando estas vera Turo de Babelo. Multaj inteligentaj svisoj lernas Esperanton, ĉar ili komprenas, ke ĝi solvos la lingvan problemon. Ĉu vi ne konsentas?

[3] **dialekto de romanĉa.**

**Por via ferio-
SVISLANDO
belega lando
en la mezo
de Eŭropo**

PRAKTIKO 5.4 Traduku anglen:

Ĉu vi parolas Esperanton? De kie vi venas? Ĉu vi estas anglino? Ne, mi estas skotino. Mi loĝas en Glasgovo. Kaj kie *vi* loĝas? Mi estas franco, kaj loĝas en Parizo. Mi estas Parizano, kaj mia edzino estas Parizanino. La francoj parolas la francan lingvon, kaj la italoj parolas la italan. Ĉu Esperanto similas al la itala lingvo? Ĉu vi iras norden de Germanujo al Italujo? Ne, mi iras suden, ĉar Italujo kuŝas sude de Germanujo. Kien ni iru por nia ferio? Mi pensas pri Svislando. Kia lando ĝi estas? Ĝi estas bela lando kun multaj montoj, kaj la aero estas tre pura. Pro tio multaj malsanuloj iras tien. Kiel ni iru tien? Ni veturu per fervojo ĝis la maro, poste per ŝipo ĝis Francujo, kaj de tie per fervojo en Svislandon. Kion ni faros dum ni estos tie? Ni vizitos diversajn interesajn urbojn, kaj vidos la Alpojn.

PRAKTIKO 5.5 Traduku esperanten:

Have you thought about your holiday? Have you thought about Switzerland? Do you know that in Switzerland you will find four official languages? Do you speak German? French? Italian? Romanche? Dutch? Russian? Are you a Londoner (*feminine*)? A Mancunian? A Glaswegian? How shall we go to Switzerland? Shall we travel by car, bicycle, bus or rail? Shall we travel across Switzerland to other countries? Where shall we go? To the north, south, east or west?

PRAKTIKO 5.6 Vera aŭ malvera?

1 Svislando ne havas montojn.
2 Svislando ne havas maron.
3 La Bernanoj parolas la francan lingvon.
4 Oni iras suden de Germanujo al Svedujo.
5 Popolfestoj ne okazas en Svislando.
6 En Svislando estas kvar oficialaj lingvoj.
7 La romanĉa estas la lingvo de Rumanujo.
8 Nur kvardek mil homoj parolas la romanĉan lingvon.
9 La kuirarto de la svisaj hoteloj estas mondfama.
10 Homo kiu loĝas en Romo estas urbano.

Dialogo

La Esperanto-grupo

Mr Lang is visiting the local Esperanto group for the first time, and meets the chairman.

Prezidanto Bonan vesperon, kaj bonvenon al la grupo. Ĉu vi loĝas en Newtown, aŭ ĉu vi nur vizitas nian urbon?

S-ro Lang Mi loĝas ĉi tie. Mia edzino kaj mi lernas Esperanton hejme, sed ĝis nun ni ne estis liberaj je la vesperoj de viaj kunvenoj. Ni ne venas kune, ĉar unu restas kun la infanoj.

Prezidanto Mi tre ĝojas, ke vi venis, kaj mi esperas, ke vi estos membro de la grupo. Kio estas via nomo, mi petas? Mi estas John Danby, kaj mi estas la prezidanto de la grupo.

S-ro Lang Mi estas Rikardo Lang.

Prezidanto Bone, sinjoro Lang. (*He turns to another member.*) Fraŭlino Jones, jen sinjoro Lang.

F-ino Jones Bonan vesperon, sinjoro Lang! Kiel vi fartas?

S-ro Lang Tre bone, dankon. Kaj vi?

F-ino Jones Bonege, dankon. Ĉu tiu ĉi estas via unua vizito al la grupo?

S-ro Lang Jes.

F-ino Jones Vi parolas Esperanton tre bone. Kie vi lernis?

S-ro Lang Dankon. Mi lernas ĝin hejme. Kion vi faras en la kunvenoj?

F-ino Jones Ho, diversajn aferojn. Ni komencas per mallongaj lecionoj, en klasoj, kaj poste ni havas ludojn en Esperanto, aŭ membro parolas al ni, kelkfoje pri vizito al alia lando. Je aliaj vesperoj ni havas diskutojn, aŭ kune tradukas interesan tekston.

S-ro Lang Kaj kio okazos hodiaŭ?

F-ino Jones Hodiaŭ sinjoro Franks parolos pri Norvegujo kaj Svedujo, kiujn li vizitis.

S-ro Lang Ho, tio estos tre interesa al mi, ĉar mi korespondas kun norvego, kaj li vizitis nin en nia hejmo!

F-ino Jones Do, la kunveno vere estos interesa al vi!

Demandoj

1 Kiun s-ro Lang renkontas unue en la grupo?
2 Ĉu li nur vizitas la urbon Newtown?
3 Kie li lernas Esperanton?
4 Kial li ne vizitis la grupon ĝis nun?
5 Kio estas la nomo de la prezidanto?
6 Kun kiu s-ro Lang poste parolas?
7 Per kio la grupo komencas la kunvenojn?
8 Kio okazos hodiaŭ?
9 Al kiu tio estos interesa?
10 Kial ĝi estos interesa al li?

---

aero *air*
afero *matter, affair, thing*
(al)logas *attracts*;
allogo *attraction*
anstataŭ *instead of*
aviado *aviation*; **aviadilo** *aircraft*
biblioteko *library*
biciklo *bicycle*
butiko *shop*
decidas *decides*
dialekto *dialect*
Dio *God*
diskuto *discussion*
diversa *different, diverse*
egala *equal* (cf. *egalitarian*)
ekspozicio *exhibition*
fama *famous*
faras *makes, does*
ferio *holiday*
festo *festival*; **popolfesto** *folk festival*
flugas *flies*
formas *forms*
gazeto *periodical, magazine*
glaso *(drinking) glass*
grava *important, serious*
hodiaŭ *today*
hoko *hook*
homo *human being (man, woman or child)*; **homoj** *people*
ideala *ideal*
industrio *industry*
instruo *instruction*;
instruas *teaches*
inteligenta *intelligent*
jako *jacket*
kalendaro *calendar*
kelkfoje *sometimes*
kiam *when*
komencas *begins*
komprenas *understands*
koncerto *concert*
konsentas *agree*
konstante *constantly, continually*
kostumo *costume*
kuir-arto *cuisine, art of cookery*
kune *together*
kunveno *meeting; coming together*
kuras *runs*
kvankam *although*
leciono *lesson*
linio *line*
longa *long*
ludo *game*
luksa *luxurious*
mankas *is lacking*; **la maro mankas** *the sea is lacking* (i.e. *there is no sea*)
maro *sea* (cf. *marine, maritime*)
membro *member*
mencias *mentions*
mondo *world* (cf. *mundane*)

muso *mouse*
muzeo *museum*
nacio *nation*
naturo *nature*
oficiala *official*
okazas *occurs, takes place*
ordinara *ordinary*
pensas *thinks* (cf. *pensive*)
per *by means of*
poemo *poem*
popolo *people* in sense of *nation;* **la svisa popolo** *the Swiss (people)*. But **kelkaj homoj** *some people*
poste *afterwards*
prenas *takes, picks up*
prezidanto *chairman*
problemo *problem*
restas *remains, stays*
romanĉa *Romanche (a language of Switzerland)*
saltas *jumps* (cf. *somersault*)
se *if*
sen *without*
simila *similar*; **similas** *resembles*
solvas *solves*; **solvo** *solution*
sono *sound* (cf. *resonant*)
spektaklo *spectacle, display*
ŝipo *ship*
ŝtato *state (country)*
tamen *however, nevertheless*
teatro *theatre*
trans *across (*at *the other side of)*
trans . . . -n *across (to the other side of)*
trinkas *drinks*
turo *tower*
tuta *whole, entire*
universitato *university*
unua *first*
vera *true* (cf. *veracity*); **vere** *truly, really*
vespero *evening*

Esprimoj:
Bonan vesperon! *Good evening!*
la pasintan jaron *last year*

6 La veter-prognozo

Impersonal verbs

1 If we want to describe something we can say, for example, 'It is large; it is beautiful,' etc., and clearly 'it' stands for the object referred to. But there are times when 'it' does not stand for a particular noun, for example, 'It is raining; it is sunny'. In such cases, 'it' is used as a kind of artificial subject, and Esperanto omits it, thus: **Pluvas** *It is raining*. Such verbs used without a subject are called *impersonal verbs*.

Pluvas. *It is raining.*
Pluvis. *It was raining.*
Pluvos. *It is going to rain.*

Frostas. *It is freezing.*
Frostis. *It was freezing.*
Frostos. *It is going to freeze.*

Neĝas. *It is snowing.*
Neĝis. *It was snowing.*
Neĝos. *It is going to snow.*

Hajlas. *It is hailing.*
Hajlis. *It was hailing.*
Hajlos. *It is going to hail.*

Note also that to make these negative or interrogative, we simply put **ne** or **ĉu** in front of them:

Ne neĝis. *It wasn't snowing.*

Ĉu pluvos? *Is it going to rain?*

2 In the same way we say:

Estas varm**e**. *It is warm.*
Estas sun**e**. *It is sunny.*

Estas malvarm**e**. *It is cold.*
Estas bel**e**. *It is fine.*

But note that as there is no subject expressed in Esperanto, **estas** is followed by an adverb (**varm**e, **malvarm**e, **sun**e, **bel**e), and not an adjective.

It is usual to say in Esperanto: **Estas varme al mi** for *I am warm*, instead of **Mi estas varma**, although it is not wrong (perhaps preferable) to use the latter form.

3 *Oni*

When we do not refer to anyone in particular, we use the indefinite pronoun **oni**, which is similar to the English 'one':

Oni ripetas, kion **oni** legas.
One *repeats what* one *reads.*

In modern English, it is perhaps more usual to use 'they':

Oni diras, ke vi estas malfeliĉa.
They *say that you are unhappy.*

In the same way we also use 'it' in English:

Oni diras, ke vi estas riĉa.
It *is said that you are rich.*

In very many instances, however, we use 'you':

Kiam **oni** estas riĉa, **oni** baldaŭ trovas amikojn.
When you *are rich*, you *soon find friends.*

Li estas tiel malgranda, ke **oni** ne rimarkas lin.
He is so small that you *do not notice him.*

Se **oni** havas bonan edzinon, **oni** estas kontenta.
If you *have a good wife*, you *are contented.*

Oni, then, is used a great deal in Esperanto, for it translates a variety of English expressions.

Correlatives

4 With *ĉi-*

You have learned a number of correlative words (see Unit 2, note **10**) beginning with **ki-** and **ti-**, and have probably noticed that the **ki-** words can generally be expressed as 'what + something', for example:

kiu *who (what person)*
kie *where (in what place)*
kiel *how (in what manner)*

and similarly, the **ti-** words can be expressed by 'that':

tiu *that one; that person*
tiel *thus (like that; in that way)*
tial *therefore (for that reason)*

In the same way, all the **ĉi** words express 'all' or 'every', and the ending tells us whether it refers to a person, thing, place, reason, etc.

ĉiu *every person (everybody, everyone)*
ĉio *everything*
ĉiel *in every way*
ĉial *for every reason*

5 With *neni-*

Just as **ĉi-** expresses 'all' or 'every', **neni-** expresses 'no' plus the appropriate ending:

nenio *nothing*
neniu *nobody; no one*
neniel *in no way*

PRAKTIKO 6.1 Traduku anglen:

Ĉu neĝas hodiaŭ? Ĉu pluvis hieraŭ? Ne, hieraŭ ne pluvis, sed eble pluvos hodiaŭ. Kia estas la vetero (*weather*) nun? Estas sune, kaj la ĉielo estas blua, sed ne estas varme. Oni diras, ke Esperanto similas la italan lingvon. Se oni havas feriojn, oni deziras havi belan veteron. Ĉiu scias, ke Svislando estas monta lando. Ĉu vi ricevis leteron hodiaŭ? Ne, neniu en la familio ricevis leteron hodiaŭ, sed mi ricevis unu hieraŭ de mia frato. Kio estas en ĉi tiu tirkesto? Estas nenio en ĝi; ĝi estas malplena. Mi ĵus rigardis en ĝin, sed mi vidis nenion. Kio estas en la karbujo? Tio ne estas malplena; estas karbo en ĝi.

PRAKTIKO 6.2 Traduku Esperanten:

This cupboard is full of all-kinds-of books. Where did you go (to) yesterday? I went (to) nowhere; I stayed at home. I have just received a letter from my sister. She says (that) it is very cold there. It is cold everywhere today. It-is-freezing. They say (that) it-is-going-to-snow. Where was it raining yesterday? Everywhere! If it is sunny, everybody is pleased. Have you a purse? What is in it? There is nothing in it; it is empty. Every room in the house is at your disposal. Thank you! You are a good friend.

PRAKTIKO 6.3 Using one correlative word for each of the following phrases, translate into Esperanto:

What? Where? In what manner? That person. There. Therefore. Everyone. Every kind of. Nobody. For no reason. What kind of? In that place. Everywhere. (In) no way! Who? Why? That kind of. Thus. For that reason. Nowhere. Like that. Such a . . . Which one? How? What a . . . ! That one. Every. Nothing. For what reason? In that way. Everybody. In every way. No one. Everything. For every reason.

More about adverbs

6 Esperanto is particularly rich in adverbs, as any root, if the sense permits, may be made into an adverb by the ending **-e**. Adverbs are therefore more widely used in Esperanto than in English, and we may express in one word what may take two or three words in English.

Generally speaking, we may use an adverb in Esperanto where we might use a preposition plus noun in English:

Li parolas saĝ**e**.	*He speaks wisely.* (*He speaks* with wisdom.)
Mi dormas nokt**e**.	*I sleep at (during the) night.*
Li laboras tag**e**.	*He works by (during the) day.*
maten**e**	*in the morning*
vesper**e**	*in the evening*
fakt**e**	*in fact, as a matter of fact*
ceter**e**	*as for the rest, moreover*
ekzempl**e**	*for example*

Days, months, etc.

7 ***La tagoj de la semajno*** (*The days of the week*)
lundo *Monday*, **mardo** *Tuesday*, **merkredo** *Wednesday*, **ĵaŭdo** *Thursday*, **vendredo** *Friday*, **sabato** *Saturday*, **dimanĉo** *Sunday*.

Note: The days of the week are not usually written with a capital letter.

8 ***La monatoj de la jaro*** (*The months of the year*)
januaro *January*, **februaro** *February*,
marto *March*, **aprilo** *April*, **majo** *May*, **junio** *June*,
julio *July*, **aŭgusto** *August*, **septembro** *September*,
oktobro *October*, **novembro** *November*,
decembro *December*.

Note: Although the names of the months are similar to the English forms, do not forget that the pronunciation is usually quite different, according to Esperanto rules: e.g. **aprilo (ah-*pree*-lo)**, **julio (yoo-*lee*-o)**, **januaro (ya-noo-*ah*-ro)**.

9 Further uses of *-n*

We saw that in expressing movement *to* (Unit 5), **-n** is added to the noun. This **-n** can be said to take the place of the preposition **al**:

La kato saltas sur la tablo**n**. = La kato saltas **al** sur la tablo.
La viro iras en la domo**n**. = La viro iras **al** en la domo.

In fact, **-n** may be used in place of any preposition, and the following are some of the practical uses:

Time

Mi venos lundo**n**.	= Mi venos **je** lundo.
I shall come Monday.	*I shall come* on *Monday.*
Mi atendos semajno**n**.	= Mi atendos **dum** semajno.
I shall wait a week.	*I shall wait* for *a week.*

Note that **lund**on means ***on** Monday*, but if we wish to indicate repetition rather than a single day, we use the adverb form: **lund**e ***on** Mondays*.

Mi iris lund**on**, kvankam kutime mi iras mard**e**.
I went on Monday, although I usually go on Tuesdays.

In accordance with this use of **-n**, when writing the date (at the top of a letter for instance), we write:

Dimanĉon la duan (2an) de marto
or simply
La 2an de marto

Weights and measures

10 Here again, it is better to use **-n**:

La monto estas mil metroj**n** alta. (La monto estas alta **je** mil metroj.)
The mountain is a thousand metres high.

La pakaĵo pezas du kilogramoj**n**. (. . . **je/ĝis** du kilogramoj)

However, if **-n** is already used to show the object, it might be ambiguous to have two **-ns** together. In such cases, the expression of time or measure may be put first, or a preposition may be used: instead of **Mi atendis lin du semajnojn**, it would be better to say **Du semajnojn mi atendis lin**, or **Mi atendis lin** dum **du semajnoj.**

Suffix

11 *-er-*

The suffix **-er-** is used to denote a unit of the whole which is indicated in the root, or one of the objects of the same kind:

neĝo	*snow*	neĝ**ero**	*snowflake*
ĉeno	*a chain*	ĉen**ero**	*a link*
fajro	*a fire*	fajr**ero**	*a spark*
mono	*money*	mon**ero**	*coin*
hajlo	*hail*	hajl**ero**	*hailstone*

Note: An **-er-** word usually denotes something complete in itself. For a mere fragment of something, use **fragmento de**.

Teksto

LA VETER-PROGNOZO

por morgaŭ, la 2a de marto

Londono, lundon, 1an de Marto

Sune; tre malvarme

Verŝajna vetero hodiaŭ je la 12ª tagmezo

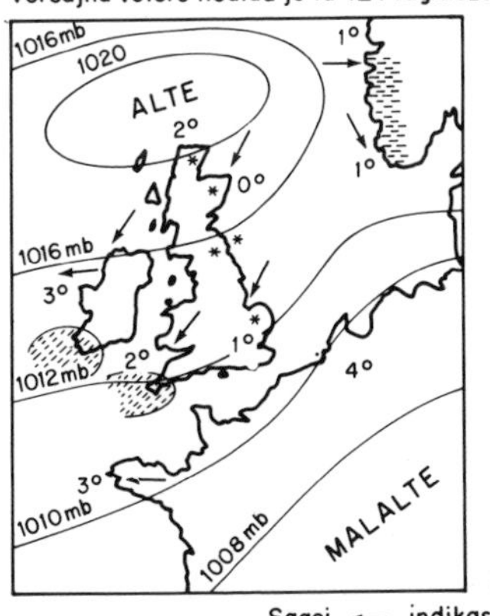

Sagoj ← indikas direkton de la vento.

pluvo neĝo nebulo

La orienta aŭ nordorienta vento daŭre blovos super la Britaj Insuloj. En Skotlando kaj orienta Anglujo neĝos ofte kaj, en kelkaj lokoj, forte. En okcidento estos sune, sed pluvetos de tempo al tempo.

Prognozo por la periodo ĝis noktomezo—

Londono, Orienta kaj Mezlanda Anglujo: Orienta vento; neĝos, kun sunaj periodoj, estos tre malvarme; frostos aŭ frostegos frumatene kaj nokte.

Cornwall kaj Devon: Nebulos aŭ nebuletos matene; poste, estos sune, kun pluveto aŭ neĝeto. Malvarme, sed verŝajne sen frosto.

Cetera Anglujo, Kimrujo: Estos sune kun sporada neĝo. Frostos vespere.

Skotlando: Intense malvarme; forte neĝos kaj frostos.

NOVA NEĜODANĜERO EN SKOTLANDO

Helikopteroj helpas

En norda Skotlando la neĝo denove izolis plurajn vilaĝojn. Helikopteroj denove helpis izolulojn, kaj portis malsanulojn al malsanulejo. Hodiaŭ ili portos nutraĵon por homoj kaj bestoj. Oni diras, ke la situacio estas tiel malbona kiel dum la lasta semajno. Sur la insulo Mull falis hajlo kun grandegaj hajleroj.

VETERO TRA EŬROPO

Aŭstrujo kaj Svisujo: Neĝis konstante dum la lastaj tagoj. La sporturboj raportas – kiel dum la tuta vintro – bonegajn kondiĉojn por la ski-sporto.

TEMPERATURO DUM LASTA SEMAJNO

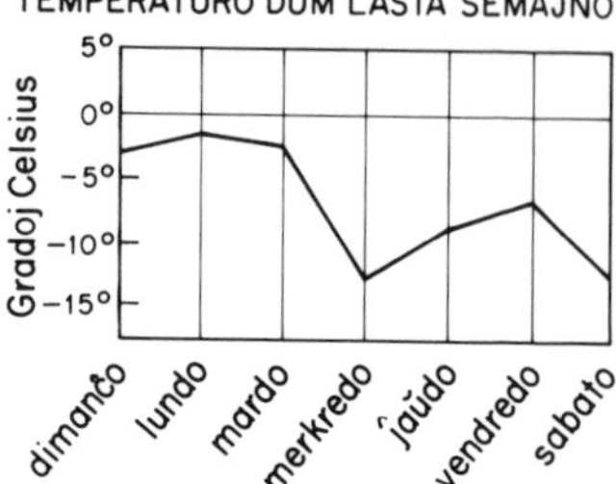

Francujo: En Parizo, malvarme, sed sen neĝo. El Cannes, oni raportas varman kaj dolĉan printempan veteron.

Italujo: Pluvis en multaj lokoj. Vetero, kiun oni ordinare ricevas dum la aŭtuno.

Hispanujo: Granda kontrasto! Ĉi tie, la vetero estis varma kaj suna kiel en somero. Dum pluraj semajnoj, ne unu pluvero aŭ neĝero falis en suda Hispanujo.

PRAKTIKO 6.4 Traduku anglen:

Kia estas la vetero en via urbo? Ĉu ofte pluvas? En Hispanujo ne ofte pluvas. Kia estas la somero en Italujo? Kutime dum la somero estas varme tie. En Skotlando ofte estas neĝo dum la vintro, kaj de tempo al tempo ĝi izolas plurajn vilaĝojn. Mi vizitos vin merkredon. Mi atendis tri semajnojn, sed ne ricevis respondon. Tiu muro estas du metrojn alta. Lundon mi iros en la urbon. La stacidomo estas unu kilometron for de mia domo. Kia estas la vetero hodiaŭ? Estas sune, kun dolĉa vento. Ĉu vi laboras sabate? Ne, mi laboras de lundo ĝis vendredo ĉiusemajne.

PRAKTIKO 6.5 Traduku Esperanten:

In Italy during the summer it is usually hot. What is the weather like in Paris during the summer? Is it warm, or is it cold? It does not often snow in my town. Do you read the weather forecast? It is usually warm here during the day, and cold during the night. They say it is sunny in Italy during March. Do you often see snow in Spain? February comes after January. Which month comes before June? Do people (does one) usually work on Sundays? No, people usually work during five days of the week, but not on Saturdays or Sundays.

PRAKTIKO 6.6 Complete these sentences by filling in the endings (one ending may consist of one, two or three letters):

1 La ludiloj de Maria estas nov– kaj bel–.
2 Ili kuŝ– sur la grand– tabl–.
3 Hieraŭ mi vid– mi– amik–.
4 S-ro Lang ricev– leter– el Norveg– hieraŭ.
5 La kato saltis de la plank– sur la tabl–.
6 Morgaŭ mi ir– en la urb– kaj sid– en la park–.
7 Trajno oft –ir –tre rapid –.
8 Mi ĵus leg– ti– libr–. Fakte, mi leg– ĉi– el ili.

Dialogo

Nova ideo

Richard Lang has returned from the group meeting, and is chatting with his wife, Clare.

Klara Nu, kiel vi ĝuis la kunvenon?

Rikardo Ho, ĝi estis tre interesa, kaj ĉiuj estis tre afablaj.

Klara Bone; mi ĝojas. Kaj kion oni faris?

Rikardo Nu, komence estis mallonga leciono, kaj oni dividis nin en klasojn. Mi estis en la altgrada klaso. Poste unu membro, sinjoro Franks, parolis pri Norvegujo kaj Svedujo.

Klara Ho, tio certe interesis vin, post la vizito de Edvard! Ĉu li menciis lokojn pri kiuj Edvard jam parolis al ni?

Rikardo Jes, mi rekonis plurajn nomojn. Kaj li veturis per la fervojo de Bergen ĝis Oslo, do li certe iris tra Voss! Li ankaŭ vizitis fervojan muzeon en Hamar, kiu uzas Esperanton en klarigaj tekstoj.

Klara Jes, Edvard diris, ke ankaŭ la fervojoj uzas ĝin en klarigoj sur la hortabeloj.

Rikardo Antaŭ la fino de la kunveno mi aŭdis alian interesan aferon. En Francujo estas kastelo kiu apartenas al la francaj esperantistoj*, kaj esperantistoj el diversaj landoj vizitas ĝin por ferioj aŭ lecionoj.

Klara Tio estas tre interesa. Kie ĝi estas, kaj kio estas ĝia nomo?

Rikardo Ĝi estas la kastelo Grésillon, aŭ Grezijono, kaj ĝi situas apud urbeto Baugé, sude de Le Mans.

Klara H'm, ĉu ni iru tien por niaj ferioj?

Rikardo Mi ĝojas, ke vi diris tion, ĉar ankaŭ mi havis tiun ideon!

Klara Do, ni diskutos la aferon poste. Nun estas malfrue; ni iru al la lito. Venu!

* esperantistoj – homoj, kiuj parolas Esperanton.

Demandoj

1 De kie Rikardo revenis?
2 Kia estis la kunveno?
3 Kiaj estis la membroj?
4 Dum la lecionoj, en kiu klaso estis Rikardo?
5 Kiu poste parolis, kaj pri kio?
6 Kien s-ro Franks veturis de Bergen?
7 Kiu muzeo uzas Esperanton en klarigaj tekstoj?
8 Al kiu apartenas la Kastelo Grezijono?
9 Kie ĝi situas?
10 Kial Rikardo kaj Klara ne diskutas la aferon nun?

afabla *kind*
altgrada *advanced* (lit. *high-grade*)
apartenas *belongs*
aŭtuno *autumn*
blovas *blows*
brilo *shine, brilliance*
cetera *remaining*
daŭras *lasts, endures*; **daŭre** *continually*
denove *again*
dividas *divides*
dolĉa *sweet, gentle*
eble *possibly, perhaps*
ekzemplo *example*
fakto *fact*
falas *falls*
for *away*
frua *early*; **fru-matene** *early in the morning*
grado *grade*
ĝuas *enjoys*
helikoptero *helicopter*
hor-tabelo *time-table*
insulo *island* (cf. *insular*)
intense *intensely*
izolas *isolates*
kastelo *castle, château*
klarigas *explain*; **klarigo** *explanation*; **klariga** *explanatory*
kondiĉo *condition*
kontrasto *contrast*
kutime *usually*
lasta *last (just gone)*
loko *place, spot* (cf. *local*)
mateno *morning* (cf. *mattins*)
metro *metre*
monato *month*
nebulo *fog* (cf. *nebulous*)
noktomezo *midnight*
nutraĵo *food, nourishment*
oni *'one', people in general*; **oni diras** *it is said*
periodo *period*
pluraj *several*
pluvo *rain*; **pluvero** *raindrop*
printempo *spring (season)*
raportas *reports*
rekonas *recognises (knows again)*
rivero *river*
sago *arrow*
semajno *week*
situas *is situated*; **situo** *situation (place)*
situacio *situation, state of affairs*
skatolo *box*
somero *summer*
sporada *sporadic*
suno *sun*; **sunbrilo** *sunshine*
ŝajnas *seems*
temperaturo *temperature*
vento *wind*
verŝajne *probably ('seemingly-true')*
vintro *winter*

7 Televido kaj radio

Parts of the day

1 To say 'on Monday morning', etc., we use the **-n** form to express 'on Monday', with the *adverb* form of the part of the day: **lundon matene** (lit. *on Monday in the morning*). For 'this morning' we say 'today in the morning': **hodiaŭ matene**. (Note that **hodiaŭ** does not take **-n**.)

mardo**n** maten**e**	*on Tuesday morning*
hodiaŭ posttagmez**e**	*this afternoon*
hieraŭ vesper**e**	*yesterday (last) evening*
morgaŭ nokt**e**	*tomorrow night*

post-tag-mezo *after midday* (lit. *after the day's middle*)

Numerals

2 To obtain the numbers 'first', 'second', 'third', etc., we put **-a** on to the numbers given in the Introduction:

unu**a** *first*	ses**a** *sixth*
du**a** *second*	sep**a** *seventh*
tri**a** *third*	ok**a** *eighth*
kvar**a** *fourth*	naŭ**a** *ninth*
kvin**a** *fifth*	dek**a** *tenth*
dudek**a** *twentieth*	tridek**a** *thirtieth* etc.

With the intermediate numbers which, you will remember, are written as two separate words (**dek unu**, **dudek unu**, etc.) the **-a** is added to the last word, but the numbers are joined by a hyphen to show that it relates to the whole figure:

dek-unu**a** *eleventh* dudek-kvin**a** *twenty-fifth*
cent-tridek-naŭ**a** *hundred and thirty-ninth*

These numbers are now adjectives, and must therefore 'agree' with their nouns:

la unu**aj** tag**oj** de la jaro
the first days of the year

lundo**n**, la dek-unu**an** de februaro
on Monday, the eleventh of February

3 The numbers can be made into nouns by the addition of **-o**:

unu**o**	du**o**	tri**o**	dek-du**o**	dudek**o**
a unit	*a couple*	*a trio*	*a dozen*	*a score*

. . . and also into adverbs by the ending **-e**:

unu**e**	du**e**	tri**e**	kvar**e**
firstly	*secondly*	*thirdly*	*fourthly*
kvin**e**	ses**e**	sep**e**	ok**e**
fifthly	*sixthly*	*seventhly*	*eighthly*
	naŭ**e**	dek**e**	
	ninthly	*tenthly*	

4 To express *how many times* a thing has happened, we add the word **foje** to the numbers:

unu**foje**	du**foje**	tri**foje**	dek**foje**
once	*twice*	*three times*	*ten times*

With an adjective, the noun **fojo** is used:

la unua **fojo**	la dua **fojo**	la lasta **fojo**
the first time	*the second time*	*the last time*

Do not confuse this with **tempo** (Unit 4), which refers to time as a whole. **Fojo** refers to an occasion when something happens.

5 The following three suffixes are all used with numerals:

(*i*) **-obl-** is used to denote multiples of the number:

du *two*	du**obl**a *double (two times)*
tri *three*	tri**obl**a *treble, triple, threefold*
kvar *four*	kvar**obl**a *quadruple (four times)*
dek *ten*	dek**obl**a *tenfold (ten times)*

(*ii*) **-on-** is used to denote fractions:

du**on**o *a half*, tri**on**o *a third*, kvar**on**o *a quarter*,
tri kvar**on**oj *three-quarters*

(*iii*) **-op-** is used to denote a numeral collective (so many together):

du**op**e *two at a time, in twos*, ses**op**e *in sixes*,
dudek**op**e *in twenties*

Telling the time

6 To ask and tell the time in Esperanto is very simple, and should present no difficulty:

Kioma horo estas? *What time is it?*

In English, the reply can be given in more than one way. For example, for 1.15 we can say 'quarter past one' or 'fifteen minutes past one' or 'one fifteen'; likewise in Esperanto. However, we advise you to learn just one method thoroughly, as you will have no difficulty in understanding the other forms when you meet them.

Estas la unua (horo). *It is one o'clock.*
1.10 La unua (kaj) dek (minutoj)
2.15 La dua (kaj) dek kvin (*or* . . . kaj kvarono)
4.30 La kvara (kaj) tridek (*or* . . . kaj duono)
6.45 La sesa (kaj) kvardek kvin
11.50 La dek-unua (kaj) kvindek

Note: The 'hour' figure always ends in **-a**; i.e. for 'one o'clock' we say 'the first hour'. The words **horo** and **minutoj** may be used, but are normally omitted. Similarly, **kaj** may be omitted, except before **kvarono** and **duono**.

If using the twenty-four hour clock, the same method can be used: 21.35 **la dudek-unua (kaj) tridek kvin**.

When we want to say *at* a certain time, we use **je**:

Mi renkontos vin **je** la sepa kaj kvarono.
I'll meet you at *quarter past seven.*

Note that **atm. (antaŭtagmeze)** = a.m.,
ptm. (posttagmeze) = p.m.

7 **Antaŭ** before an expression of time is often translated *ago*:

Mi vidis lin **antaŭ** du jaroj.
I saw him two years ago.

Antaŭ tri horoj mi estis en la butiko.
Three hours ago *I was in the shop.*

Similarly, **post** is often translated by *in*:

Li estos libera **post** du jaroj.
He will be free in *two years.*
Post du horoj mi estos en Londono.
In *two hours I shall be in London.*

PRAKTIKO 7.1 Traduku anglen:

Kioma horo estas? Ĉu estas la sepa? Ankoraŭ ne; estas nur la sesa (kaj) kvardek kvin. Kion vi faros hodiaŭ? Hodiaŭ matene mi iros en la urbon. Unue mi iros al la poŝto kaj aĉetos poŝtmarkojn. Poste mi iros al la stacidomo por informoj pri vagonaroj al Londono. Ĉu vi ne iris tien hieraŭ posttagmeze? Jes, sed mi forgesis pri la poŝtmarkoj. Hieraŭ matene mi renkontis malnovan amikon. Mi unue renkontis lin antaŭ tri jaroj en Francujo. Post tridek minutoj estos la deka horo. Do, nun estas la naŭa kaj duono.

PRAKTIKO 7.2 Traduku esperanten:

I am going to the station this morning. When will you come back? I shall not come back until twelve o'clock. I met Mr and Mrs Lang yesterday evening. Yesterday was the twenty-first of January. What will the date be tomorrow? I have been there three times. I was there four years ago. I shall be there again in three months. Where is the meeting-place of the Esperanto group? It is near the town hall. The group meets on Monday evening at half past seven. How long do the meetings last? Usually they last two hours.

PRAKTIKO 7.3 Kioma horo estas? Respondu Esperante (**Estas la . . .**)

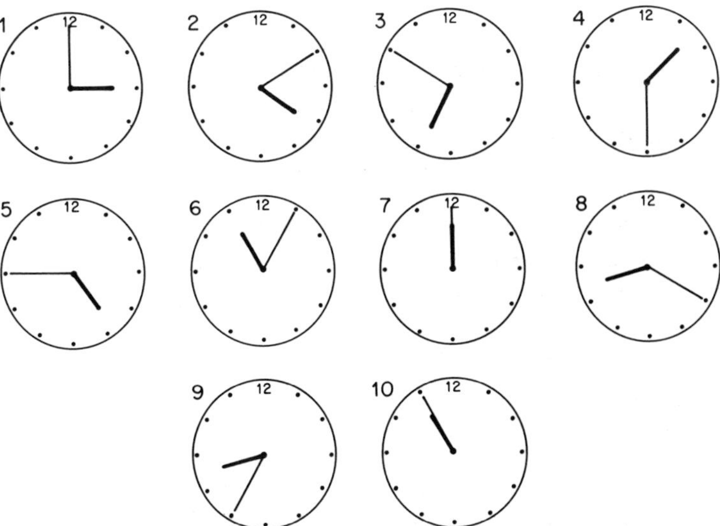

Quantity

8 *Da, de* and *el*

When we wish to indicate the quantity or number of something, the 'of' is translated by **da**:

tuno **da** karbo *a tonne* of *coal*	glaso **da** akvo *a glass* of *water*
dudeko **da** pilkoj *a score* of *balls*	kilogramo **da** teo *a kilogram* of *tea*

In other words, **da** is used if the previous word answers the question 'How much?' or 'How many?' Notice the difference between

taso **de** teo *a cup of tea (not coffee, etc.)*
and taso **da** teo *a cup(ful) of tea (not a pot)*

However, **da** is used only when we are talking about a quantity or number of something in general. If we are speaking of some particular substance, i.e., if it is defined by **la**, **tiu**, 'of' is translated by **de**:

kilogramo **de tiu** teo *a kilogram* of that *tea*	sako **de tiuj** pomoj *a bag* of those *apples*

Sometimes we use **da** when 'of' is not used in English:

pli **da** pano *more bread*

When we are talking about a few *out of* a known number, **el** may be used in place of **de**:

duo **el la** kukoj *a couple* of the *cakes*	tri **el tiuj** libroj *three* of those *books*

9 *Kiom, tiom*, etc.

Kiom (*kee-om*)? = *how much? how many?* **tiom** = *so much, so many*; **ĉiom** (hardly used) = *all the lot, all of*; **neniom** (*ne-**nee**-om*) = *none, none at all.*

Kiom mi ŝuldas? *How much do I owe?*	Tiom mi ŝuldas. *I owe so much.*

Kiom el la papero vi deziras?
How much of the paper do you want?

Mi deziras ĉiom. *or* Mi deziras neniom.
I want all of it. *I want none of it.*

When **tiom**, **kiom** are used together, they are translated by *as much as/as many as*:

Helpu lin **tiom**, **kiom** vi povas.
Help him as much as *you can.*

Mi havas **tiom**, **kiom** vi.
I have as many as *you.*

When we ask 'How much?/How many?' or express 'So much/So many' *of* a named article, the *of* is always included – even though it is omitted in English – and is translated by **da**:

Kiom da akvo vi havas?
How much water have you?

Ni vidis tiom da neĝo.
We saw so much snow.

Kiom da jaroj vi havas?
How old are you? (How many years have you?)

Ŝi havis tiom da infanoj.
She had so many children.

Expressions of time

10 *Kiam, tiam,* etc.

Kiam (*kee-am*) = *when*; **tiam** = *then (at that time)*; **ĉiam** = *always (all the time)*; **neniam** (*ne-**nee**-am*) = *never (at no time)*.

Kiam vi venos?
When will you come?

Tiam li loĝis en Londono.
Then (at that time) he lived in London.

Li ĉiam estas preta.
He is always ready.

Ŝi neniam parolas al mi.
She never speaks to me.

Suffix

11 *-aĵ-*

The suffix **-aĵ-** is used to denote some concrete thing made from, or possessing the quality of the root:

pakas *packs*	pak**aĵ**o *package, piece of luggage*
manĝas *eats*	manĝ**aĵ**o *food*
lano *wool*	lan**aĵ**oj *woollens*
konstruas *builds*	konstru**aĵ**o *a building*

In particular, it indicates the flesh of an animal used for food:

porko *a pig*	pork**aĵ**o *pork*
ŝafo *a sheep*	ŝaf**aĵ**o *mutton*
bovido *a calf*	bovid**aĵ**o *veal*
fiŝo *a fish*	fiŝ**aĵ**o *fish (as food)*

It often also gives the idea of 'a piece of':

muziko *music*	muzik**aĵ**o *piece of music*
nova *new*	nov**aĵ**o *piece of news*
teatro *theatre*	teatr**aĵ**o *a play, piece*
majstro *maestro*	majstr**aĵ**o *masterpiece*

Teksto

TELEVIDO-PROGRAMO

Por hodiaŭ vespere, lundo 1a marto.

4.30 **Por la Infanoj**
- 4.35 *La Aventuroj de Tom Sawyer*, 5.
- 4.55 Sub la Ĉielo, 2. Promenoj en la kamparo.
- 5.10 *La familio Jones.*

5.30 **La Mondo de Morgaŭ**
Charles Shaw prezentas: Ideojn el la mondo de la sciencoj.

6.00 **Horsignalo, Novaĵoj kaj Veterprognozo**

6.30 **La Supraj Dek**
Viaj preferataj pop-steloj kaj grupoj.

7.00 **Loka Gazeto**
Kio okazas en via regiono, kun John Russell.

7.30 **Varieteo**
kun akrobatoj, komikuloj, kantoj, dancoj, kaj aliaj.

8.30 **Studlokoj**
Numero 8 en nia serio: Kastelo en Francujo. (Vidu artikolon sube.)

9.00 **Horsignalo, Novaĵoj kaj Veterprognozo**

9.30 Filmo: *La Verda Fajro*, kun Derek Bourne kaj Francine Marmont.

11.30 **Rigardu la Stelojn**
La noktomeza ĉielo en marto.

12.00 Fermo

RADIO

4.30 Teatraĵo: *La 39 Ŝtupoj* de John Buchan, aranĝita por radio de Tim Rourke.

5.30 **Por via Plezuro**
Preferataj muzikaĵoj.

6.00 **Horsignalo, Novaĵoj kaj Veterprognozo**

6.30 **Tra la Mondo**
Rigardo al Aŭstrujo. Flora Lloyd raportas el Vieno.

7.00 **En via Ĝardeno**
Will Broome diskutas taskojn por marto.

7.30 **Muzika Horo**
Haydn kaj Beethoven.

8.30 **Hodiaŭ Vespere**
Aktualaj aferoj.

9.00 **Respondu tiun Demandon!**
Teamludo prezentata de George Denver.

9.45 **La Urbega Ĝangalo**
Alia kazo por la Londona polico.

10.30 **Dankon pro la Memoro**
Linda Green memoras Sir Alexander Fleming.

11.00 **Nokta Muziko**

12.00 **Fermo**

Artikolo:

STUDLOKO EN FRANCUJO

(*Televido:* 8.30 *ptm.*)

Hodiaŭ nia programo 'Studlokoj' vizitas, ne universitaton aŭ kolegion kiel kutime, sed kastelon en Francujo, kiu apartenas al la francaj esperantistoj. Do, ne surprize, oni studas tie ne la francan lingvon, sed Esperanton! Kutime okazas tri diversgradaj kursoj, el kiuj unu ĉiam estas por komencantoj, kun geknaboj kaj plenkreskuloi, aŭ geknaboj aparte. Tiuj kursoj ofte estas per rekta metodo (nur en Esperanto) ĉar diverslandanoj (*divers-land-anoj*) ofte vizitas la kastelon Grésillon.

Sed de tempo al tempo, dum la posttagmezoj, okazas kursoj pri diversaj aliaj aferoj, ekzemple: foto-rivelado aŭ farado de korboj, emajlitaj kupraĵoj, kolĉenoj per bidoj, sakoj el 'makramo', aŭ artaj desegnaĵoj per streĉitaj fadenoj ĉirkaŭ najletoj. Tiaj kursoj, kompreneble, dependas de la ĉeesto de kapabla respondeculo. Pro tiuj kursoj, la kastelo nomiĝas 'Esperantista Kulturdomo'.

La kastelo Grésillon situas en la bela valo de la rivero Loire, kaj staras en 17-hektara parko kun lageto, insuleto, banejo, infanludejo kaj ludkampoj. Esperantistoj vizitas ĝin el la tuta mondo, do oni ekkonas tie esperantistojn el multaj landoj, kaj multaj el ili vizitas la kastelon, aŭ kulturdomon, jaro post jaro. Kiam ili ne studas, ili vizitas pitoreskajn vilaĝojn, belajn urbojn, zoologian ĝardenon, aŭ la famajn kastelojn de la Loire-valo. Oni ankaŭ naĝas en la naĝejo, fiŝkaptas en la rivero, aŭ ludas tenison, tablotenison, retpilkon, kartludojn, ŝakon, k.t.p.*

Nu, rigardu la filmon hodiaŭ vespere, kaj vidu ĉi tiun vere internacian studlokon!

* **k.t.p.: kaj tiel plu** *and so on.*

Note the pronunciation of **radio** (*ra*-**dee**-*oh*), **teamo** (*teh*-**ah**-*mo*), **zoologia** (*zo*-*oh*-*log*-**ee**-*a*).

PRAKTIKO 7.4 Traduku anglen:

Kioma horo estas? Estas la sepa kaj duono. Post unu horo kaj duono estos la naŭa horo. Antaŭ du horoj li estis en la lernejo. Post du monatoj mi estos en Svedujo. Ĉu plaĉas al vi teo? Jes, ĝi tre plaĉas al mi. Kiom da kafo vi deziras? Unu kilogramon, mi petas. Hieraŭ estis la unua de majo. Kiam mi vizitu vin? Venu lundon aŭ mardon; mi estos libera je la sepa. Hieraŭ mi ricevis novaĵon de mia amiko en Francujo. Ĉu vi preferas porkaĵon aŭ bovidaĵon? Ĉu vi aŭdis la novaĵojn hodiaŭ matene? Je kioma horo ni vidos la filmon *La Verda Fajro?* Ni vidos ĝin je la naŭa kaj duono, post la novaĵoj. La programo 'Studlokoj' plaĉas al mi. Kutime ĝi estas pri universitatoj kaj kolegioj, sed hodiaŭ ĝi estos pri kastelo en Francujo.

PRAKTIKO 7.5 Traduku esperanten:

At what time do you hear the weather forecast? When did you hear the news? Will you come on Monday or Friday? We heard an orchestra at three o'clock. We will come at half past four or quarter to five. What is half of six? What is a quarter of a dozen? Three days ago I saw a play. In seven weeks I shall receive permission. How many clocks have you got? We heard an hour of music on records.

PRAKTIKO 7.6 Respondu en Esperanto:

(All questions refer to the text in this unit. Answer using complete sentences in Esperanto, writing all the times in words.)

1 Je kioma horo estas la novaĵoj je la televido?
2 Kiam oni diskutos ideojn el la mondo de la sciencoj?
3 En kiu programo oni vidos pop-grupojn?

4 Kiu prezentos la programon 'Loka Gazeto'?
5 Kio okazos je la televido je la naŭa kaj duono?
6 Kiu estos la stelino en tio?
7 Kiun teatraĵon ni aŭdos je la kvara kaj duono?
8 El kiu urbo raportos Flora Lloyd je la sesa kaj duono?
9 Je kioma horo ni aŭdos pri 'La Urbega Ĝangalo'?
10 Al kiuj apartenas la kastelo de Grésillon?

Dialogo

Diskuto pri veturo

La familio Lang diskutas la veturon al Grésillon.

Andreo Kiel ni veturos al Grezijono, Paĉjo?

Rikardo Ho, mi opinias, ke estos plej bone se ni iros aŭtomobile. Kun kvar personoj en aŭtomobilo, kostos malpli ol per vagonaro, kaj ni vidos la pejzaĝon survoje (sur la vojo).

Klara Jes, tio estas bona ideo, se ni ne veturos tro longe dum unu tago.

Rikardo Ho, tio ne necesos. Ni rigardu la mapon . . . Nu, se ni ekiros, ni diru, sabaton fru-matene, ni estos en Dovro (*Dover*) tagmeze.

Klara Kaj kiam ni iros sur la ŝipon?

Rikardo Certe estos ŝipo kiu ekiros al Bulonjo (*Boulogne*) ĉirkaŭ la mezo de la tago, kaj ni manĝos surŝipe . . .

Andreo Ho, bone!

Rikardo Ni rigardu la mapon denove. Jen Bulonjo! Sabaton posttagmeze ni veturos de tie ĝis Abbeville, kaj poste sur tiu vojo en la direkto al Rouen, sed ni tranoktos survoje, eble tie, en Neufchâtel, kaj dimanĉon matene ni denove ekveturos.

Klara Kiom da mejloj estas de Bulonjo ĝis Neufchâtel?

Rikardo Nu . . . mi kalkulu! . . . inter cent kaj cent dek.

Klara Bone. Tio ne estas tro longa veturo. Kaj kie estas Grezijono?

Rikardo Mi vidu; Jen Bauĝé, la apuda urbeto. Rigardu la vojon. Neufchâtel estas tie. Ni iros tra Rouen; poste laŭ tiu ĉi vojo ĝis Alençon. Poste al le Mans, La Flèche kaj ĝis Bauĝé.

Andreo Cu ni vidos la aŭtomobilan vetkurejon de Le Mans, kie okazas la dudek-kvar-hora vetkuro?
Rikardo Jes, mi opinias, ke ni veturos ĉirkaŭ kvin mejlojn laŭ la vetkurejo!
Andreo Ho, bonege!
Klara Kaj kiom da mejloj estos de Neufchâtel ĝis Grezijono?
Rikardo Ho, ĉirkaŭ cent naŭdek.
Klara Do, ni certe estos en Grezijono dum la posttagmezo!
Rikardo Jes, certe.
Andreo Kaj kion ni faros tiam?
Rikardo Unue ni trovos la dormĉambron, kaj poste ni ĉirkaŭrigardos la lokon!

Demandoj

1 Kiel la familio veturos de Newtown ĝis Grezijono?
2 Kiam ili ekveturos?
3 Kie ili suriros (= iros sur) la ŝipon?
4 Kie ili manĝos?
5 En kiu urbo ili eble tranoktos?
6 Kiom da mejloj estas de Bulonjo ĝis Neufchâtel?
7 Kaj kiom de Neufchâtel ĝis Grezijono?
8 Kio okazas en Le Mans ĉiun jaron? (ĉiujare)
9 Ĉu la familio vidos la vetkurejon?
10 Kion ili faros kiam ili alvenos (*arrive*) en Grezijono?

aktuala *topical, up-to-date*
akvo *water* (cf. *aquatic*)
ankoraŭ *still (continuing)*;
ankoraŭ ne *not yet (still not)*
aparta *separate*
aŭdas *hears*
bidoj *beads*
certe *certainly*
ĉeestas (ĉe-estas) *is present (at)*
da (see note **8**)
dato *date*
desegnas *draws*; **desegnaĵo** *a drawing*
do *so, therefore, then*
eble *possibly, perhaps*
ekiras *sets off, sets out*
ekkonas *gets to know, makes the acquaintance of*
emajlita *enamelled*
fadeno *thread*
farado *doing, making*
fermas *closes*; **fermo** *close*
fotorivelado *photo-developing*
ĝangalo *jungle*
hektaro *hectare (nearly 2½ acres)*
horo *hour*
horloĝo *clock, watch*
inter *between, among*;
internacia *international*
kampo *field*;
kamparo *country(side)*
kantas *sings*; **kanto** *song*
karto *card*; **kartludo** *card-game*
kazo *case (medical, law, etc.)*
kolo *neck*; **kolĉeno** *necklace*
komencanto (pron. **ko-ment-*san*-to**) *beginner*
korbo *basket*
kreskas *grows*
kulturdomo *cultural centre*
kupro *copper*
kurso *course (of lessons)*
laŭ *along, according to*
makramo *macramé*
matenmanĝo *breakfast*
mejlo *mile*
memoras *remembers*;
memoro *memory*
miras *is amazed, wonders*
najlo *nail*
necesas *is necessary*
noktomezo *midnight*
nomiĝas *is called*
opinias *thinks (has an opinion)*
pano *bread*
pejzaĝo *landscape, scenery*
pitoreska *picturesque*
plej *most*
plenkreskulo *grown-up*
pli *more*
preferas *prefers*;
preferata *favourite*
prezentas *presents, introduces*
respondeca *responsible*
retpilko *netball*
sako *bag*
stelo *star*
streĉita *stretched, taut*
studas *studies*
supro *top*; **supra** *top(most), highest*
ŝako *chess*
ŝtupo *a step*; **ŝtuparo** *flight of stairs*
teamo *team*
tranoktas *spends the night*
tro *too, too much*
vagono *(railway) coach, carriage*;
vagonaro (= trajno) *train*
valo *valley*
varieteo *variety show*
verda *green*
vetkuro *race*; **vetkurejo** *race-track*
vivo *life*; **vivas** *lives*

Esprimoj:
dependas de *depends on*
jaro post jaro *year after year*
rekta metodo *direct method (of language teaching)*

8 Notoj pri la naturo

Comparison

1 All adjectives of quality each have three forms which are sometimes called *degrees*. As the different degrees are compared, this is called the 'comparison of adjectives.' The three degrees are: the positive degree, the comparative degree, and the superlative degree.

Adding the suffixes '-er' and '-est' is the usual way in English to compare adjectives:

Positive	*Comparative*	*Superlative*
tall	taller	tallest

However, for long words we use 'more' and 'most':

beautiful	more beautiful	most beautiful

A few adjectives have quite irregular forms:

good	better	best

In Esperanto, there is one form to cover all three:

alta	**pli** alta	**plej** alta
bela	**pli** bela	**plej** bela
bona	**pli** bona	**plej** bona

Mi havas **pli** bonan hundon.
I have a better dog.

Everest estas la **plej** alta monto en la mondo.
Everest is the highest mountain in the world.

Ŝi estas mia **plej** bela amikino.
She is my most beautiful friend.

Li estas mia **plej** bona amiko.
He is my best friend.

2 **Ol** is used with **pli** to translate 'than':

Li estas **pli** alta **ol** vi.
He is taller than you.

Ŝi estas **pli** bela **ol** ŝia patrino.
She is more beautiful than her mother.

Mia hundo estas **pli** bona **ol** la via.
My dog is better than yours.

El is used with **plej** to translate 'of' when it means 'out of':

Li estas la **plej** alta **el** la fratoj.
He is the tallest of the brothers.

Mi havas tri **el** la **plej** belaj.
I have three of the most beautiful.

Jen la **plej** bona **el** miaj libroj.
Here is the best (one) of my books.

3 Adverbs are compared in the same way:

alte *highly*	pli alte *more highly*	plej alte *most highly*
bele *beautifully*	pli bele *more beautifully*	plej bele *most beautifully*
bone *well*	pli bone *better*	plej bone *best*

Ŝi kantas plej bele.
She sings most beautifully.

Li faris ĝin **pli** bone **ol** vi.
He did it better than *you.*

Word order

4 The normal order of the words in Esperanto is similar to that in English: subject–verb–object. However, in order to throw special emphasis on the object or some other part of the sentence, the word order is often changed:

La edzon mi ne konas, sed mi ofte vidas lian edzinon.
The husband I do not know, but I often see his wife (= I do not know the husband).

Al infanoj mi ne donas monon.
To children I do not give money (= I do not give money to children).

Al ni en Britujo mankas leonoj.
To us in Britain are lacking lions (= We do not have lions in Britain).

5 Note also that a sentence never ends with a preposition, as it often does in English:

Kun kiu vi korespondas?
With whom do you correspond? (Who do you correspond with?*)*
Pri kio vi parolas?
About what are you speaking? (What are you speaking about?*)*

PRAKTIKO 8.1 Traduku anglen:

Li estas pli afabla ol ŝi. Mi havas pli bonan hundon ol vi. Mia frato estas pli alta ol mi. Li estas la plej alta el la familio. Andreo iras al la lito pli frue ol Maria. Tigro estas pli danĝera ol kato. Tiu libro estas plej interesa. Stefano estas la plej inteligenta el tiuj tri knaboj. Vagonaro veturas pli rapide ol aŭtobuso. Mi esperas, ke vi estas pli sana nun. Kiu estas la plej rekta vojo al la urbocentro? Ŝi kantas la plej bele el ĉiuj la knabinoj. Kun kiu vi vizitis Londonon? En kiu ĉambro vi manĝas? Mi ne scias pri kio vi parolas.

PRAKTIKO 8.2 Match the answers to these questions:

1	Kiu estas la plej granda urbo en Anglujo?	(*a*)	Ne, ŝi ne estas pli bela.
2	Kun kiu ŝi venis al via domo?	(*b*)	Ne, mi dormas en mia dormoĉambro.
3	Kiu estas la plej granda knabo el via familio?	(*c*)	Jes, ŝi estas pli juna ol mi.
4	En kiu ĉambro vi dormas?	(*d*)	Londono estas la plej granda urbo en Anglujo.
5	Ĉu via frato estas pli alta ol vi?	(*e*)	Mi dormas en mia dormoĉambro.
6	Ĉu vi dormas en la kuirejo?	(*f*)	Ŝi venis kun s-ro Smith.
7	Sur kio vi sidis dum vi parolis?	(*g*)	Mia fratino estas pli juna ol mi.
8	Ĉu via fratino estas pli bela ol vi?	(*h*)	Mi sidis sur seĝo.
9	Ĉu via fratino estas pli juna ol vi?	(*i*)	Mia frato estas la plej granda knabo.
10	Kiu estas pli juna ol vi?	(*j*)	Ne, mi estas pli alta ol li.

PRAKTIKO 8.3 Traduku esperanten:

Our house is smaller than yours. That girl is the most beautiful in the class, but she is not the happiest. I am stronger than my brother because he is younger than I. That street is wider than this one. It is the widest street in the town. Which is the most direct (straightest) way to the town hall? Andrew was ill yesterday, but he is better now. Who was the most famous English poet? What are you talking about? Which town are you going to? Who did you come with? I came with my younger brother.

6 In negative sentences, **ne** usually stands before the verb, but it may be placed before another word for emphasis:

Mi ne skribis leteron.
I did not write a letter.

Ne mi skribis leteron.
It was not I who wrote a letter (but someone else).

Mi skribis ne leteron, sed poŝtkarton.
It wasn't a letter I wrote, but a postcard.

Suffixes

7 ***-ad-***
The suffix **-ad-** is used to denote the continuation or constant repetition of an action. In the noun form it equals the English '-ing':

pafas *shoots* — paf**ad**o *a firing (fusillade)*
legas *reads* — leg**ad**o *reading (the process)*
iras *goes* — ir**ad**as *keeps on going*
kantas *sings* — kant**ad**o *singing (the act)*
uzas *uses* — uz**ad**o *usage*
dancas *dances* — danc**ad**o *dancing*

It is also used with the names of some instruments to name the action of that tool:

martelo *a hammer* — martel**ad**o *hammering*
broso *a brush* — bros**ad**o *brushing*
krono *a crown* — kron**ad**o *crowning*

8 ***-ar-***
The suffix **-ar-** is used to denote a collection or assemblage of the persons or objects indicated by the root:

kampo *field*	kamp**aro** *countryside*
monto *mountain*	mont**aro** *range of mountains*
arbo *tree*	arb**aro** *a wood*
ŝafo *a sheep*	ŝaf**aro** *flock of sheep*
homo *a man (human being)*	hom**aro** *mankind*
hirundo *a swallow*	hirund**aro** *a flight of swallows*
besto *animal*	best**aro** *fauna, the animal kingdom*
birdo *bird*	bird**aro** *flock of birds*

9 *-ebl-*

The suffix **-ebl-** is used to denote possibility (like '-able', '-ible'):

komprenas *understand*	kompren**ebl**a *understandable*
movas *move*	mov**ebl**a *movable*
legas *read*	leg**ebl**a *legible*
vidas *see*	vid**ebl**a *visible*
sentas *feel, have a sense of*	sent**ebl**a *perceptible*
kredas *believe*	kred**ebl**a *credible, probable*
kalkulas *calculate*	nekalkul**ebl**a *incalculable*

10 *-ind-*

The suffix **-ind-** is used to denote worthiness, merit, deserving of something:

amas *love*	am**ind**a *lovable*
faras *do*	far**ind**a *worth doing*
laŭdas *praise*	laŭd**ind**a *praiseworthy*
miras *marvel, be surprised at*	mir**ind**a *marvellous, wonderful, astonishing*
rimarkas *notice, remark, observe*	rimark**ind**a *remarkable, worth noticing*
vizitas *visits*	vizit**ind**a *worth visiting*

11 *-id-*

The suffix **-id-** is used to denote the young or offspring of:

ŝafo *sheep*	ŝaf**id**o *lamb*
koko *cock*	kok**id**o *chicken*
kato *cat*	kat**id**o *kitten*
hundo *dog*	hund**id**o *puppy*
bovo *ox*	bov**id**o *calf*
leono *lion*	leon**id**o *lion-cub*

Teksto

NOTOJ PRI LA NATURO

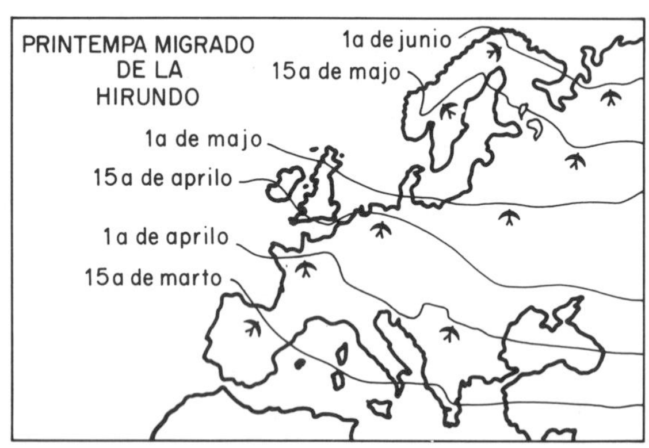

Pri la Birdmigrado

La unuaj krokusoj jam estas videblaj; sur la kampoj, ŝafidoj kaj bovidoj saltas. Printempo estas sentebla en la aero. Baldaŭ ni atendas la revenon de la migraj birdoj.

La migrado estas plej mirinda fenomeno, kiun ni ankoraŭ ne perfekte komprenas. Ni pensu pri la *hirundo.* Kredeble vi scias, ke la hirundaro flugas en aŭtuno al Afriko; sed ĉu vi scias, al kiu parto de Afriko? Ne al la nordo, sed al *Suda* Afriko, al la ĉirkaŭaĵo de Johannesburg!

Tiu birdeto, do, flugas 6500 mejlojn en la aŭtuno, kaj denove 6500 mejlojn en la frua printempo! Sed eĉ pli kurioza estas la reveno al Eŭropo. Ili revenas ne nur al la sama lando, ne nur al la sama parto de la lando, sed al la sama farmdomo en la sama vilaĝo, kie ili vivis dum la antaŭa somero! Kaj ili venas tre akurate. La mapo montras kiel ili, tago post tago, flugas trans Eŭropon al Britujo kaj Skandinavio.

Alia rimarkinda fakto estas, ke la pli junaj birdoj ofte flugas *antaŭ* la pli aĝaj – sur vojo, do, kiun ili tute ne konas, kaj al celo 6500 mejlojn for.

Eble pli mirinda estas marbirdo nomata Arkta Marhirundo, kvankam ĝi vere ne estas hirundo (anglalingve: *Arctic Tern*), kiu vivas dum nia somero en la Arkta regiono, kaj dum nia vintro en la Antarkto! Tiu birdo, do, preskaŭ neniam konas la nokton; por ĝi, preskaŭ ĉiam estas tage.

Pri Ŝtataj Parkoj

La ideo pri ŝtatparkoj venas al ni el Usono. La plej rimarkinda el la pioniraj ŝtatparkoj estas tiu de Yellowstone (= 'Flava Ŝtono') en Wyoming, kiu estas publika parkego jam de 1872, kaj enhavas pli ol 3800 kvadratmejlojn. (Tio signifas, ke ĝi estas duone tiel granda, kiel la tuta lando Kimrujo.) Ĝi estas fama pro belegaj pejzaĝoj kaj pro varmegaj akvofontoj.

En multaj landoj nun ekzistas similaj naturparkoj, en kiuj la bestaro kaj birdaro ricevas protektadon. Ekzemple, en Sud-Afriko la grandega ŝtatparko Kruger, tra kiu homoj veturas laŭ vojoj, apud kiuj ludas leonoj, ĝirafoj kaj elefantoj.

Al ni en Britujo mankas leonoj, escepte de en zoologiaj ĝardenoj kaj tiel-nomataj 'safari-parkoj', sed ankaŭ ni havas jam niajn ŝtatparkojn – danke al longa laborado kaj klopodado de multaj entuziasmuloj. Du el la plej grandaj estas tiuj de Norda Kimrujo kaj de la Laga Regiono. Tiuj parkoj donas, kaj ĉiam donos, nekalkuleblan plezuron al la brita popolo kaj al eksterlandanoj kiuj vizitas nin. Ili konservos por ĉiam la plej belajn regionojn de nia lando; en ili ni ĉiam libere studos la naturon, kaj ĝuos ripozon en belegaj ĉirkaŭaĵoj.

Vidaĵo en la ŝtatparko de Nord-Kimrujo: ŝafaro, kun ŝafidoj, antaŭ la alta montaro Snowdonia

PRAKTIKO 8.4 Traduku anglen:

Ĉu bovido estas pli granda ol ŝafido? Oni vidas pli da ŝafidoj kaj bovidoj dum la printempo ol dum la aŭtuno. Oni ofte vidas florojn en la kamparo dum somero. En niaj ŝtatparkoj oni ne vidas leonojn, ĝirafojn kaj elefantojn. Juna leono estas leonido. Kiuj floroj estas videblaj frue en printempo? Kio estas rimarkinda pri la migrado de la hirundoj? En aŭtuno la hirundoj flugas de Britujo ĝis suda Afriko. Ĉu plaĉas al vi promeni tra arbaro? Jes, arbaroj ofte estas vizitindaj. La dancado ne tre plaĉas al mi; mi preferas la kantadon. La ŝtatparkoj estas ĉiam vidindaj. Ili donas nekalkuleblan plezuron al ĉiuj, kiuj vizitas ilin. Niaj ŝtatparkoj donas plezuron ne nur al la brita popolo, sed ankaŭ al tiuj eksterlandanoj, kiuj vizitas nin. La uzado de Esperanto estas pli facila ol la uzado de aliaj lingvoj.

PRAKTIKO 8.5 Traduku esperanten:

What do you know about bird migration?[1] Which is taller, a puppy or a kitten? You don't see herds of elephants in this country. Flocks of swallows migrate in autumn. The national park is a praiseworthy idea. What is noteworthy about the national park in Wyoming? Is the Kruger national park[2] the biggest in the world? I don't know, but I know that two of the biggest in Britain are those of North Wales and the Lake District. The arctic tern migrates from the Arctic to the Antarctic.

PRAKTIKO 8.6 Vera aŭ malvera?

1 Oni jam plene komprenas le fenomenon de la birdmigrado.
2 La hirundo migras printempe de Suda Afriko.
3 La pli junaj birdoj ofte flugas antaŭ la pli aĝaj.
4 La ŝtatparko de Yellowstone estas publika parkego jam de la jaro mil okcent sesdek du.
5 Ĝi estas tiel granda kiel la tuta lando Kimrujo.
6 Ĝi estas fama pro varmegaj akvofontoj.
7 En malmultaj landoj ekzistas similaj naturparkoj.
8 La Nord-Kimruja ŝtatparko estas unu el la plej grandaj en Britujo.
9 Ĝi estas tiel granda kiel la ŝtatparko de Yellowstone.
10 La ŝtatparkoj konservas por ĉiam la plej belajn regionojn de nia lando.

[1] **la birdmigrado** *bird migration*; **la kantado** *singing*; **la dancado** *dancing*. The word **la** is often used (but not translated) when a noun is used in a general sense: **Mi amas la hundojn** *I like dogs.*

[2] **La ŝtatparko Kruger.** 'Kruger' is the name of the park.

Dialogo

En la Kastelo Grésillon (Grezijono)

La matenon post la alveno al Grésillon. La familio jam matenmanĝis.

Rikardo Nu, ni alvenis nur hieraŭ posttagmeze, kaj mi sentas, ke mi estas ĉi tie* jam dum kelkaj tagoj!

Klara Jes, ni jam konas tiom da homoj, ke mi sentas min kvazaŭ hejme! Nu, kion ni faru hodiaŭ?

Rikardo Unue, estos bone se ni decidos pri kursoj . . .

Andreo Mi jam decidis!

Rikardo Ho, jes? Kaj kion vi decidis?

Andreo Nu, miaj novaj amikoj, Petro el Francujo kaj Fulvio el Italujo, ĉeestos la Esperanto-kurson por geknaboj, do ankaŭ mi iros al tiu!

Klara Bona ideo! Kaj ĉu ankaŭ vi tion faros, Maria?

Maria Jes, kun mia germana amikino Trudi!

Rikardo Niaj infanoj jam havas internacian amikaron, ĉu ne?

Klara Jes; tre bona afero! Mi provos la kurson pri makramo. Tiuj ekzemploj, kiujn la instruistino alportis, estis tre belaj.

Rikardo Se la instruisto pri foto-rivelado venos, mi aniĝos al tiu kurso, sed mi ne scios tion ĝis hodiaŭ vespere. Se li ne alvenos, mi venos kun vi al la makramo!

(Franco, Robert Chabot, alproksimiĝas al ili.)

Roberto Bonan matenon, geamikoj! Mi estas Roberto Chabot. Vi estas el Anglujo, ĉu ne?

Rikardo Jes, Rikardo kaj Klara Lang, el Newtown, kaj niaj gefiloj, Andreo kaj Maria. Kaj laŭ via nomo vi estas franco.

Roberto Vi pravas. Se vi ankoraŭ ne decidis pri io alia, ĉu plaĉos al vi promeno tra la arbaro ĝis Baugé?

Klara Volonte. Estas nia unua mateno ĉi tie, kaj ĝis nun ni iris nenien!

Andreo Mi restos tie ĉi se vi permesas, Panjo, kaj ludos kun miaj du amikoj.

Maria Ankaŭ mi volonte ludos kun Trudi!

Klara Nu, mi kredas, ke vi estos sekuraj ĉi tie . . .

Roberto Certe ili estos, inter tiom da geamikoj!

Klara Do, bone! Ni ekiru, Roberto!

* In a phrase such as 'I have been here for a week', implying 'and still am', Esperanto uses the present tense: *I have been learning Esperanto for six months.* **Mi lern**as **Esperanton de ses monatoj.**

(Post aniĝo al la kursoj, Rikardo kaj Klara promenas kun Roberto tra la arbaro al Baugé, kaj post kafo tie, vizitas muzeon en la Kastelo de Baugé. Kiam ili estas pretaj eliri, la kuratoro parolas al ili.)

Kuratoro Nu, gesinjoroj, mi esperas, ke vi trovis vian viziton interesa?
Rikardo Jes, ĝi estis interesega, sinjoro, dankon!
Kuratoro Mi tre ĝojas pri tio. Kaj nun, gesinjoroj, se vin interesos alia vizito dum vi estas en nia urbeto, mi rekomendas al vi la farmaciejon.
Klara La farmaciejon? Kial ni vizitu farmaciejon? Ni ne bezonas medikamentojn!
Kuratoro Mi esperas, ke ne, sinjorino. Sed eĉ se jes, oni ne vendos ilin tie!
Rikardo Ĉu vere? Kia farmaciejo estas tiu, kie oni ne vendas medikamentojn?
Kuratoro Ĝi estas farmaciejo de la dek-sepa jarcento, kiun oni konservas en ĝia tiama stato!
Klara Ho, kiel interese! Ni devas vidi tion!
Roberto Do, ni vidos ĝin kune. Mi jam konas ĝin; ĝi situas en la malsanulejo, ĉu ne?
Kuratoro Vi pravas, sinjoro. Do, gesinjoroj, bonan viziton, kaj ĝis revido!
Ĉiuj Ĝis revido, sinjoro, kaj dankon!

Reminder! Did you remember to pronounce **franco** as *frant-so*?

Demandoj

1 Kial Klara sentas sin kvazaŭ hejme?
2 Kial Andreo ĉeestos la kurson por geknaboj?
3 El kiuj landoj venas la geamikoj de Andreo kaj Maria?
4 Kial Klara provos la kurson pri makramo?
5 Kiuj akompanas Roberton al Baugé?
6 Tra kio ili promenas?
7 Kion ili unue vizitas tie?
8 Kiu rekomendas viziton al la farmaciejo?
9 Kial la farmaciejo ne vendas medikamentojn?
10 Kiu jam vizitis ĝin?

aĝo *age*
akompanas *accompanies*
alportas *brings*
alproksimiĝas *approaches*
alvenas *arrives*
aniĝas *joins*
Antarkto *the Antarctic*
Arkto *the Arctic*
bezonas *needs;* **bezono** *need*
celo *aim, goal, destination*
ĉe-estas *is at, attends*
ĉirkaŭaĵoj *surroundings*
danko *gratitude*; **dankon!** *thank you!*; **danke al** *thanks to*
enhavas *has in, contains*
escepte de *except*
farmaciejo *pharmacy*
farmdomo *farmhouse*
flava *yellow*
fonto *spring, source*
hirundo *swallow*
instruisto *teacher*
jarcento *century*
klopodas *takes steps (to), endeavours*
konservas *preserves*
kredas *believes*
kuratoro *curator, guardian*
kurioza *curious, quaint*
kvadratmejlo *square mile*
kvazaŭ *as if*
makramo *macramé (knotted thread-work)*
migras *migrates*
ol *than*
permesas *permits, allows*
pravas *is right (in an opinion)*
provas *tries out, tries on*
sekura *safe, secure*
signifas *means* (**Kion signifas. . .?** *What does. . . mean?*)
ŝtatparko *state/national park*
tra *through*
tute *quite*; **ne tute** *not quite*; **tute ne** *not at all*
vendas *sells*
vivas *lives, is alive*
volonte *willingly, would like to*

Esprimoj:
ĉu ne? *haven't they? isn't it? don't we?* etc.
ĉu vere? *really?*
devas vidi *must see*
mi esperas, ke jes *I hope so*
pli aĝa *older*
se jes *if so*; **se ne** *if not*
tago post tago *day after day*
tiel-nomata (t.n.) *so-called*

9 Hejma paĝo

The infinitive

1 When we merely wish to *name* an action or state – that is, without reference to person or time – we use a form of the verb called the infinitive. In English, we usually – but not always –use 'to' to indicate the infinitive, but in Esperanto, as in French and other languages, it is shown by a distinctive ending. In French, there are four such endings, but in Esperanto *all* infinitives end in **-i**:

esti *to be*	**paroli** *to speak*
manĝi *to eat*	**sidi** *to sit*
meti *to put*	**stari** *to stand*

Note: Do not confuse this 'to' with **al**, which expresses *direction* only. Do not say **al manĝi** for 'to eat'.

2 In Esperanto, as in English, there are a few verbs which need another verb in the infinitive to complete their meaning. For example, we do not say: 'I must something', 'I can something', or 'I am able something', but: 'I must *do* something', 'I can *do* something', 'I am able *to do* something'.

This 'do' – with or without 'to' – is the infinitive, and is translated by **fari**:

Mi devas **fari** ion.
I must (am obliged to) do *something.*
Mi povas **fari** ion.
I can (am able to) do *something.*

It is worth remembering that if two verbs (other than participles, dealt with in Unit 11) come together, the second one must be infinitive (i.e. must end in **-i**).

Prepositions with an infinitive

3 The ending '-ing' in English is very often equal to an infinitive; so a preposition before an infinitive in Esperanto is usually translated by the corresponding preposition in English plus a word ending in '-ing':

Anstataŭ Anstataŭ **ripozi**, li laboris.
Instead of *Instead of resting, he worked.*

Anstataŭ **iri** hejmen, mi iris en kafejon.
Instead of going home, I went into a café.

Krom Li vizitis min krom **viziti** vin.
Besides *He visited me besides visiting you.*

Krom **kanti** li volis fajfi.
Besides singing he wanted to whistle.

Por Mi ne havas la tempon por **ludi**.
For *I haven't the time to play (for playing).*

Oni bezonas horojn por **prepari** manĝon.
You need (one needs) hours to prepare a meal.

Mi iras al la butikoj por **aĉeti** viandon kaj terpomojn.
I'm going to the shops to buy meat and potatoes.

Note: **Por** with an infinitive means *in order to*, and is not usually translated.

Sen Li foriris sen **diri** ion.
Without *He went away without saying anything.*

Mi ne povas movi la tablon sen **fari** bruon.
I cannot move the table without making a noise.

The ending *-us*

4 The endings **-as**, **-is**, **-os** are used to express a fact:

Mi est**as** viro. *I am a man.*
Mi don**is** la monon al li. *I gave the money to him.*
Ni atend**os** vin. *We shall wait for you.*

There are three endings, because when we speak of facts we are interested in the time of the action or state.

When, however, we express a supposition – a mere thought or a flight of fancy – we use the one ending **-us** because, as the action or state is imaginary anyway, time does not usually enter into it:

Ho, se mi nur est**us** riĉa!
Oh, if only I were rich! (I am not, so it is just fancy)

Ho, se mi nur hav**us** la propran domon!
Oh, if only I had my own house! (but I haven't)

(See note **7**.)

5 **-us** is used particularly in conditional sentences, i.e. where the fulfilment of an action or state is dependent on another supposed, imagined condition:

Se mi est**us** riĉa, mi loĝ**us** en Kanado.
If I were rich, I should live in Canada.

Se vi lav**us** ĝin, ĝi est**us** pura.
If you washed it, it would be clean.

6 As in English, it is also used as a polite form to express a wish or request, as if it were just a passing thought:

Mi volus aĉeti tiun jupon!
I should like to buy that skirt!
Ĉu mi povus havi tason da teo?
Could I have a cup of tea?
Ĉu vi povus prunti al mi du pundojn?
Could you lend me two pounds?

Word order with *nur* and *ankaŭ*

7 It should be noticed that the position of these two words makes a difference to the meaning of a sentence. Consider the basic statement:

Mi manĝas ovojn dimanĉon matene.
I eat eggs on Sunday morning.

If we now put **nur** before each word in turn, we get five different meanings, as follows:

(*i*) **Nur mi** manĝas ovojn dimanĉon matene.
Only I (and nobody else) eat eggs on Sunday morning.
(*ii*) Mi **nur manĝas** ovojn dimanĉon matene.
I only eat eggs (but don't cook them etc.) on Sunday morning.
(*iii*) Mi manĝas **nur ovojn** dimanĉon matene.
I eat only eggs (and nothing else) on Sunday morning.
(*iv*) Mi manĝas ovojn **nur dimanĉon** matene.
I eat them only on Sunday (and on no other day) morning.
(*v*) Mi manĝas ovojn dimanĉon **nur matene**.
I eat eggs on Sunday, but only in the morning.

The position of **ankaŭ** similarly affects the meaning:

Maria vidos Andreon morgaŭ matene.
Mary will see Andrew tomorrow morning.

(*i*) **Ankaŭ Maria** vidos Andreon morgaŭ matene.
Mary, too, (as well as her father) will see Andrew tomorrow morning.

(*ii*) Maria **ankaŭ vidos** Andreon morgaŭ matene.
Mary will see Andrew (as well as hearing him) tomorrow morning.

(*iii*) Maria vidos **ankaŭ Andreon** morgaŭ matene.
Mary will see Andrew (as well as seeing others) tomorrow morning.

(*iv*) Maria vidos Andreon **ankaŭ morgaŭ** matene.
She will see Andrew tomorrow, too, (as well as today).

(*v*) Maria vidos Andreon morgaŭ **ankaŭ matene**.
She will see Andrew tomorrow, in the morning (as well as in the afternoon).

PRAKTIKO 9.1 Traduku anglen:

Mi devas iri al la urbo hodiaŭ matene. Ĉu vi deziras aĉeti kolĉenon? Fermu la pordon, mi petas. Se mi havus aŭtomobilon, mi povus veturi pli rapide ol per biciklo. Dankon pro via letero. Mi ne havas tempon nun por respondi plene, sed mi baldaŭ povos tion fari. Anstataŭ labori en la ĝardeno, li sidas kaj legas. Tiu jupo estas tre bela, ĉu ne? Mi volus aĉeti ĝin, se mi havus la monon. Ankaŭ al mi ĝi plaĉas. Se mi estus riĉa, mi aĉetus tiom da aferoj! Jes, se oni estus riĉa, oni povus aĉeti multajn aferojn sen pensi pri la kosto, ĉu ne?

PRAKTIKO 9.2 Traduku esperanten:

Instead of beginning yesterday, he waited until today. I'll see you this afternoon (in order) to help you. If I were you, I would go without waiting for him. Besides learning Esperanto she is also learning French (*Careful! Where does* **ankaŭ** *go?*). Could you help me (to) carry this, please? If I had time I could walk (**piediri**) to your house. I only go to (the) church on Sundays (*i.e. not on other days*). I went to the cinema on Saturday, and Andrew came too. I like to go to a cinema when I am free.

PRAKTIKO 9.3
Add **nur**, and then **ankaŭ**, in five different positions in the following sentence, and indicate the meaning of each, as shown in note **7**:

Mi rigardos la gazeton hodiaŭ vespere.

Correlatives with *i-*

8 Correlatives starting with **ki-**, **ti-**, **ĉi-** and **neni-** can usually be expressed respectively as 'what something', 'that something', 'every something' and 'no something', e.g. **kie** *what place (where)*, **tie** *that place (there)*, **ĉie** *every place (everywhere)* and **nenie** *no place (nowhere)*. Correlatives starting with **i-** are indefinite, and mean 'some . . . ' or 'any . . . ', e.g. **ie** *somewhere, anywhere*, **ial** *for some reason*, **iom** *some quantity*.

Iel, mi perdis mian mansakon.
Somehow (in some way) I've lost my handbag.
Ĝi devas esti ie!
It must be somewhere!
Mi iam faros ĝin.
I'll do it some time.

–and a favourite opening for a fairy tale:

Iam estis reĝo . . .
Once (upon a time) there was a king . . .

If you now turn to the Appendix on p. 000, you will see the full set of forty-five correlatives: nine sets of five. The beginnings show what . . . , that . . . , some . . . , every . . . and no . . . ; and the endings add . . . one, . . . thing, . . . kind, . . . place, etc. (For the only ending you have not yet met, see note **11**.)

Affixes as independent words

9 Many of the prefixes and suffixes whose sense permits may be used as independent roots, taking the appropriate ending. Here are the most important of those we have learned so far:

Li faris la **malon**.	*He did* the opposite.
Male, mi venos kun vi.	On the contrary, *I shall come with you.*
La **ina** intuicio.	Feminine *intuition.*
Mi vidis **etan** muson.	*I saw a* tiny *mouse.*
Li **ege** miris.	*He was* greatly *surprised.*
Mi estas **ano**.	*I am a* member.
Kie estas la **ejo**?	*Where is the* place?
Tie estas la **ujo**.	*There is the* container.

Aro da infanoj.	A party *of children.*
Aro da birdoj.	A flock *of birds.*
Aro da bovoj.	A herd *of cattle.*
La proksima **ero** estos . . .	*The next* item *will be . . .*
Li iris tien kaj **reen**.	*He went there and* back.
Inda je pli bona sorto.	Worthy *of a better fate.*
Mi ne **indas** tian honoron.	*I am not* worthy of *such an honour.*
Tio ne estas **ebla**.	*That is not* possible.
Eble ni farus same.	Possibly *we should do the same.*

10 Similarly, the use of the particles (i.e. words normally used without an ending – correlatives, prepositions, etc.) may also be enlarged by the use of an appropriate ending. In fact, a very great number of words can be derived in this way; here is just a small selection to give you some idea of the wealth of words latent in quite a small vocabulary:

ĉiam *always*	ĉiam**a** *permanent, constant*
tiam *then*	tiam**a** *of that time*
	tiam**ulo** *a man of that time, a contemporary*
iam *some time*	iam**a** *one-time* (adj.)
tie *there*	tie**a** *of that place, local*
	tie**ulo** *a native of the place*
kial *why*	kial**o** *reason*
antaŭ *before*	antaŭ**a** *previous*
	antaŭ**e** *previously*
	antaŭ**ulo** *predecessor*
ĉirkaŭ *about*	ĉirkaŭ**i** *to surround*
	ĉirkaŭ**aĵo** *surroundings*
ekster *outside*	ekster**a** *outer, external*
	ekster**aĵo** *outer part*
super *above*	super**a** *superior*
	super**ulo** *a superior*
	nesuper**ebla** *insuperable*
nun *now*	nun**a** *present, instant*
ne *no, not*	ne**i** *to deny, say no to*
	ne**ebla** *impossible*
jes *yes*	jes**i** *to reply in the affirmative*

Correlatives with *-es*

11 These words show *possession*, as follows:

Kies (*kee-ess*) *whose (what person's)*; **ties** *that one's (of that person)*; **ies** *someone's, somebody's*; **ĉies** *everyone's*; **nenies** *no one's.*

Kies libro estas tiu? *Whose book is that?*	Eble ĝi estas ties. *Perhaps it is that person's.*
Jen ies biciklo. *There's someone's bicycle.*	Esperanto estas ĉies propraĵo. *Esperanto is everybody's property*

Li estas nenies malamiko.
He is nobody's enemy.

Note: **Kies** is not only used as a question word: **la lando, kies gastoj ni estas** *the country whose guests we are.*

Ties is sometimes found with the meaning of 'the latter's': **Johano renkontis Arturon kaj ties amikon** *John met Arthur and the latter's friend.*

The past participle

12 ***-ita***

This is the ending of the (passive) past participle. It is an adjective (note the **-a** ending!) formed from a verb, with the meaning '(having been) -ed'.

fermi *to close*	ferm**ita** *closed (having been closed)*
fari *to do, make*	far**ita** *(having been) done, made*
miksi *to mix*	miks**ita** *(having been) mixed*

Kiam mi alvenis, la pordo estis ferm**ita**.
When I arrived, the door was closed.

Mi aĉetis skatolon de miks**itaj** legomoj.
I bought a tin (can) of mixed vegetables.

Note 1 The participle, being an adjective, must 'agree' with its noun (hence: **miks**itaj **legom**oj).

2 *Never* put **havi** before this type of participle, since it is always passive (having been done). *I have closed the door:* **Mi fermis la pordon**. (See Unit 4, note **6**.)

Teksto

HEJMA PAĜO

En via kuirejo

Jen recepto por vi el Germanujo!

Por ĉi tiu salato ne ekzistas sezono! Preparita el freŝaj legomoj, ĝi estas aparte delikata kaj valora, sed ankaŭ dum-vintre, farita el konservitaj legomoj, ĝi bongustas. Sola ĝi estas bela antaŭmanĝo; kun blanka pano aŭ rizo ĝi fariĝas leĝera tag- aŭ vespermanĝo.

Oni bezonas: 200 g da kokidaĵo, 100 g da kuirita ŝinko, 100 g (aŭ malgrandan skatolon) da agarikoj, 750 g da miksitaj freŝaj legomoj (aŭ en skatolo), 100 g da majonezo, 1 sup-kuleron da acida aŭ dolĉa kremo, citronsukon, salon, pipron, petroselon, skatolon da artiŝokaj koroj.*

** gramojn*

Procedu jene:

La freŝajn legomojn (karotojn, pizojn, verdajn fazeolojn, florbrasikon, brokolon, k.t.p.) purigu, lavu, pecetigu se necese kaj kuiru en salita akvo, ĝis ili estas preskaŭ molaj. Forverŝu la akvon kaj tenu por momento sub fluanta, malvarma akvo. Lasu malvarmiĝi.

La viandon, la ŝinkon kaj la fungojn tranĉu laŭplaĉe en kubetojn aŭ striojn. Maldensigu la majonezon per citronsuko kaj kremo. Spicu per salo kaj pipro kaj verŝu sur la preparitajn legomojn kaj viandon. Zorge miksu kaj metu en fridujon por unu horo.

Ornamu la pladon per malmolige kuiritaj ovotranĉaĵoj, artiŝokokoroj kaj tomatotranĉaĵoj.

Se vi uzas konservitajn legomojn el skatolo, forverŝu la likvaĵon kaj metu la legomojn por kelkaj minutoj en freŝan akvon.

Special vocabulary of food items mentioned in this recipe:

agariko *mushroom*
artiŝoko *artichoke*
brasiko *cabbage*
brokolo *broccoli*
citrono *lemon*
citronsuko *lemon juice*
fazeoloj *beans*
florbrasiko *cauliflower*
majonezo *mayonnaise*
ovo *egg*
petroselo *parsley*
pipro *pepper*
pizoj *peas*
rizo *rice*
salo *salt*
supo *soup*
ŝinko *ham*

En ĉina kuirejo

Tradicia kuirado en Ĉinujo

Ĉinaj kuiristinoj, kies arto estas tre subtila, ankoraŭ obeas regulojn, kiujn Konfucio proponis jam antaŭ 2500 jaroj! Tio ŝajnas stranga; sed se ni loĝus en Ĉinujo, eble ni farus same kiel la tieuloj.

Oni manĝas ĉefe legomojn. Viando (porkaĵo, bovidaĵo, tre malofte ŝafaĵo) estas altekosta, do oni malmulte manĝas ĝin.

La Ĉinoj neniam *boligas* manĝaĵojn – ili rostas, stufas en tre malmulte[1] da akvo, kaj fritas (rapide, je alta temperaturo, kaj en iomete[2] da graso). Oni ŝanĝas la kuirmetodon laŭ la manĝaĵo – ekzemple, grasan porkaĵon oni stufas, sed malgrasan porkaĵon oni fritas.

Laŭ Konfucio, oni devas ĉiam *spici* la manĝaĵojn. La celo de la spicado estas, forpreni malagrablajn odorojn (ekzemple *fiŝan* odoron) kaj emfazi la naturan guston de la manĝaĵo. Ofte oni bezonas horojn por prepari manĝon, sed nur kelkajn minutojn por manĝi ĝin.

[1] **multe da** *a lot of*; so **malmulte da** *a small quantity of.*
[2] **iomete da** *a little.*

KONSILETOJ EN LA HEJMO

Por forpreni[1] globkrajonan inkon de vestoj, verŝu iom da[2] lakto sur la makulon kaj leĝere, cirkle frotu per pura tolo. Poste lavu la veston.

[1] *'away-take'; remove.*
[2] **iom da** *some.*

Por forpreni sangon de naztuko, tuj metu la tukon en malvarman akvon. Se vi volas tuj lavi ĝin, agitu ĝin en la malvarma akvo ĝis la makuloj preskaŭ malaperis.

Por teni vin sana

1 Por la brusto kaj brakoj.

Jen kelkaj korpaj ekzercoj por helpi ĉiun kiu deziras esti kaj resti sana.

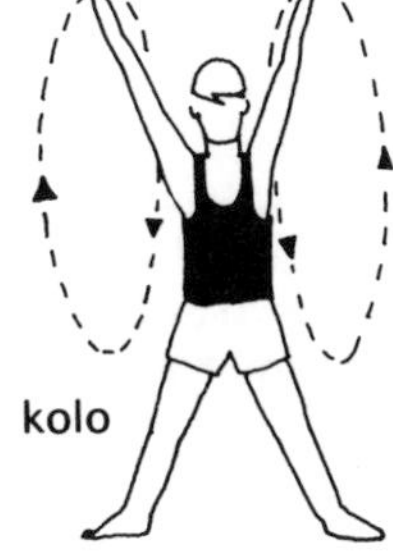

4 Por la kolo kaj ŝultroj.

2 Por la trunko.

5 Por la spino, dorso kaj kruroj.

3 Por la brakoj, manoj, fingroj, kaj ventro.

6 Por la piedoj, kruroj kaj dorso.

Kion vi farus, se vi ricevus £50,000?

Ĉu vi aĉetus idealan domon? Ĉu vi vojaĝus ĉirkaŭ la mondo?

Ĉu vi dediĉus monon al la edukado de viaj infanoj?

Ĉu vi donus monon al persono, kies bezono estas pli granda ol via?

Ĉu vi aĉetus belan pianon, aŭ luksan aŭtomobilon?

Ĉu vi helpus iun helpindan societon?

Sendu al ni viajn ideojn. Post du semajnoj, ni presos la plej interesajn el ili.

PRAKTIKO 9.4 Traduku anglen:

Se mi ricevus kvindekmil pundojn, mi aĉetus novan domon. Se Rikardo ricevus tiom da mono, li vojaĝus ĉirkaŭ la mondo. Kion vi farus? Ĉu vi dediĉus monon al la edukado de viaj infanoj, aŭ helpus iun helpindan societon? Klara deziras esti kaj resti sana. Ŝi faras korpajn ekzercojn ĉiutage. Mi perdis mian globkrajonon; ĝi devas esti ie, sed mi ne scias kie. Eble iu trovos ĝin kaj redonos ĝin al mi. Io nekutima okazis al mi hieraŭ. Ial, li forkuris. Kial la pordo estas fermita? La tasko estis jam farita. Anstataŭ fermi la pordon, li faris la malon. Tiu sinjoro estas ano de nia grupo. La arto de la ĉinaj kuiristinoj estas tre subtila. Antaŭ dumil kvincent jaroj, Konfucio proponis regulojn, kiujn oni ankoraŭ obeas. En Ĉinujo oni manĝas ĉefe legomojn, ĉar la viando estas multekosta. Ĉu vi preferas rostitan bovaĵon aŭ rostitan porkaĵon? Ĉu plaĉas al vi salato? Oni bezonas multe pli longan tempon por prepari manĝon ol por manĝi ĝin!

PRAKTIKO 9.5 Traduku esperanten:

What would you do if you were rich? I hope (that) I should use my money wisely. Every day I do physical exercises in front of an open window. This salad is prepared from (out of) fresh vegetables. The vegetables must be carefully washed (one must . . .). Would you like (*use* **plaĉi**) a cup of tea? Can I go there and back in one day? That could be the reason. Can I do anything to help (**por helpi**)? That river flows very quickly. I hope (that) the children will behave well.

PRAKTIKO 9.6 Respondu esperante:

Kio estas la celo de la korpaj ekzercoj sur la Hejma Paĝo? Por kiu sezono estas la salato en la recepto? Kion oni devas fari unue pri la freŝaj legomoj? En kia akvo oni devas kuiri ilin? Ĝis kiam oni kuiras ilin? Kion oni devas fari pri la likvaĵo, se oni uzas konservitajn legomojn el skatolo? En Ĉinujo, kiu proponis la regulojn, laŭ kiuj la kuiristinoj ankoraŭ kuiras? Kiam li proponis ilin? Kial oni manĝas ĉefe legomojn? Kial oni spicas la manĝaĵojn? Kiel la ĉinaj kuiristinoj kuiras grasan porkaĵon? Kiel ili kuiras malgrasan porkaĵon?

Dialogo

Interesaj vizitoj

Kelkajn tagojn poste, dum la vespermanĝo, Klara kaj Rikardo Lang babilas kun franca paro, Martin kaj Chantal, kiuj dum la posttagmezo akompanis Andreon kaj Marian al la bestĝardeno en La Flèche.

Klara Nu, geamikoj, ni kore dankas vin pro via afabla zorgo pri niaj infanoj. Mi esperas, ke ili kondutis bone.

Chantal Tute bone! Kaj ili tiom ĝuis la viziton al la bestĝardeno! Ĝi vere estas mirinda loko.

Rikardo Jes, mi supozis, ke tio plaĉos al ili.

Marteno Maria tre amis la elefanton, kiu estis tiel granda sed tiel milda. Andreo preferis la tigron, sed ili ambaŭ amis la ĉimpanzojn. Mi estas certa, ke ili ĉirkaŭiris la tutan lokon dufoje! Ili absolute ne deziris foriri (= **iri for**) de la bestoj.

Klara Nu, ĉar vi tiel afable kondukis ilin tien, ni estis liberaj viziti Angers, kiun ni longe volis vidi.

Rikardo Jes. La kastelo tie estas mirinda. Kia situo! Tridek metrojn alte sur tiu grandega roko! Kaj la vidaĵo de ĝi trans la riveron! Grandioza!

Klara Sed tio, kio plej plaĉis al mi, estis la grandiozaj tapetoj faritaj inter la 14a kaj la 18a jarcentoj. Kaj la plej mirinda el ĉiuj certe estis tiu de la Apokalipso! Ĝi estis farita en la dek-kvara jarcento, kaj konsistas el sepdek paneloj. Entute ĝi estas longa 150 metrojn, kaj alta preskaŭ kvin metrojn. Kiom da laboro por fari ĝin!

Marteno Jes, kaj mi vetus, ke post tiu vizito vi volis sidi kaj ripozi!

Klara Ho, miaj piedoj! Sed estas multaj belaj ĝardenoj en Angers, do ni ripozis en bela ĉirkaŭaĵo. Mi aŭdis, ke oni nomas Angers 'la urbo de la floroj', kaj tio ja estas vera.

Rikardo Ni vizitis ankaŭ la Katedralon de Sankta Maŭrico, kiu estas de la 12a kaj 13a jarcentoj.

Klara Kaj la 'Logis Barrault', kie ni rigardis multajn skulptaĵojn kaj pentraĵojn de francaj artistoj de la 18a jarcento.

Marteno Nu, ni nun diskutu la vesperon. Se vi ne kontraŭas, ke la infanoj restu tre malfrue el la litoj, mi volus sugesti, ke ni kvar, kaj viaj infanoj, iru al la Kastelo de Le Lude, kie nokte okazas unika spektaklo.

Chantal Per 'Sono kaj Lumo' oni aŭdas kaj vidas la historion de la kastelo. Oni aŭdas muzikon kaj vidas eventojn, dancojn, k.t.p. (= **kaj tiel plu**) laŭ la epoko.

Marteno Mi estas certa, ke ni ĉiuj multe ĝuos tion. Sed la spektaklo okazas inter la naŭa kaj tridek kaj la dek-unua kaj tridek. Ĉu vi estos kontentaj, se la infanoj estos ekster la litoj tiom malfrue?

Rikardo H'm, tio ja estas malfrua fino. Kion vi opinias, karulino?

Klara Nu, ĝi estas unika okazo, kaj certe interesos ilin. Mi kredas, ke ankaŭ ili ĝuos ĝin.

Chantal Mi estas certa pri tio.

Marteno Do, mi sugestas, ke ni veturu en nia aŭto, kiu havas spacon por ni ĉiuj. Sed jam estas la horo por ekveturi, se ni deziras havi bonajn sidlokojn! Ni iru!

Demandoj

1 Pro kio ges-roj Lang dankas la francajn geamikojn?
2 Kion ambaŭ infanoj amis en la zoologia ĝardeno?
3 Kion faris Rikardo kaj Klara dum la infanoj vizitis la zoologian ĝardenon?
4 Kio plej plaĉis al Klara en la urbo Angers?
5 Kion Klara kaj Rikardo rigardis en la 'Logis Barrault'?
6 Kion sugestas Marteno pri la vespero?
7 Kio okazas nokte en la Kastelo de Le Lude?
8 Je kioma horo oni komencas la spektaklon tie?
9 Kaj kiomlonge ĝi daŭras?
10 Kial oni devas tuj ekveturi?

agiti *to agitate, shake*
agrabla *pleasant*
ambaŭ *both*
aperi *to appear*; **malaperi** *to disappear*
aŭskulti *to listen (to)*
babili *to chat, chatter*
bestĝardeno *zoo*
blanka *white*
boligi *to boil (something)*
brusto *chest*
dediĉi *dedicate, set aside*
densa *dense, concentrated;* **maldensigi** *to dilute*
dorso *back* (cf. *dorsal fin*)
ekzerco *exercise*
ekveturi *to set off*
fariĝi *to become*
flui *to flow*; **fluanta** *flowing*
fridujo *refrigerator, fridge*
friti *to fry*
froti *to rub*
globkrajono *ball point pen* (lit. *globe pencil*)
grandioza *grand, magnificent*
graso *fat*
gusto *taste*; **bongusta** *tasty*
ja *indeed*
jene *as follows, thus*
konduti *to behave*
konsilo *advice*; **konsileto** *a hint*
kontraŭi *to oppose*
korpo *body*
kruro *leg*
kuirist(in)o *a cook*
kulero *spoon*
lakto *milk*
laŭplaĉe *to your liking*
lavi *to wash*
legomo *vegetable*
leĝera *light (not heavy), slight*
likvaĵo *liquid*
lumo *light (not dark)*
makulo *a stain* (cf. *immaculate*)
malvarmigi *to cool*
mano *hand*
meti *to put*
miksi *to mix*
mola *soft*
nazo *nose*; **naztuko** *handkerchief*
ornami *adorn, decorate*
paro *pair, couple*
pecetigi (pec-et-igi) *to break, cut into small pieces*
pentri *to paint (picture)*; **pentraĵo** *a painting*
piedo *foot*
plado *dish*
propra *(one's) own*
pundo *pound, £*
recepto *recipe*
regulo *rule, regulation*
roko *rock*
salato *salad*
sezono *season*
sola *alone*
spaco *space, room*
spici *to spice, season*
strio *strip, stripe*
stufi *to stew*
subtila *subtle*
ŝanĝi *to change (something)*
ŝultro *shoulder*
tapeto *tapestry*
teni *to hold, keep*
tieulo *a person of that place*
tolo *cloth, linen*
tranĉi *to cut (with knife)*; **tranĉaĵo** *slice*
tuj *immediately*
unika *unique*
valora *valuable*
ventro *belly, abdomen*
verŝi *to pour*
vesto *garment*
zorga *careful*; **zorgi** *to take care*

Note that verbs are now given in the infinitive form.

10 La vivo de Einstein

The reflexive pronoun

1 The majority of verbs show that someone or something (the subject) does something to someone or something (the object):

Subject	*Verb*	*Object*
la knabo	trinkas	la lakto**n**
the boy	*drinks*	*the milk*

However, with some verbs it is possible to do the action not only to someone or something else, but also to *oneself*: in such cases, 'myself', 'yourself', 'yourselves', 'ourselves' are translated as 'me', 'you', 'us':

Mi	lavas	**min**.
I	*wash*	myself.
Vi	flatas	**vin**.
You	*flatter*	yourself.
Ni	amuzis	**nin**.
We	*amused*	ourselves.

2 In the above cases, there is no doubt about who the object is. But with **li**, **ŝi**, **ĝi** and **ili**, there is a doubt: **li lavas lin** means *he washes him*, and we don't know who 'him' refers to.

This problem is solved by the special reflexive pronoun **si**, (or **sin**, when it is the object.) 'Himself', 'herself', 'itself' and 'themselves' are all translated by **si(n)**:

Li	vidis	**sin**.
He	*saw*	himself.
Ŝi	admiris	**sin**.
She	*admired*	herself.
Ĝi	lekis	**sin**.
It	*licked*	itself.
Ili	amuzis	**sin**.
They	*amused*	themselves.

La viro	diris	**al si**.
The man	*said*	to himself.
La virino	parolis	**al si**.
The woman	*spoke*	to herself.
La hundo	rigardis	**al si**.
The dog	*looked*	at itself.
La infanoj	legis	**al si**.
The children	*read*	to themselves.

Note: When a verb is followed by 'myself', 'yourself', 'himself', etc., it is said to be used *reflexively*, because the action done reflects back on the doer.

3 ***Sia***

We saw (Unit 4, note **8**) that **-a** is added to the personal pronouns to translate 'my', 'your', 'our', etc. **-A** may be added to the reflexive pronoun **si** to show that the object belongs to the subject, and **sia** is translated by 'his', 'her', 'its', or 'their' depending on the subject:

Subject		*Subject*		
Li trinkis	**sian**	bieron kaj ŝi trinkis	**sian**	teon.
He drank	his	*beer and she drank*	her	*tea*.

The first **sian** = *his*, because it refers to **li**; and the second **sian** = *her*, because it refers to **ŝi**.

It follows that if we say **Li trinkis lian bieron**, this would mean he drank somebody else's beer, not his own.

Johano ne estis kontenta ĉar Georgo trinkis lian bieron.
John was not pleased because George drank his (John's) beer.
(George did the drinking, but it was *not* his own beer)

Subject		*Subject*		
Li	diras ke lia	hundo	lavas	**sian** vizagon.
He	*says that his*	*dog*	*is washing*	its *face*.

Here **sian** = *its*, because it refers to **hundo**.

Subject			*Subject*		
Li	vidis	ke	ili	finis	**sian** laboron.
He	*saw*	*that*	*they*	*had finished*	their *work*.

Here **sian** = *their*, because it refers to **ili**.
Of course, if the noun is plural, **sia** must agree with it:

Ili legis sia**jn** libro**jn**.
They were reading their books.

Note: The main thing to remember is that **sia** must not be used to directly qualify a subject; it may only refer to it. For example, in the second example it would be wrong to say **Li diris, ke** sia **hundo** . . . , because **hundo** is a subject.

Suffixes

4 *-ig-*

The suffix **-ig-** is used to form words which express the causing or bringing about of the action or state indicated in the root or formation to which it is attached. As an independent word, **igi** = *to cause*.

kompleta *complete*	komplet**igi** *to (cause to be) complete*
seka *dry*	sek**igi** *to (cause to be) dry*
pura *clean*	pur**igi** *to clean, cleanse, purify*
klara *clear*	klar**igi** *to explain, clarify, elucidate*
nigra *black*	nigr**igi** *to blacken*
ruĝa *red*	ruĝ**igi** *to redden (make red)*
blanka *white*	blank**igi** *to whiten*
facila *easy*	facil**igi** *to make easy, facilitate*
sana *healthy*	san**igi** *to make well, heal*
kun *with*	kun**igi** *to connect, unite, join together*
sub *under*	sub**igi** *to subdue, overwhelm*
nulo *nought*	nul**igi** *to nullify, annul, cancel*

Verbs which express an act that is *caused* to something or someone are called *causative verbs*. The suffix **-ig-** is used to form causative verbs from non-causative verbs:

fali *to fall*	fal**igi** *to fell (a tree, etc.), to drop*
kuŝi *to lie*	kuŝ**igi** *to lay (cause to lie)*
timi *to fear*	tim**igi** *to frighten (cause to fear)*
daŭri *to go on*	daŭr**igi** *to continue (cause to go on)*
iri *to go*	ir**igi** *to propel (cause to go)*
miri *to marvel, be amazed*	mir**igi** *to astonish (make one marvel)*
veni *to come*	ven**igi** *to summon (cause to come)*

In some cases, English uses the same verb for the non-causative and causative senses, but note that in Esperanto we use **-ig-** for the latter:

boli *to boil*	bol**igi** *to boil (cause to boil)*
droni *to drown (perish)*	dron**igi** *to drown (kill by drowning)*

bruli	*to burn (be on fire)*	bru**ligi**	*to burn (set on fire)*
flosi	*to float*	flos**igi**	*to float (cause to float)*

PRAKTIKO 10.1 Traduku anglen:

Tiu viro parolas al si. Mi lavas min antaŭ mia matenmanĝo. Mi vidis lin hieraŭ. Mi vidis min en la spegulo (*mirror*). Li ne flatis min, sed li flatis sin. La infanoj legis al si kiam mi vidis ilin. Andreo ne estas kontenta ĉar lia patro trinkis lian lakton. (*Careful! Whose milk?*) La patrino ne sciis, ĉu Maria trinkas ŝian lakton, ău la sian. Sed Maria diris al ŝi, ke ŝi trinkas sian lakton. Tio kontentigis ŝian patrinon. Mi klarigis al mia frato, kiel mi faris la laboron. Mi faris ĝin tiel por faciligi ĝin. La knabo kuŝigis sin sur la lito. La knabinoj ludis per siaj ludiloj.

PRAKTIKO 10.2 Traduku esperanten:

The teacher spoke to the class, but he did not amuse them. They amused themselves. John says that his friend is drinking his beer (i.e. his own beer). John says that his friend is drinking his beer (i.e. John's beer). I saw that the children (had) finished their work. The child was playing with (**per**) red ink, and reddened his hands. He also reddened his clothes. Can you explain this to me? Have you cleaned the floor? Dry your clothes and then (**poste**) dress yourself.

PRAKTIKO 10.3 Express each of these words by an Esperanto verb ending in **-igi**. You may have to use an affix or preposition. A clue in brackets gives the meaning.

1	to cure	(to make well again)
2	to improve	(to make better)
3	to facilitate	(to make easy)
4	to compel	(to cause to have to)
5	to diversify	(to make diverse)
6	to equalise	(to make equal)
7	to rejuvenate	(to make young again)
8	to liberate	(to cause to be free)
9	to necessitate	(to make necessary)
10	to post	(to cause to be in the post)

5 *-iĝ-*

The suffix **-iĝ-** is used to form words indicating that the state expressed in the root has come into being. As an independent word, **iĝi** = *to become.*

From adjectives:

evidenta	*evident*	eviden**tiĝi**	*to become evident*
malseka	*wet*	malsek**iĝi**	*to become (get) wet*
malpura	*dirty*	malpur**iĝi**	*to become (get) dirty*
pala	*pale*	pal**iĝi**	*to grow (turn) pale*
plena	*full*	plen**iĝi**	*to become full*

From nouns, prepositions, affixes and adverbs:

amiko	*friend*	amik**iĝi**	*to become friends*
lumo	*light*	lum**iĝi**	*to become (grow) light*
edzo	*husband*	edz**iĝi**	*to marry (become a husband)*
edzino	*wife*	edzin**iĝi**	*to marry (become a wife)*
kun	*with*	kun**iĝi**	*to unite, become joined*
ano	*a member*	an**iĝi**	*to join (a society etc.)*

From verbs:

sidi	*to sit*	sid**iĝi**	*to become seated, sit down*
stari	*to stand*	star**iĝi**	*to get on one's feet, stand up*

The suffix **-iĝ-** is used in particular with verbs that show that the action is done *to something* or *someone*, in order to show that the action is taking place without affecting anyone or anything other than the subject:

naski	*to bear, give birth to*	nask**iĝi**	*to be born*
eduki	*to educate (someone)*	eduk**iĝi**	*to be educated*
montri	*to show (something)*	montr**iĝi**	*to appear, be shown*
detrui	*to destroy (something)*	detru**iĝi**	*to be destroyed*
komenci	*to begin (something)*	komenc**iĝi**	*to be started*
fini	*to finish (something)*	fin**iĝi**	*to come to an end*
renkonti	*to meet (someone)*	renkont**iĝi**	*to come together*
trovi	*to find (something)*	trov**iĝi**	*to be found*

6 *-ec-*

The suffix **-ec-** is used to form abstract nouns expressing the quality or characteristic of that indicated in the root, like the English '-ness', '-hood', '-ship':

bona	*good*	bon**eco**	*goodness*
patrino	*mother*	patrin**eco**	*motherhood*

amiko *friend*	amik**ec**o *friendship*
juna *young*	jun**ec**o *youth, youthfulness*
relativa *relative*	relativ**ec**o *relativity*
granda *great, large*	grand**ec**o *greatness, magnitude, size*
vera *true*	ver**ec**o *truth*
ebla *possible*	ebl**ec**o *possibility*
bonkora *kind*	bonkor**ec**o *kindness*

7 ***-ist-***

The suffix **-ist-** is used to denote one who is occupied, either professionally or as a hobby, with the thing or matter named in the root:

tajpi *to type*	tajp**ist**o *typist (male)*
	tajp**istin**o *typist (female)*
dento *tooth*	dent**ist(in)**o *dentist*
arto *art*	art**ist(in)**o *artist*
instrui *to teach*	instru**ist(in)**o *teacher*
scienco *science*	scienc**ist(in)**o *scientist*
muziko *music*	muzik**ist(in)**o *musician*
labori *to work*	labor**ist(in)**o *worker; workman/woman*
plumbo *lead (metal)*	plumb**ist(in)**o *plumber*
ĵurnalo *newspaper*	ĵurnal**ist(in)**o *journalist*

8 ***-ism-***

The suffix **-ism-** denotes a doctrine, practice, or school of thought (like English '-ism'):

katoliko *a Catholic*	katolik**ism**o *Catholicism*
kanibalo *cannibal*	kanibal**ism**o *cannibalism*
angla *English*	angl**ism**o *anglicism*
internacia *international*	internaci**ism**o *internationalism*

Please

9 You already know how to use **mi petas** for **please**, but this is often not convenient at the beginning of a sentence. In this case, we use **Bonvolu** followed by an infinitive:

Bonvolu veni ĉi tien.	*Please come here.*
Bonvolu helpi min.	*please help me.*

We also often use **Bonvolu** by itself when offering something to somebody, inviting somebody to sit down, etc., i.e. where it is obvious what you want the person to do.

Teksto

LA VIVO DE EINSTEIN

REVOLUCIISTO DE LA SCIENCO

La 14a de Marto estas la datreveno[1] de granda homo. Je tiu ĉi tago, en la jaro 1879, naskiĝis **Albert Einstein.** Li edukiĝis en München kaj en Aarau. En frua juneco evidentiĝis lia genio pri matematiko. Lia onklo tre simple klarigis al li pri algebro: kaj la eta knabo, sen ia helpo, solvis tutan libron de algebraj problemoj. Li eniris[2] la universitaton de Zürich, kaj deziris fariĝi instruisto. Sed fakte, en 1902, li fariĝis teknika fakulo en la svisa patentejo.

En 1903 li edziĝis al slava fraŭlino: sed poste oni nuligis tiun geedziĝon, kaj en 1916 li reedziĝis, al sia kuzino Else. Unu filino naskiĝis al ili.

La junulo kiu revoluciigis la sciencan mondon

Dum sia libera tempo li konstante studis la misteron de la universo, kaj doktoriĝis[3] ĉe la universitato de Zürich. Fine, en la memorinda jaro 1905, li verkis plurajn gravegajn artikolojn. La ĉefa el ili estis tiel originala, ke eĉ grandaj sciencistoj ne povis kompreni ĝin. Nur en 1915 li kompletigis sian 'Ĝeneralan Teorion pri Relativeco.'

La grandeco de tiu teorio konsistas en tio: ke ĝi radikale ŝanĝis niajn konceptojn pri la leĝoj de la universo. Ni trovas, ke la principoj de Newton kaj de Eŭklid estas nur oportunaĵoj, kaj ne reprezentas la realan verecon! Ni devas, do, kvazaŭ rekomenci de la komenco: kaj longa laborado estas ankoraŭ necesa por plene esplori ĉiujn eblecojn[4] de tia grandioza teorio.

Germanujo forpelis[5] sian grandan filon

De 1914 ĝis 1933 Einstein laboris en sia patrolando Germanujo. La registaro[6] de Hitler atakis lin ĉar li estis Judo; do en 1933 li lasis Germanujon kaj elmigris, unue al Svislando, poste al Usono. Li loĝis en Princeton, kie li mortis je la 18a de Aprilo, 1955.

Einstein: humila, simpla homo

Krom sciencisto, Einstein estis ankaŭ bona muzikisto, per piano kaj violono. Li havis, cetere, profundan religian senton. Persone, li estis homo simpla kaj humila, de granda bonkoreco[7]. Ĉiuj homoj ne nur respektis, sed amis lin. Li diris, ke se li povus revivi sian vivon, li preferus esti simpla laboristo, ekzemple plumbisto. Politike, li estis socialisto kaj pacifisto, kiu abomenis militon. Dum la lastaj jaroj li malgajiĝis[8],

[1] *return-of-the-date': birthday, anniversary.*
[2] *'went-in', entered.*
[3] *'became-a-doctor': graduated.*
[4] **ebla + eco**: *'possibility'.*
[5] **for-pelis**: *drove away.*
[6] *'group of rulers': government.*
[7] *'good-heartedness': kindness.*
[8] **mal-gaj-iĝ-is**: *became sad.*

ĉar li timis, ke liaj propraj eltrovoj[9] kondukis al situacio, en kiu la homoj povas detrui sin per atombomboj. Ĵurnalisto iam demandis al Einstein: 'Ĉu vi povas antaŭdiri'[10], kiajn armilojn oni uzos en tria mondmilito?' Li respondis: 'Ne; sed mi ja povas antaŭdiri, kiajn armilojn oni uzus en *kvara* mondmilito–rokojn kaj bastonojn!'

[9] **el-trovo**: *finding out, discovery.*
[10] **antaŭ-diri**: *'before-say', foretell.*

PRAKTIKO 10.4 Traduku anglen:

Kion vi diris al vi? Ili lavas sin ĉiumatene, ĉu ne? Einstein estis la plej fama matematikisto. Lia genio pri matematiko evidentiĝis en frua juneco. Li estis ankaŭ bona pianisto kaj violonisto, ĉu ne? Eble ie, iam, estos eĉ pli mirinda matematikisto, kies nomon ni ankoraŭ ne scias. Ĉu vi opinias, ke la homaro detruos sin per atombomboj? Einstein timis, ke tio povus okazi. Neniu povas scii ĉion, sed ĉiu povas lerni, kaj tiel scii pli ol antaŭe. Bonvolu daŭrigi vian laboron. La kato iris en la ĝardenon kaj timigis la birdojn. Hieraŭ mi forigis grandan amason da paperoj de mia skribotablo, kaj bruligis ilin ĉiujn.

PRAKTIKO 10.5 Traduku esperanten:

Mary is reading her book. The children love their lessons, don't they? The sun soon dried the clothes. You must always clean your teeth. He completed his task yesterday morning, didn't he? Have you boiled the water? Then please make the tea. I went out in(to) the rain, and got wet. My brother was married in March, and my sister will be married in September. John and Mary were married in June. I am a member of the society, and my friend will join tomorrow. When was he born?

PRAKTIKO 10.6 Vera aŭ malvera?

1 Einstein naskiĝis en majo, 1879.
2 Kiel eta knabo li senhelpe solvis tutan libron de algebraj problemoj.
3 Li eniris la Universitaton de Zürich por fariĝi instruistino.
4 Li edziĝis dufoje, sed havis nur unu infanon.
5 Li verkis plurajn gravegajn artikolojn tri jarojn post sia unua edziĝo.
6 La 'Ĝenerala Teorio pri Relativeco' ŝanĝis niajn konceptojn pri la leĝoj de la universo.
7 Einstein laboris en Germanujo ĝis 1939.
8 Li estis tre religia homo.
9 Li ludis nenian muzikan instrumenton.
10 Li mortis en Svislando en 1955.

Dialogo

Amikoj kaj najbaroj

Hejme denove, Rikardo kaj Klara babilas vespere, post la enlitiĝo de la infanoj.

Rikardo Ha, estas agrable esti en la propra hejmo denove, kvankam mi tre ĝuis nian restadon en la Kulturdomo!
Klara Jes! Almenaŭ estas pli trankvile ĉi tie, aparte kiam la infanoj jam enlitiĝis.
Rikardo Nu, mi kredas, ke ili ambaŭ tre ĝuis siajn feriojn; ĉu vi ne konsentas?
Klara Jes, ja! Cetere, la ferioj faris al ili multe da bono. La restado en Grezijono kutimigis ilin al la kunesto de alilandanoj, kaj komprenigis ilin, ke ni ĉiuj estas similaj.
Rikardo Vere, la amikeco de homoj el diversaj landoj ĉiam devas esti bona. Multaj internaciaj amikecoj devis jam komenciĝi en la Kulturdomo!
Klara Ni devos instigi ilin skribi al siaj novaj geamikoj, por ke ili daŭrigu la amikecon.
Rikardo Kaj, cetere, ankaŭ ni devos skribi al la niaj!
Klara Ne *ni*, karulo; *vi*!
Rikardo Ho! Kial mi? Ni ambaŭ amikiĝis kun ili!
Klara (*kaĵole*) Sed estas vi, kiu ĉiam faras la korespondadon. Vi faras ĝin multe pli bone ol mi!
Rikardo Flatado, flatado! Do, mi faros ĝin, sed vi devos skribi al Chantal, kiu donis al vi tiun belan kolĉenon kiel memorigilon.
Klara Ho, nu, se vi insistas . . . !

(Du tagojn poste. Rikardo hejmenvenas de kunveno de la Esperanto-Grupo.)

Klara Saluton, kara! Ĉu vi ĝuis la kunvenon?
Rikardo Jes, ĝi estis tre interesa. Sed divenu, kio okazis!
Klara Kiel mi povas diveni? Ne atendigu min; diru!
Rikardo Ili deziras, ke mi faru paroladon al la grupo pri niaj ferioj. Imagu, fari paroladon! Mi!
Klara Vi ne timas, ĉu?
Rikardo Mi timegas! Mi neniam antaŭe faris publikan paroladon!
Klara Ho, ne troigu! La Esperantogrupo apenaŭ estas la publiko! Pensu nur, vi estas inter geamikoj. Vi konas ilin

ĉiujn, kaj ili konas vin. Simple imagu, ke vi parolas al unu aŭ du el ili, kaj parolu kiel vi parolis al Marteno kaj Chantal.

Rikardo H'm, ni vidos.

Klara Dum vi ĉeestis vian kunvenon, iu vizitis min.

Rikardo Ho, kiu?

Klara Nia najbarino, s-ino Smith. Ŝi volis demandi nin pri niaj ferioj. Vi memoras, ke ili vizitis Francujon ĉi-jare, sed ili estis kun angle-parolanta turisma grupo, kaj ŝi diris, ke ne necesis al ili paroli france.

Rikardo Supozeble ili neniam parolis kun franco aŭ francino!

Klara Nu, ŝi konfesis, ke iun tagon ŝi promenis kun sia edzo, kaj ili vojeraris. Ŝi diris, ke ili devis alparoli kelkajn homojn antaŭ ol ili trovis iun kiu parolis angle!

Rikardo Mi supozas, ke post tio ili ne volis promeni sen aliaj membroj de la grupo.

Klara Pri tio ŝi nenion diris. Sed ŝi volis scii, ĉu ni vere parolis Esperanton la tutan tempon dum ni estis tie, kaj ŝi tre miris kiam mi diris, ke en Grezijono ni parolis Esperantlingve kun homoj el almenaŭ ses landoj, kaj komprenis unu la alian perfekte!

Rikardo Ĉu vi sugestis, ke ili lernu Esperanton?

Klara Ankoraŭ ne. Kiel diras la proverbo: 'Kiu tro pelas, nur malakcelas'.

Rikardo Aŭ eĉ pli mallonga proverbo: 'Rapidu malrapide'!

Klara Ĝuste!

Demandoj

1 Kiom el la familio ĝuis siajn feriojn?
2 Kiel la ferioj faris bonon al la infanoj?
3 Kion la gepatroj instigos la infanojn fari?
4 Kial Rikardo devos skribi al la geamikoj de la gepatroj?
5 Kial Klara devos skribi al Chantal?
6 Kio okazis al Rikardo en la kunveno de la Esperantogrupo?
7 Kial li timas?
8 Kio okazis al ges-roj Smith kiam ili promenis sole en Francujo?
9 Kion s-ino Smith demandis al Klara?
10 Kio mirigis ŝin?

abomeni *to abhor, loathe*
akceli *to accelerate*;
malakceli *to slow down*
almenaŭ *at least*
alparoli *to address, speak to*
aparte *especially*
apenaŭ *hardly, scarcely*
armiloj *arms, weapons*
atombombo *atomic bomb*
bastono *stick*
cetere *besides, moreover*
ĉu? *are you? is it? etc.* (cf. *ĉu ne?*)
detrui *to destroy*
diveni *to guess*
enlitiĝi *to go to/get into bed*
esplori *to investigate, explore*
fako *compartment, department, specialisation*; **fakulo** *specialist*
fariĝi *to become*
flatado *flattery*
fraŭlino *unmarried girl or woman, Miss*
ĝuste *exactly, precisely*
humila *humble*
imagi *to imagine*
instigi *to prompt, spur, urge*
judo *Jew*
kaĵole *coaxingly*
krom *besides, apart from*
kunesto *'being-with': company*
kutimigi *to accustom*
kuzo *cousin*
leĝo *law*
memorigilo *memento, souvenir*
milito *war*
mistero *mystery*
morti *to die*
najbaro *neighbour*
naski *to give birth to*; **naskiĝi** *to be born*
onklo *uncle*; **onklino** *aunt*
oportuna *convenient*;
oportunaĵoj *things of convenience*
peli *to drive* (cf. *impel, expel etc.*)
perfekta *perfect*
politiko *politics*;
politika *political*
profunda *deep, profound*
regi *to rule, govern, control*;
registaro *government*
religio *religion*; **religia** *religious*
restado *stay*
revivi *to relive*
revolucio *revolution (political)*
supozeble *presumably*
timi *to fear, be afraid*
trankvila *calm, tranquil*
troigi *to exaggerate*
turismo *tourism*
verki *to compose, write (original work)*
violono *violin* (note spelling)
vojerari *to lose one's way*

Esprimoj:
angle-parolanta *English-speaking*
antaŭ ol *before* (when followed by an action)
ĉi-jare *this year*
devis jam *must have already*
iun tagon *one day*
pensu nur! *just think!*
por ke *in order that*
unu la alian *one another, each other*

11 Kelkaj reklamoj

Active participles

1 You have seen that a noun can be made into an adjective by simply changing the ending **-o** to **-a:**

flor**o** *a flower* flor**a** *floral*

However, if we wish to give some idea of action to the simple describing word, we use the fuller ending **-anta**:

flor**anta** *flowering, flourishing*

Floranta is the *active present participle* of the verb **flori** *to flower, flourish.* It is active and present because it describes what something is doing at the present time.

Note that it still remains an adjective describing a noun, although it differs from an ordinary adjective in that it also suggests action.

The *active past participle* has the ending **-inta**, which means 'having done (in the past)' whatever action is indicated in the root:

ferm**inta** *having closed*

You should notice the difference between this *active* past participle and the *passive* one which you met in Unit 9, note **12**:

ferm**inta** *having closed*; ferm**ita** *having* been *closed*

(You will meet the rest of the passive participles in Unit 13.)

Now compare the meanings of these present and past active participles:

falanta *falling* falinta *fallen*
fluganta *flying* fluginta *flown*
kreskanta *growing* kreskinta *grown*
mortanta *dying* mortinta *dead*
pasanta *passing* pasinta *passed, past*
pendanta *hanging* pendinta *hung, hanged*

Mi vidis falantan arbon. *I saw a falling tree.*
Li sidis sur falinta arbo. *He sat on a fallen tree.*

Mi vidis mortantan muson. *I saw a dying mouse.*
Ŝi trovis mortintan muson. *She found a dead mouse.*

Rapide pasantaj tagoj *quickly passing days*
Ne parolu pri pasintaj jaroj. *Do not speak of past years.*

Note: Like adjectives, the participles take **-n** and/or **-j** when required.

The perfect tenses

2 In order to emphasise that an action is finished and complete, we use in English the past participle with 'have'/'has'/'had' to show the time. In Esperanto, we also use the past participle, but we use **estas/estis/estos** to show the time. These 'compound' tenses (formed with the verb **esti** and a participle ending in **-inta**) are called *perfect* tenses, as follows:

(*i*) The present perfect tense:

mi estas falinta *I have fallen*
vi estas falinta *you have fallen*
li estas falinta *he has fallen*
ŝi estas falinta *she has fallen*
ĝi estas falinta *it has fallen*
ni estas falintaj *we have fallen*
vi estas falintaj *you (plural) have fallen*
ili estas falintaj *they have fallen*

This tense is, in fact, little used, except for emphasis, as we prefer to use the simple past tense in **-is**.

(*ii*) The past perfect (pluperfect) tense:

mi estis falinta *I had fallen*
vi estis falinta *you had fallen*
li estis falinta *he had fallen*
ŝi estis falinta *she had fallen*
ĝi estis falinta *it had fallen*
ni estis falintaj *we had fallen*
vi estis falintaj *you (plural) had fallen*
ili estis falintaj *they had fallen*

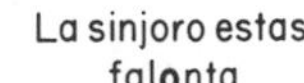

La sinjoro estas fal**o**nta

La sinjoro estas fal**a**nta

La sinjoro estas fal**i**nta

(*iii*) The future perfect tense:

mi estos falinta	*I shall have fallen*
vi estos falinta	*you will have fallen*
li estos falinta	*he will have fallen*
ŝi estos falinta	*she will have fallen*
ĝi estos falinta	*it will have fallen*
ni estos falintaj	*we shall have fallen*
vi estos falintaj	*you (plural) will have fallen*
ili estos falintaj	*they will have fallen*

Note 1 In such sentences, 'have' is never translated by **havi**, which means 'to have' in the sense of 'to possess'.

Mi estas falinta = lit. *I am having-fallen: I have fallen.*

2 The participle, like an adjective, takes **-j** if the subject is plural (**ni estas falint**aj).

3 *-onta*

There is also a third participle in Esperanto, not found in English. This is used to describe an action which has not yet started but is on the point of starting, and it gives the idea of 'about to' or 'going to':

La viro **ironta** en la domon estas mia edzo.
The man about to go into the house is my husband.

La arbo estis **falonta**.
The tree was about to fall.

La fantomo estas **aperonta**.
The ghost is about to appear.

Mi venos en la **venonta** vintro.
I shall come in the coming winter (about-to-come winter).
Estonta tempo.
Future time (about-to-be time).

PRAKTIKO 11.1 Traduku anglen:

Mi vidis la kurantan knabon. La maljuna viro sidis kaj rigardis la pasantajn homojn. La knabino rigardis la falintan arbon. La politikisto alparolis la ĉeestantajn homojn. La enlitiĝantaj infanoj diris 'bonan nokton' al siaj gepatroj. La viroj foriris de la falonta arbo. Mi esperas, ke la vetero estas varmiĝonta. Mi estis aŭdinta la novaĵon. Je la dua horo Andreo estos fininta sian tagmanĝon. Mi estas lerninta multon el ĉi tiu libro. Ili estis ĝuintaj la feriojn. Maria estas kreskinta multe dum la jaro. Kiam vi venos, mi estos preparinta la tagmanĝon. Miaj gepatroj estis vizitintaj min la antaŭan tagon.

PRAKTIKO 11.2 Traduku esperanten:

(*Note*: Use compound verbs where possible.)
I have bought a new jacket. At three o'clock he will have finished the task. At half past seven I was about to pack my clothes. I had long (**longe**) admired that writer (**verk-**). I was going to inform him about that, but I forgot. She will have decided that before tomorrow. I had announced it when he came in. The show is going to last two hours.

PRAKTIKO 11.3 Make all nine possible combinations from the following table, and translate each into English:

Ŝi	est is est as est os	lud inta lud anta lud onta

Participle-nouns

4 The participles can take the ending **-o** in place of **-a**, and such nouns indicate a person performing the action (English '-er', '-or'):

ami *to love*	am**anto** *lover*
detrui *to destroy*	detru**anto** *destroyer*
helpi *to help*	help**anto** *helper*
komenci *to begin*	komenc**anto** *beginner*
krei *to create*	kre**anto** *creator*
legi *to read*	leg**anto** *reader*
loĝi *to live, dwell*	loĝ**anto** *dweller, inhabitant*
protekti *to protect*	protekt**anto** *protector*
okupi *to occupy*	okup**anto** *occupier, occupant*
venki *to conquer*	venk**anto** *conqueror, victor*
vendi *to sell*	vend**anto** *seller, vendor*

(This is how Esperanto got its name! Dr Zamenhof, to avoid 'tying' the language to himself, adopted the pseudonym 'Doktoro Esperanto', from the verb **esperi** *to hope*.)

Note also that the past and future participles can take the ending **-o**:

posedi *to possess*	posed**into** *one who has possessed, ex-owner*
korespondi *to correspond*	korespond**into** *one who has corresponded, ex-correspondent*
konduki *to conduct*	konduk**onto** *one who is going to conduct, conductor*
vojaĝi *to travel*	vojaĝ**onto** one who is going to travel

Comparison

5 ***Ju. . .des. . .***

The expression 'the (more/less) . . . the (more/less)', used in the comparison between two acts or states, is translated by **ju (pli/malpli) . . . des (pli/malpli)**:

Ju pli vi rigardos ĝin, **des pli** vi ŝatos ĝin.
The more you look at it, the more you will like it.

Ju pli rapide, **des pli** bone.
The quicker, the better.

Ju pli mi legas ĝin, **des malpli** mi komprenas ĝin.
The more I read it, the less I understand it.

Ju malpli mi laboras, **des malpli** mi volas labori.
The less I work, the less I want to work.

Occasionally **des pli** is used in the sense 'all the more', 'so much the more':

Mi kuris **des pli** rapide.
I ran all the quicker.
Des pli bone.
So much the better.

Any, -ever

6 ***Ajn***

The word **ajn** is used to give a generalising sense to the expression. Placed after a correlative beginning with **k-**, it corresponds to the English '-ever:'

kiu ajn	*whoever, whichever*	kie ajn	*wherever*
kio ajn	*whatever*	kiam ajn	*whenever*
kia ajn	*whatever kind of*	kiom ajn	*however much*

Li atendu, kiu ajn li estas.
Let him wait, whoever he is.

Kion ajn vi trovas, vi rajtas reteni.
Whatever you find, you may keep.

Mi iros, kia ajn estos la vetero.
I shall go whatever the weather is like.

Li sidas, kie ajn li volas.
He sits wherever he wants.

Kiam ajn li venos, li estos bonvena.
Whenever he comes, he will be welcome.

When **ajn** is used with a correlative beginning with **i-**, it is usually translated by *any* (*at all, whatever*):

iu ajn	*any(one)*	ie ajn	*anywhere*
io ajn	*anything*	iam ajn	*any time*
ia ajn	*any kind of*	iom ajn	*any amount*

Mi ne konis iun ajn en la ĉambro.
I did not know anyone (at all) in the room.

Donu al mi ion ajn por trinki.
Give me anything (at all) to drink.

Mi estas preta iri en ia ajn vetero.
I am ready to go in any kind of weather.

Ŝi povas dormi ie ajn.
She can sleep anywhere.

Suffix/prefix

7 *-il-*

The suffix **-il-** is used to denote the *instrument* by which the action expressed by the 'root' is carried out:

tranĉi	*to cut*	tranĉ**il**o	*knife*
ŝlosi	*to lock*	ŝlos**il**o	*key*
kombi	*to comb*	komb**il**o	*a comb*
boligas	*boils*	bolig**il**o	*boiler, kettle*
kuiri	*to cook*	kuir**il**o	*cooking utensil*
flugi	*to fly*	flug**il**o	*wing*
aviado	*aviation*	aviad**il**o	*aircraft, plane*

8 ***ek-***

The prefix **ek-** is used to denote the beginning of an action, or to show that it is just momentary:

vidi *to see*	**ek**vidi *to catch sight of*
iri *to go*	**ek**iri *to set off, start*
dormi *to sleep*	**ek**dormi *to fall asleep*
bruli *to burn, be on fire*	**ek**bruli *to catch fire*
posedi *to possess*	**ek**posedi *to take possession of*
flugi *to fly*	**ek**flugi *to take flight*
brili *to shine*	**ek**brili *to flash*
rigardi *to look (at)*	**ek**rigardi *to glance (at)*
scii *to know*	**ek**scii *to get to know, find out*

Teksto

KELKAJ REKLAMOJ

Komercistoj-Turistoj-kaj ĉiuj vojaĝontoj-

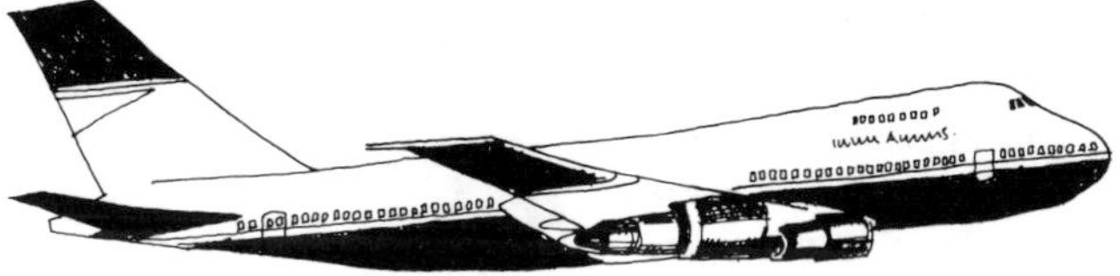

Uzu 'FULMO' aviadil-servojn! Per niaj 'flugantaj aŭtobusoj', kiuj ekflugas je ĉiu horo, vi atingos iun ajn parton de la mondo, plej rapide kaj komforte, je minimuma kosto.

Kun plezuro ni aranĝos ankaŭ vian eksterlandan ferion en la venonta somero. Ni garantias, ke ĉiu el niaj multaj vojaĝplanoj nepre plaĉos al vi!

FULMO AVIADILSERVOJ – OLDAM STRATO
LONDONO

NOVAJ GEEDZOJ!

Baldaŭ vi ekposedos vian hejmon, kaj estas aĉetontaj meblaron. Pripensu tion: ĝi estas akompanonta vin dum multaj jaroj! Do: ne oferu la avantaĝojn de longa spertado por ŝpari iom da mono. Niaj spertegaj laboristoj konas nur **unu** kvaliton: la PLEJ BONAN! Ju pli vi rigardos iun ajn meblon el nia fabriko, des pli vi ŝatos ĝin.

Ni invitas vin kontroli tion per la propraj okuloj – vizitu nian magazenon!

'IDEALHEJMO' MEBLISTOJ–BRISTOL

Eleganta meblaro por la manĝoĉambro kun 3 seĝoj kaj 1 brakseĝo

SPORTISTOJ!

Kiuj Sportoj Interesas Vin?

Ĉu teniso? biciklado? naĝado? subakva naĝado? akvo-skiado? velado? montgrim-pado? skiado? rajdado?

Kian ajn sporton vi preferas, ne aĉetu viajn novajn vestojn aŭ ekipaĵon sen konsulti nin!

Ni havas ampleksan stokon de vestoj kaj ekipaĵo por ĉiuj el ili.

VI NOMU ĜIN–NI HAVAS ĜIN!

***'SPORTEKIPO'*: LONDONO MANĈESTRO EDINBURGO**

ELEKTRO

HELPANTO

Ĉiu bezonas elektron en la hejmo. Sed ĉu vi jam ekspluatas ĉiujn ĝiajn eblecojn? Ni havas grandajn stokojn de ĉiaj elektraj aparatoj je malaltaj prezoj!

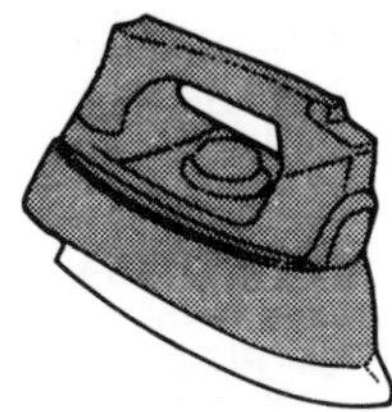

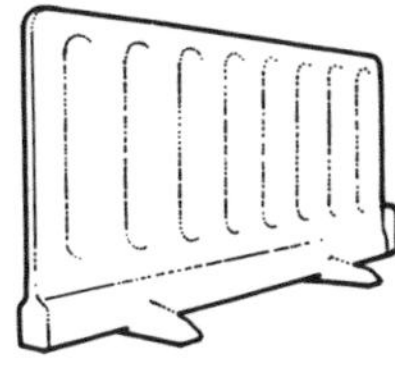

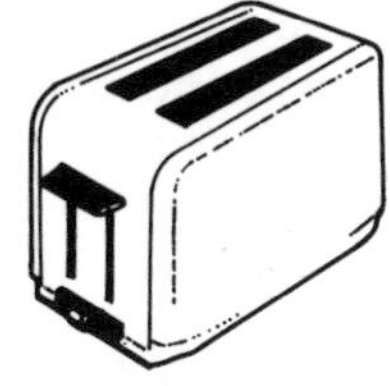

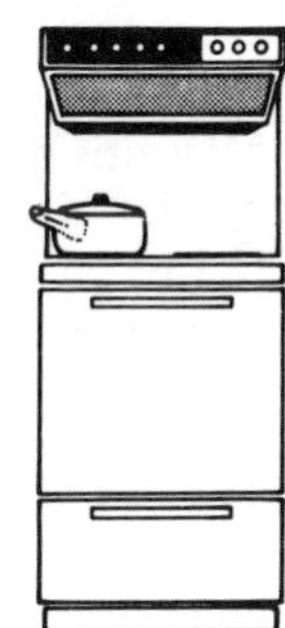

boligiloj
gladiloj
kuirfornoj
fridujoj
frostigiloj
harar-sekigiloj
komputoroj
lavmaŝinoj
magnetofonoj
manĝilarlaviloj
mikro-ondaj bakujoj
miksiloj
panrostiloj
polvosuĉiloj
radiofonoj
raziloj
sekigiloj (agitaj kaj centrifugaj)
stereo-aŭdigiloj
televidiloj
varmigiloj ĉiuspecaj
vidbendaparatoj

Nia komerco estas kreskinta el unu simpla butiko; ni nun havas 128 butikojn tra la tuta lando. Ni staros ĉiam je via servo en venontaj jaroj, kiel en la pasintaj

PRAKTIKO 11.4 Traduku anglen:

Per niaj 'flugantaj aŭtobusoj' vi atingos iun ajn parton de la mondo. Ni aranĝos viajn eksterlandajn feriojn en la venonta somero. Ĉu vi estas aĉetonta meblaron? Ju pli vi rigardos iun ajn meblon el nia fabriko, des pli vi ŝatos ĝin. Ĉu vi havas elektran gladilon? Ĉu vi havas elektran lavmaŝinon? En kiu ĉambro troviĝas via kuirforno? Ĉu via kuirforno estas elektra? Nia komerco estas kreskinta el unu simpla butiko. Ni staros ĉiam je via servo en venontaj jaroj, kiel en la pasintaj. Ju pli vi uzos niajn servojn, des pli da mono vi ŝparos. Ju pli rapide vi veturos, des pli bone. Baldaŭ ni ekposedos novan domon. Ni ekiris frue por atingi la butikon.

PRAKTIKO 11.5 Traduku esperanten:

The plane has flown northwards. Our business is growing very quickly. It has grown from a small shop. We are at your service as in past years. I have seen your store. We had already bought our furniture. He was about to travel to Germany. She set off early. What will you do in the coming winter? The more I look at it, the less I like it. Where is the key? Do you have (possess) a knife? I haven't got a comb. He passed in front of the woman without a glance.

PRAKTIKO 11.6 Complete the following sentences by filling in the missing endings. Endings can be one, two or three letters, but there is only one correct ending in each case:

1 Hieraŭ ni ekvetur– al Italujo por ni– ferioj.
2 Mi vizitis butik – por aĉet – jup–, sed vid – bel – rob – kiu tre plaĉ – al mi.
3 Help– mi–, mi petas. Bonvol– ne forir–!
4 Kiam mi iris en la kuirej– mi vid– mi– du fratin–.
5 Rigardu ti– falint– arb– !

Dialogo

Venontjaraj ferioj

Klara kaj Rikardo vespermanĝas.

Klara Hodiaŭ matene venis letero de Chantal kaj Marteno. Jen ĝi.

Rikardo Mi legos ĝin kiam mi estos fininta la vespermanĝon. Ĉu ĝi enhavas ion aparte interesan?

Klara Nu, ĝi konsistas ĉefe el rakonto pri iliaj agadoj, sed ĉe la fino ili diras, ke venontjare ili iros al la Universala Kongreso de Esperanto, en Belurbo[1]. Ili demandas, ĉu ni intencas partopreni en ĝi.

Rikardo Mi tute ne pensis pri ĝi! Kion vi opinias?

Klara Mi vere bezonas scii pli pri ĝi. Mi scias, ke tiuj kongresoj okazas ĉiujare en diversaj landoj, kaj ke kelkaj miloj da homoj partoprenas en ili.

Rikardo Kaj mi memoras, ke iam, kiam oni menciis ĝin en la Esperantogrupo, oni diris, ke kutime estas partoprenantoj el pli ol kvardek landoj.

Klara Sed ne allogas min la ideo pasigi plurajn tagojn en enuigaj kunvenoj. Tio ne estas mia ideo pri feriado!

Rikardo Ho, sed la kongresoj ne konsistas nur el kunvenoj. Kompreneble, ja okazas kunvenoj, de homoj kun similaj interesoj; ekzemple, sciencistoj, anoj de diversaj religiaj kredoj, instruistoj, fervojistoj, kaj multaj aliaj. Sed estas ankaŭ sociaj eventoj, teatraĵoj, kaj tiel plu.

Klara Nu, tio ŝajnas pli interesa . . . se ni povas toleri la elspezon! Sed . . . ĉu tio vere estus taŭga feriado por la infanoj?

Rikardo Mi iom dubas pri tio. Sed hodiaŭ la Esperantogrupo kunvenos, kaj estos via vico iri, dum mi prizorgas la infanojn. Do, vi povos demandi, kaj eble ricevos ankaŭ multajn aliajn informojn[2]. Ju pli ni ekscios, des pli bone!

Klara Jes, mi demandos pri la tuta afero.

(Pli malfrue en la vespero.)

Rikardo Nu, ĉu vi ricevis la necesajn informojn pri la kongresoj?

Klara Jes, mi eksciis multon pri ili.

Rikardo Kaj kion pri la infanoj? Se la kongreso ne taŭgas por ili, ni malŝparas tempon diskuti ĝin!

Klara La kongreso mem ne taŭgos por ili, sed ĉiujare, okazas je la sama tempo tiel-nomata Infana Kongreseto, en iu loko ne tro malproksima de la Universala Kongreso. Tiel, kongresanoj, kies infanoj komprenas Esperanton, scias, ke oni bone prizorgas ilin.

Rikardo Bonŝance, niaj infanoj jam bone komprenas ĝin. Sed mi scivolas, kiel ili pasigos la tempon.

Klara Johano Danby diris al mi, ke la kongresetoj kutime okazas en la kamparo aŭ ĉe la marbordo, kaj la infanoj dividiĝas en malgrandajn grupojn, ĉiu kun sia plenkreska gvidanto. Oni organizas ludojn, promenojn, ekskursojn, kaj tiel plu.

Rikardo Kiel oni dividas ilin? ĉu en naciajn grupojn?

Klara Male, ĉiu grupo konsistas, laŭeble, el infanoj el diversaj landoj, tiel, ke ili devas paroli Esperanton.

Rikardo Kia bona ideo! Kaj ĉu vi eksciis ion pli pri la Universala Kongreso mem? Ekzemple, kiomlonge ĝi daŭras?

Klara La kongreso daŭras unu semajnon, sed tiuj, kiuj deziras ferii dum du semajnoj, povas aniĝi ankaŭ al 'antaŭkongreso' aŭ 'postkongreso', kiu estas feria semajno okazanta, kiel la nomo indikas, antaŭ aŭ post la kongreso.

Rikardo Nu, tio dependos de la kosto, ĉu ne? Kaj ni volos ekscii, ĉu Marteno kaj Chantal intencas partopreni en ambaŭ aferoj.

[1] **Belurbo** – a fictitious town.

[2] **Informo** is really a piece of information, hence the plural in this case.

Demandoj

1 Kial Rikardo ne tuj legas la leteron?
2 Kion demandas Chantal kaj Marteno en la letero?
3 Kiam kaj kie okazas la Universalaj Kongresoj de Esperanto?
4 Ĉu ili konsistas nur el kunvenoj?
5 Pri kio Klara kaj Rikardo dubas?
6 Kial Klara kaj Rikardo ne iras kune al la Esperantogrupo?
7 En kio la infanoj povas partopreni?
8 Kie la Infanaj Kongresetoj kutime okazas?
9 Kiel la infanoj dividiĝas?
10 Ĉu oni organizas ilin en naciajn grupojn?

agado *action, activity*
agita sekigilo *tumble-drier*
ampleksa *extensive*
atingi *to attain, reach*
bakujo *oven*
boli *boil* (intrans.); **boligi** *to boil (something)*; **boligilo** *kettle*
bonŝanca *lucky*
bruna *brown*
centrifuga sekigilo *spin-drier*
dubi *to doubt, be doubtful*
ekipaĵo *equipment*
ekspluati *to exploit*
enui *to be bored*; **enuigi** *to bore (someone)*
fabriki *to manufacture*; **fabriko** *factory*
frosti *to freeze*; **frostigilo** *freezer*
fulmo *lightning*
gladi *to iron*
grimpi *to climb*
gvidi *to guide, lead*
haro *a hair*; **hararo** *the hair (of head, etc.)*
indiki *to indicate*
intenci *to intend*
kontroli *to check* (not *control*)
kudri *to sew*
kuirforno *cooker*
kvalito *quality*
laŭeble *as far as possible*
magazeno *store, large shop*
magnetofono *tape recorder*
manĝilaro *crockery, dishes*
marbordo *coast, seaside*
mem *oneself, itself, themselves, etc.*
mikro-onda *microwave*
naĝi *to swim*
nepre *without fail*
nome *namely*
oferi *to sacrifice* (not *offer*)
okulo *eye*
pan-rostilo *toaster*
pantalono *pair of trousers* (note: singular)
partopreni *to take part*
pasi *to pass (by)*; **pasigi** *to spend (time)*
polvo *dust*; **polvosuĉilo** *vacuum-cleaner*
poŝo *pocket*
prezo *price*
prizorgi *to look after*
proksima *near*; **malproksima** *distant*; **proksimume** *approximately*
radiofono *radio*
rajdi *to ride (horse, cycle, etc.)*
rajti *to be entitled to*; **Ĉu mi rajtas?** *May I?*
rakonto *story, account*
razi *to shave*
robo *dress, robe*
ruĝa *red*
scivoli *to wonder (want to know)*
sperti *to experience*
ŝati *to appreciate, think highly of*
ŝlosi *to lock*
ŝpari *to save*; **malŝpari** *to waste*
taŭga *suitable*; **taŭgi** *to be suitable*
velado *sailing*
vico *(someone's) turn*
vidbendaparato *video recorder*

Esprimo:
toleri la elspezon de *to afford*

12 Paĝo de flank-okupoj

Verbs preceding their subjects

1 When the verb precedes its subject in English, we use the word 'there' or 'it' to introduce or draw attention to the subject. Neither of these words is translated in Esperanto.

Estas bildo sur la muro.
There is a picture on the wall.
Estis multaj hundoj en la parko.
There were many dogs in the park.
Estos pli da viroj ol virinoj tie.
There will be more men than women there.

Note: This use of 'there' should not be confused with **tie**, which means *there* in the sense of *in that place*.

Estas mi.
It is I.
Estis Maria, ne Arturo, en la ĝardeno.
It was Mary, not Arthur, in the garden.
Estos lundo morgaŭ.
It will be Monday tomorrow.

Note: This use of 'it' should not be confused with **ĝi**, which stands in place of a noun (cf. Unit 6, note **1**).

The introductory 'It'

2 As shown above, the word 'it' is translated only when it represents some definite noun. In the following sentences, 'it' introduces and is equal to the part beginning with 'that' or with an infinitive:

Estas vere, ke vi estas frua. = Ke vi estas frua estas vere.
It is true that you are early. *That you are early is true.*
(It = That you are early)

Ne estas eble, nei la ekziston de Dio. =	Nei la ekziston de Dio ne estas eble.
It is not possible to deny the existence of God.	*To deny the existence of God is not possible.*

(It = To deny the existence of God)

Plaĉis al ŝi, ke vi povis resti. =	Ke vi povis resti plaĉis al ŝi.
It pleased her that you were able to stay.	*That you were able to stay pleased her.*

(It = That you were able to stay)

Note that because the 'it' is not translated, what is an adjective in English (It is *true*; It is not *possible*) becomes an adverb in Esperanto (**Estas vere; Ne estas eble**).

Myself, himself, etc.

3 *Mem*

The word **mem** is used to throw emphasis on the noun or pronoun it follows:

Mi mem ne estas surda.
I myself am not deaf.

Li mem ne povas iri.
He himself cannot go.

Mi renkontis la reĝinon mem.
I met the queen herself.

La kato mem rifuzis trinki ĝin.
The cat itself refused to drink it.

Ni mem neniam aŭskultas al la radio.
We ourselves never listen to the radio.

Ŝi parolis al la viroj mem.
She spoke to the men themselves.

Note that although **mem** is translated by *myself, himself, ourselves, themselves*, etc., it is in no way reflexive and should not be confused with **si**. In fact, it is often used with the reflexive pronoun to give added emphasis, though this is not translated in English:

Li razas sin mem.
He shaves himself (no one else does it).

Mem is also used as a prefix to show that a condition is independent by itself without outside help:

memevidenta *self-evident (without further explanation).*
meminstruita *self-taught (without the aid of a teacher).*
memstara *independent (by itself without support).*

Word-building

4 You have seen how words may be changed or built up in various ways:

(*a*) by changing the grammatical ending:

lok**o** *place, locality* lok**a** *local*

(*b*) by putting a prefix before the root*:

bona *good* **mal**bona *bad*

(*c*) by adding a suffix between the root and the grammatical ending:

manĝi *to eat* manĝ**aĵ**o *food*

(*d*) by using a preposition as a prefix:

iri *to go* **trans**iri *to go across (to cross)*

You may also have noticed for yourself how we can put two roots together to make a compound word. In this case the main word stands at the end:

libroŝranko (ŝranko por libroj) *bookcase*
dormoĉambro (ĉambro por dormi) *bedroom*

The ending **-o** is usually omitted from the first root, provided the resulting group of consonants is easy to pronounce:

horsignalo (signalo de la horo) *time signal*
semajnfino (fino de la semajno) *weekend*

A number of useful words can be made from **sama** (*same*) by using **sam-** as a prefix:

samtempe *at the same time*
sammaniere *in the same way*
samlandano *fellow countryman*
samklasano *classmate*
samideano *fellow member,* lit. *'member of the same idea' (often used to denote a fellow esperantist)*

* The *root* is that part of a word which does not change, and to which prefixes, suffixes and grammatical endings are attached.

PRAKTIKO 12.1 Traduku anglen:

Estas vere, ke nia komerco rapide kreskas. Necesas, ke ni tuj iru tien. Estas eble, ke li estas surda. Nur li mem scias tion. Estas vere, ke Esperanto estas pli simpla ol aliaj lingvoj. Sed eĉ Esperanto ne lernos sin mem; oni devas labori por lerni ĝin! Ŝajnas al mi, ke tio estas memevidenta. Estas danĝere transiri la straton sen rigardi ambaŭflanken. Estas pli facile konsili, ol akcepti konsilon. Ne oportunas al mi fari tiun taskon nun; vi mem devos fari ĝin.

PRAKTIKO 12.2 Traduku esperanten:

There are a lot of trees in the park. It was I who said that. I myself met the queen. I met the queen herself. It is quite possible that he will not be able to come. It was late: I got out of bed quickly and got dressed (dressed myself). The quicker (more quickly) he ran, the sooner he arrived. It is obvious that he himself cannot go. There are two pictures on the wall of my room. The more I see them, the less I like them.

PRAKTIKO 12.3
From the roots **ban-**, **ĉambr-**, **ĉarm-**, **ĉeval-**, **erar-**, **land-**, **manĝ-**, **nov-**, **patr-**, **trov-**, **ven-**, make one word each for the following:

1	to arrive	11	old
2	bathroom	12	to return
3	charm	13	something found
4	dining-room	14	stable
5	error	15	suite of rooms
6	fatherland	16	worth finding
7	foal	17	charmingly
8	to make a mistake	18	bathing place
9	food	19	mare
10	news	20	novice

5 ***Kaj . . . kaj . . . , aŭ . . . aŭ . . . , nek . . . nek . . .***
The words **kaj**, **aŭ** and **nek** are used in pairs as follows:
kaj . . . kaj . . . = *both . . . and . . .*

> Ŝi estas **kaj** bela **kaj** bona.
> *She is* both *beautiful* and *good.*

aŭ . . . aŭ . . . = *either . . . or . . .*

> **Aŭ** pluvos **aŭ** neĝos.
> *It will* either *rain* or *snow.*

nek . . . nek . . . = *neither . . . nor . . .*

Li estas **nek** riĉa **nek** malriĉa.
He is neither *rich* nor *poor.*

6 *Jen . . . jen . . .*
The word **jen** is also repeated to give the meaning *now . . . now . . . (sometimes . . . sometimes . . .)*

Mi vizitas **jen** teatron **jen** kinejon.
I visit sometimes *a theatre*, sometimes *a cinema.*

7 *Ĉu . . . ĉu . . .*
By analogy, the word **ĉu** is repeated to give the meaning *whether . . . or . . .*

Ĉu knabo, **ĉu** knabino, la infano estos bonvena.
Whether *a boy* or *girl, the child will be welcome.*

But perhaps it is more usual to find **Ĉu . . . aŭ** (the second **ĉu** being understood).

Mi ne scias, **ĉu** iri **aŭ** (ĉu) resti.
I do not know whether *to go* or *(whether) to stay.*

Suffixes and prefixes

8 *-estr-*
The suffix **-estr-** is used to denote the *person in charge*. It is much used as an independent word to translate *boss.*

lernejo *school*	lernej**estr**o *headmaster*
urbo *town*	urb**estr**o *mayor*
lando *country*	land**estr**o *head of state*
imperio *empire*	imperi**estrin**o *empress*
poŝto *post, mail*	poŝt**estrin**o *postmistress*

9 *-em-*
The suffix **-em-** is used to denote a disposition, inclination or proneness to do the thing which is expressed in the root. **Emi** is much used as an independent word to translate *to be inclined to.*

paroli *to speak, talk*	parol**em**a *talkative*
ludi *to play*	lud**em**a *playful*
labori *to work*	labor**em**a *diligent*
batali *to fight*	batal**em**a *pugnacious*
kvereli *to quarrel*	kverel**em**a *quarrelsome*
plendi *to complain*	plend**em**a *querulous, complaining*
ŝpari *to save (up)*	ŝpar**em**a *thrifty*
suspekti *to suspect*	suspekt**em**a *suspicious (by nature)*
timi *to fear, be afraid*	tim**em**a *timid*

10 *fuŝ-*

Fuŝi = *to spoil, botch, make a mess of, bungle, (either intentionally or through lack of attention or stupidity)*:

Vi certe fuŝos plurajn el ili.
You will certainly spoil (make a mess of) several of them.
Li fuŝis ĉion.
He bungled everything.
Fuŝulo *a bungler.*

Note: **Fuŝ-** is used as a prefix with this meaning: fuŝ**fotografisto** *a bungling photographer.*

11 *dis-*

The prefix **dis-** expresses dispersal or separation:

sendi *to send*	**dis**sendi *to distribute, circulate*
ŝiri *to tear*	**dis**ŝiri *to tear to shreds*
fali *to fall*	**dis**fali *to fall to pieces*
bati *to beat*	**dis**bati *to dash to pieces*

12 *bo-*

The prefix **bo-** is used to denote relationship by marriage, i.e. 'in-law':

patro *father*	**bo**patro *father-in-law*
patrino *mother*	**bo**patrino *mother-in-law*
frato *brother*	**bo**frato *brother-in-law*
fratino *sister*	**bo**fratino *sister-in-law*
filo *son*	**bo**filo *son-in-law*
filino *daughter*	**bo**filino *daughter-in-law*
parenco *relative*	**bo**parencoj *'in-laws' (relatives by marriage)*

Note also: **bo**gepatroj *parents-in-law.*

Teksto

PAĜO DE FLANKOKUPOJ

La amatora fotografisto

BIRD-FOTOGRAFADO

La birdoj estas konstruontaj – eĉ jam konstruantaj – siajn nestojn. Ĉu vi iam penis fotografi birdojn ĉe la nesto? Por tio, oni bezonas nek altekostan[1] aparaton, nek profesian lertecon; eĉ fuŝfotografisto sukcesos, se li havas unu virton: pacienco!

Komencanto prudente elektos birdon kies nesto kuŝas aŭ sur tero aŭ sur akvo – ne en alta arbo. Birdoj estas tre suspektemaj kaj timemaj; tial oni devas uzi kaŝejon. La bildo montras kiel konstrui simplan skeleton, kiun oni kovras per dubekolora[2] sak-tolo, kun truo por la lenso. Ekfiksu la kaŝejon je longa distanco de la nesto, kaj movu ĝin ĉiutage pli proksimen, ĝis, fine, ĝi estas staranta nur 2 aŭ 3 metrojn for de la nesto.

Kiam vi estas preta fari la fotojn, estu certa ke vi kunportas sufiĉe da filmo. (Vi certe fuŝos plurajn bildojn!) Vi bezonos ankaŭ notlibron kaj – amikon! Kiam vi estas sidanta komforte en la kaŝejo, la amiko formarŝas, kun bruo.

Galinolo ĉe la nesto
(foto de unu el niaj legantoj)

La birdo ne povas kalkuli: ĝi vidas, ke unu homo foriras, kaj ĝi ne suspektas, ke alia homo ankoraŭ restas en la kaŝejo. Ĝi do revenas al la nesto, kaj vi povos fari multajn belajn fotojn – se la fortuno favoras vin!

[1] *'higly-costing': expensive.*
[2] *'doubtfully-coloured': drab.*

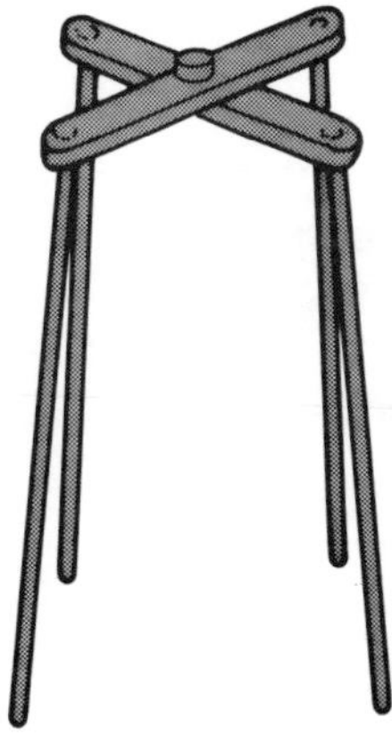

Faldebla skeleto de kaŝejo

Kaŝejo preta, kun kovrilo

En via ĝardeno:

PRINTEMPAJ TASKOJ

KONSTRUADO DE ROKĜARDENO

Laborema ĝardenamanto kaptos nun la okazon por konstrui rokĝardenon. Tia ĝardeno bonege utiligos negrandan spacon, kaj ĝiaj plantoj provizos tre kontentigajn[1] rezultojn – kaj laŭ kvanto, kaj laŭ kvalito.

La bildo (p. 142) montras kiel kuŝigi la rokojn. Ne uzu tro da rokoj! Malmultaj sufiĉas.

Inter belaj rokplantoj oni havas tre vastan elekton. Ili estas tre *rampèmaj*, do necesas severe regi ilian kreskadon.

Multajn rokplantojn oni povas ankaŭ meti en potojn kaj starigi jen en pordejoj, jen en fenestroj, kie ili kreskos kaj floros eĉ dum la vintro.

[1] *'making-satisfied': satisfactory.*

Vizito al Kew

Laŭ afabla invito de la Ĝardenestro, la anoj de nia ĝardenista klubo faros oficialan viziton al Kew, venontan sabaton je la 2.30 p.t.m. La kondukonto estas nia Prezidanto, S-ro Green.

KONSTRUADO de ROKĜARDENO

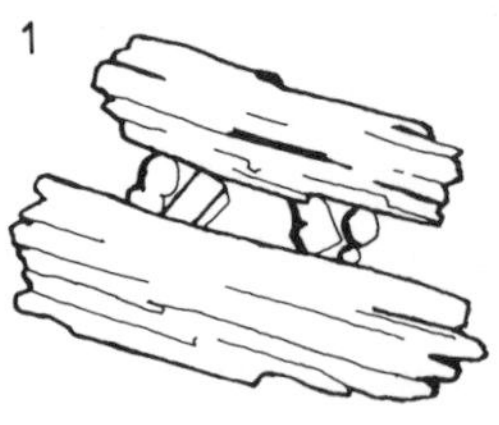

Apartigu la rokojn per roketoj aŭ brikoj

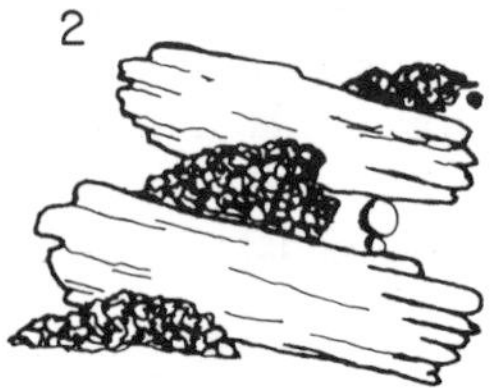

Klinu la rokojn jene, kaj plenigu la inter-spacojn per humo

Nur malmulte da roko restu videbla!

Per simpla aparato, oni povas konstrui ankaŭ akvofaleton

PRAKTIKO 12.4 Traduku anglen:

Por fotografi birdojn, oni bezonas nek altekostan aparaton, nek profesian lertecon. Nek la kvanto nek la kvalito estas kontentiga. La nesto devas esti aŭ sur tero aŭ sur akvo. Li estas aŭ tro prudenta, aŭ tro timema. Oni povas meti ilin aŭ en potojn aŭ en la ĝardenon. Ĝi estas kaj necesa kaj utila. Birdoj estas kaj suspektemaj kaj timemaj. La kaŝejo estas kaj simpla kaj malaltekosta. Oni povas starigi ilin jen en pordejo jen en fenestro. Vi sukcesos, ĉu vi estas profesia fotografisto, ĉu fuŝfotografisto. Ĉu birdoj estas tre suspektemaj kaj timemaj? Ĉu vi estas tre laborema? Ĉu rokplantoj estas tre rampemaj? Ĉu vi estas lernejestrino? Aŭ poŝtestrino? Ĉu la ĝardenestro invitis la anojn de nia ĝardenista klubo?

PRAKTIKO 12.5 Traduku esperanten:

He is neither good nor bad. Neither near nor far. It is neither the door nor the window. You can choose either one or the other. The results are good, both in quantity and in quality. Now she runs, now she walks. I do not know whether to go, or to stay. Who is the mayor? Do you know the headmaster? The kitten is very playful. He is very quarrelsome. He makes a mess of everything.

PRAKTIKO 12.6 Respondu:

1 Ĉu necesas profesia lerteco por sukcese fotografi birdojn?
2 Kian birdon elektos prudenta komencanto?
3 Kial oni devus havi multe da filmo?
4 Kion la birdo ne suspektas?
5 Kian avantaĝon havas rokĝardeno se oni havas malgrandan ĝardenon?
6 Ĉu oni bezonas multe da rokoj por fari rokĝardenon?
7 Per kio oni apartigu la rokojn?
8 Kial necesas severe regi la kreskadon de la rokplantoj?
9 Kiuj faros viziton al Kew, kaj je kiu tago?
10 Laŭ kies invito ili iros tien?

Dialogo

La Kristnaskfesto

La familio Lang gastigas siajn parencojn je la Kristnaska tago. Ĉeestas la patrino de Klara ('Avino'); Marko kaj Dorina, frato kaj bofratino de Rikardo; kaj Junia kaj Stefano, fratino kaj bofrato de Klara. Ili estas finantaj la Kristnaskan tagmanĝon.

Marko Nu, mi devas diri, ke tio estis la plej bona festmanĝo, kiun mi iam manĝis!

La gastoj Jes! Ja! (*Ili aplaŭdas.*)

Klara (*ruĝiĝas*) Dankon. Mi ĝojas, ke ĝi plaĉis al vi. Sed ankaŭ Rikardo helpis.

Junia Ho, tiu meleagraĵo estis vere rava!

Stefano Kaj kiom multe da legomoj! Mi sentas, ke mi ne volos manĝi denove dum almenaŭ du tagoj!

Rikardo Kiomofte oni diras tion! Sed post kelkaj horoj oni ree estas preta.

Avino Mi estas tute certa, ke *mi ne* povos!

Klara Ho, Panjo, vi povos kiam la tempo venos.

Marko Kaj ankaŭ la vino estis bonega. Vi bone elektis, frato mia!

Rikardo Dankon.

Klara Nu, se vi ĉiuj jam finis, eble estus bone iri en la salonon kaj vidi, kion faras la infanoj. Ili lasis la tablon antaŭ iom longa tempo!

Marko Stefano kaj mi lavos la manĝilaron, ĉu ne, Stefano?

Klara Ho, dankon, sed ne nun. Ni lasos tion ĝis post la disdono de la donacoj. Venu en la salonon!

(Ĉiuj iras en la salonon, kie ili trovas Andreon kaj Marian, kiuj rigardadas la bele ornamitan Kristnaskarbon, sub kiu estas amaso da bele volvitaj pakoj.)

Klara Nu, do, infanoj. Kion vi faras?
Andreo Nenion, Panjo. Ni nur rigardas la arbon.
Klara Do, sidiĝu ĉiuj, mi petas. Laŭ nia kutimo, Andreo kaj Maria nun disdonos la donacojn.
Andreo (*prenas pakon kaj legas la etikedon*) Ĉi tiu estas por onklo Marko, de Panjo kaj Paĉjo.
Maria Por onklino Dorina de onklo Stefano . . .

(Ili daŭrigas la disdonadon, sed post du-tri minutoj Klara komencas aspekti iomete maltrankvila. Ŝi parolas mallaŭte al Rikardo.)

Klara Estas io nekutima . . . tiuj pakoj . . .
Rikardo Kio estas?
Stefano Pardonu, sed mi kredas, ke iu eraris. Ĉi tiu pako havas etikedon 'Al Stefano, de Dorina', sed en ĝi estas mansaketo!
Junia Kaj la mia, kun etikedo 'Al Junia, de Marko', enhavas abonbileton al la futbalejo!
Avino Mi estas certa, ke ĉi tiuj tri pipoj ne estas por mi!
Klara (*laŭte*) Infanoj! Kion vi scias pri tio ĉi? Kion vi faris?
Andreo Ni nur . . . ni nur . . . (*Li ekridas, kaj ne povas daŭrigi.*)
Maria Ni . . . ŝanĝis la etikedojn, Panjo.

(Kelkaj personoj komencas ridi.)

Klara (*penas soni severa*) Vi estas tre malbonkondutaj! Mi havas fortan volon sendi vin al la litoj!
Andreo Ho, Panjo!
Klara Sed ĉar estas Kristnasko, mi ne tion faros. (*Ŝi ekridetas.*) Kaj vere, tio estis iom amuza ŝerco!

(Ĉiuj ridas.)

Rikardo Nu, Andreo, se vi kaj Maria finos la disdonadon, la donintoj povos klarigi, por kiu ĉiu donaco estis destinita.
Stefano Kaj do, 'fino bona, ĉio bona'!

Demandoj

1 Kio estas la parenceco inter Dorina kaj Rikardo?
2 . . . kaj inter Avino kaj Rikardo?
3 . . . kaj inter Avino kaj Andreo?
4 Kian viandon oni manĝis je la Kristnaska tagmanĝo?
5 Kion oni trinkis?
6 Kiu elektis tion?
7 Kiu proponas lavi la manĝilaron?
8 Kion faras la infanoj dum la adoltoj trinkas post la manĝo?
9 Kiu unue suspektas, ke estas io stranga?
10 Kial la patrino ne sendas la infanojn al la litoj?

---

abonbileto *season ticket*
adolto *adult*
aparta *separate*; **apartigi** *to separate*
aplaŭdi *to applaud*
avo *grandfather*; **avino** *grandmother*
bruo *noise*
daŭrigi *to continue (something)*
donaco *a present*
elekti *to choose*
eraro *mistake, error*
etikedo *label*
faldi *to fold*
festo *party, celebration*; **festi** *to celebrate*
galinolo *moorhen*
gastigi *to entertain, have guests*
grundo *soil, earth*
humo *humus*
kaŝi *to hide (something)*
klini *to slope, incline (something)*
konstrui *to build*
kovri *to cover*
Kristnasko *Christmas*
kvanto *quantity*
laŭta *loud*; **mallaŭta** *quiet*
lerta *clever, skilful*
maniero *way, manner*
mansaketo *handbag*
meleagro *a turkey*; **meleagraĵo** *turkey (meat)*
nepo *nephew*
pako *parcel*
pardoni *to excuse, forgive*; **Pardonu!** *Excuse me!*
peni *to try*
pipo *(tobacco)-pipe*
pordejo *doorway*
rampi *to crawl*
rava *delightful*
ree *again*
soni *to sound*
sufiĉa *enough, sufficient*; **sufiĉi** *to suffice*
ŝerco *a joke*
tero *earth, ground*
truo *hole*
utila *useful*
vasta *spacious, wide, vast*
vino *wine*
virto *virtue*
volvi *to wrap*

Esprimoj:
du-tri *two or three*
forta volo *'a good mind (to)'* (lit. *a strong will*)
'fino bona, ĉio bona' *'all's well that ends well'*

13 Leteroj al la redaktisto

Indirect or reported speech

1 When we quote what someone has said, using the exact words, this is called *direct speech*, and we use quotation marks: I said, 'I am going!'

If, however, we report what someone has said, without using the exact words, this is called *indirect* or *reported speech*. You will notice that if the verb of saying etc. is in the past tense, the tense of the 'reported' verb goes into the past in English: I said (that) I *was going*.

In Esperanto, however, indirect speech has the same tense as direct speech:

Mi diris, 'Mi ir**as**!'
Mi diris, **ke** mi ir**as**.

Study the following examples:

Direct	*Indirect*
Li diris, 'Ŝi manĝ**as**!'	Li diris, **ke** ŝi manĝ**as**.
He said, 'She is *eating!'*	*He said (that) she* was *eating.*
Li diris, 'Ŝi manĝ**is**!'	Li diris, **ke** ŝi manĝ**is**.
He said, 'She has *eaten!'*	*He said (that) she* had *eaten.*
Li diris, 'Ŝi manĝ**os**!'	Li diris, **ke** ŝi manĝ**os**.
He *said, 'She* will *eat.'*	*He said (that) she* would *eat.*

2 The same thing happens if we report a question. Note that while in English we sometimes use 'if' instead of 'whether', in Esperanto we always use **ĉu**, never **se**.

He asked, 'Do you love me?'
Li demandis, 'Ĉu vi amas min?'

He asked whether (if) she loved *him.*
Li demandis, ĉu ŝi **amas** lin.

3 Indirect speech, despite its name, does not always refer to actual speech, but is used for thinking, believing, knowing, wondering, imagining, etc.:

> *I thought (that) he was very tall.*
> (*I thought, 'He* is *very tall.*')
> Mi opiniis, **ke** li est**as** tre alta.
>
> *I wondered whether (if) she would answer.*
> (*I wondered,* 'Will *she answer?*')
> Mi scivolis, ĉu ŝi respond**os**.
>
> *I knew (that) you would understand.*
> (*I knew, 'You* will *understand.*')
> Mi sciis, **ke** vi kompren**os**.

Passive participles

4 Corresponding to the three participles ending in **-anta**, **-inta** and **-onta** (Unit 11), there are three *passive participles* ending in **-ata**, **-ita** and **-ota**.

Of these, you have already met **-ita** (Unit 9, note **12**), which shows that the action has finished, or been completed:

> pres**ita** paperfolio = *a printed sheet of paper (one which* has been *printed)*
> ferm**ita** pordo = *a closed door (one which* has been *closed)*
> io perd**ita** = *something lost (which* has been *lost)*

-ata shows that the action is still in progress, or that the state is still applicable:

> am**ata** homo = *a man, person, who is (now, still) loved*
> kon**ata** lando = *a known country, a country which everyone knows*
> estim**ata** sinjoro = *dear Sir (one who is esteemed)*

-ota shows that the action has not yet been started:

> konstru**ota** domo = *a house which has yet (is going) to be built*
> far**ota** laboro = *work which has yet to be done*
> io elpens**ota** = *something which has yet to be thought out*

PRAKTIKO 13.1 Traduku anglen:

Li diris, ke li iros tiun posttagmezon. Ŝi opiniis, ke ŝia frato estas inteligenta. Mi scivolis, ĉu li diris ion al ŝi. Mi imagis, ke mia frato iros tien. Mia kuzo demandis, ĉu mi skribis la leteron. Mi respondis, ke mi skribos ĝin poste. Ili sendis al mi presitan leteron. Mia nova domo estas konstruota venontjare. Ĉu tiu tasko estas jam farita? Ne, ĝi estas nun farata. Ĉu vi jam sendis la leteron? Ne, ĝi estas ankoraŭ skribota.

PRAKTIKO 13.2 Traduku esperanten:

I asked her where (**kien**) she was going, and she replied that she was going to the shops. My brother said he had forgotten his book. He hoped (that) he would remember it today. I hoped she had finished it. Andrew said he was learning Esperanto. I asked Mary whether she would bring her new record, but she said she had lost it. Andrew thought it was in the cupboard, and said he would look for it.

PRAKTIKO 13.3 Translate the following signs, and having checked them against the key, try to retranslate them into Esperanto:

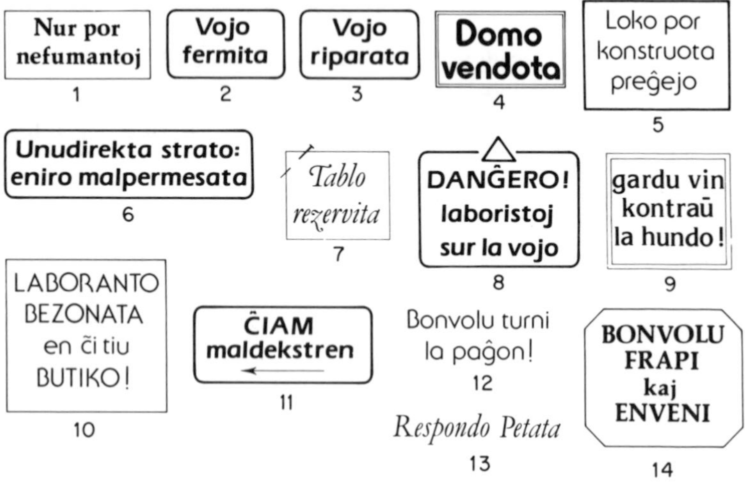

Compound tenses

5 Just as with the active participles, the passive participles can be combined with **estas**, **estis** and **estos**, for example:

Li estas edukita.	*He is educated.*
Li estas edukata.	*He is being educated.*
Li estas edukota.	*He is going to be educated.*

Li estis edukita.	*He was educated.*
Li estis edukata.	*He was being educated.*
Li estis edukota.	*He was going to be educated.*
Li estos edukita.	*He will be educated.*
Li estos edukata.	*He will be being educated.**
Li estos edukota.	*He will be going to be educated.**

6 Notice that when we say something is done *by* somebody, *by* is translated by **de**:

Mi estimas lin.	Li estas estim**ata de** mi.
I esteem him.	*He is esteemed* by *me.*
Li helpos vin.	Vi estas help**ota de** li.
He will help you.	*You are going to be helped* by *him.*

To show the 'instrument' with which an action is done, we usually use 'with' in English, but note that this is *not* **kun**, but **per** (*by means of*):

La hundo estis batata **de** la knabo **per** bastono.
The dog was being beaten by *the boy* with *a stick.*

La bildo estis desegnita **de** ŝi **per** krajono.
The picture was drawn by *her* with *a pencil.*

Note the following distinction:

La knabino ludis **kun** sia fratino.
The girl was playing with her sister.

La kato ludis **per** la muso.
The cat was playing with the mouse.

In the former case the sister was also playing, but in the latter case the mouse certainly was not! **Kun** always contains the idea of 'together with'; in fact **kune** means *together.*

Passive participles as nouns

7 The passive participles are also used as nouns, as follows:

ami *to love*	am**ato** *loved one*
instrui *to teach*	instru**ato** *trainee*
pagi *to pay*	pag**ato** *payee*
koni *to know, be acquainted with*	kon**ato** *acquaintance*

* Virtually never used.

mortigi *to kill*	mortig**ito** *someone who has been killed*
venki *to conquer*	venk**ito** *someone who has been conquered*
elekti *to choose*	elekt**oto** *someone who is going to be chosen*
viziti *to visit*	vizit**oto** *someone who is to be visited*

The relative pronoun

8 This term refers, in the main, to the pronoun **kiu**, with alternative forms **kiun**, **kiuj** and **kiujn**, (*who*, *whom*, *which*, *that*). Here are some examples of their uses as relative pronouns:

(*a*) the man *who* saw me
the man *that* saw me
(*b*) the letter *that* was on the table
the letter *which* was on the table
(*c*) the man (*whom*) I saw
the man (*that*) I saw
(*d*) the letter (*that*) I wrote
the letter (*which*) I wrote

Note that in (*c*) and (*d*) the pronouns in brackets may be omitted in English without altering the sense. Note also that in each of these cases the action is done, not by the man or the letter, as in (*a*) and (*b*), but by *me*. Since the pronoun in brackets (the relative pronoun) always refers to the word which precedes it, it refers in (*c*) and (*d*) to the *object* of the verb.

In Esperanto, these words must *always* be put in:

(*a*) la viro **kiu** vidis mi**n**
(*b*) la letero **kiu** estis sur la tablo
(*c*) la viro **kiun** mi vidis
(*d*) la letero **kiun** mi skribis

Remember that **kiu(n)** refers in each case to the word which precedes it. In (*a*) and (*b*) as we have seen, the word it refers to is the *subject* of the verb: **la viro** (subject) **vidis min**; **la letero** (subject) **estis sur la tablo**. In (*c*) and (*d*) the word referred to is the *object*: **mi** (subject) **vidis la viron** (object); **mi** (subject) **skribis la leteron** (object). This is why in the first two sets of examples, **kiu** does not take **-n**, while in the second two it does. In other words, if **kiu** refers to the object, it becomes **kiun**.

If the word preceding the relative pronoun is *plural*, the relative pronoun will have the forms **kiuj**, **kiujn**.

Note: **Ke** can *never* be used as a relative pronoun.

For the student, the main difficulty lies in recognising where to put in a relative pronoun when it is not used in English:

The book I read yesterday was good.
La libro, **kiun** mi legis hieraŭ, estis bona.

One possible consolation is that when we can miss it out in English, it will always end in **-n** in Esperanto!

9 Kies (*whose*) may also serve as a relative pronoun. **Kies** never changes; only the noun which follows it may change:

The woman whose *bag was on the table.*
La virino **kies** saketo estis sur la tablo.

The woman whose *bag he stole.*
La virino **kies** saketo**n** li ŝtelis.

Suffix/prefix

10 ***-aĉ-***

The suffix **aĉ-** is used to denote poorness of quality or condition, and forms words with a disparaging sense of that which is indicated by the root. As an independent word, **aĉa** = *rotten, poor in quality*.

domo *house*	dom**aĉ**o *hovel*
infano *child*	infan**aĉ**o *brat*
ĵurnalo *newspaper*	ĵurnal**aĉ**o *'rag'*
paroli *to speak*	parol**aĉ**i *to speak badly, murder (the language)*
skribi *to write*	skrib**aĉ**i *to scribble*
virino *woman*	virin**aĉ**o *hag, crone*

11 ***fi-***

The prefix **fi-** denotes looseness of morals, lack of principles, depravity:

homo *person*	**fi**homo *scoundrel*
virino *woman*	**fi**virino *slut, bad woman*
menso *mind*	**fi**mensa *foul-minded*
vorto *word*	**fi**vorto *bad, dirty word*
rakonto *story*	**fi**rakonto *dirty, smutty story*

Fi! as an interjection means *Fie! Shame!*: **Fi al vi!** *Shame on you!*

Teksto

LETEROJ AL LA REDAKTISTO

Virinoj kiel registoj?

Estimata Sinjoro!

Via korespondinto J.L. estas malprava se li opinias, ke virinoj regos la mondon pli saĝe ol viroj. Ĉiam en la mondhistorio, kiam virinoj estis landestroj, kun absoluta potenco, tiuj virinaĉoj estis tiel same batalemaj, kruelaj kaj stultaj, kiel viroj. Nenio indikis, ke ili amas pacon.

Kore salutas,
R.F. (Swansea)

Estimata Sinjoro!

Mi konsentas kun S-ro J.L. La[1] viro estas ofte detruanto, sed la virino estas ĉiam kreanto. Virinoj, ĝenerale, amas la homaron – viroj emas malami ĝin.

Via,
(S-ino) P.J. (Bristol)

Rasaj antaŭjuĝoj[2]

Sinjoro!

Mi estis operaciita de irlanda ĥirurgo, kies helpanto estis hinda kuracisto. La malsanulejestro estis judo. Inter miaj flegistinoj estis fraŭlinoj el Trinidad, Afriko kaj Nederlando. Post tiu sperto, miaj rasaj antaŭjuĝoj estas tuj detruitaj.

Kun kora saluto,
E.P.K. (Derby)

Ĉu kukolo jam en marto?

Estimata Sinjoro!

Hodiaŭ mi ekvidis grandetan, grizan birdon, kaj amiko opiniis, ke ĝi estas kukolo. Ĉu tio estas ebla en marto?

Via,
P.M. (Exeter)

Dulingvaj infanoj

Respektata Sinjoro!

Mi estis estro de brazila lernejo por anglaj infanoj. Mi estis mirigita kiam mi rimarkis, kiel glate funkcias la instruado en du lingvoj. Infanoj nur kvinjaraj lernis legi per anglalingvaj libroj en la mateno kaj per portugallingvaj libroj en la posttagmezo. La infanoj ŝajne apartigis la matenan kaj posttagmezan laboron inter du fakoj de la menso.

Sincere via,
J.M.C. (Plymouth)

Sinjoro!

Mi bedaŭras, sed mi ne konsentas, ke edukado en du lingvoj kaŭzas nenian malutilon al infano. Mi estis edukita trilingve (angle, france kaj itale). Mi loĝas jam de 15 jaroj en Britujo, sed malgraŭ tio, mi parolas ĉiujn tri lingvojn, eĉ la anglan, per iom 'fremda' elparolado[3], kaj mi emas misparoli kaj uzi neĝustajn parolturnojn[4]. Tio estas malavantaĝo por mi. Neniu infano devus studi duan lingvon, antaŭ ol li havas almenaŭ 15 jarojn. Multaj ja parolaĉas eĉ la propran, gepatran[5] lingvon!

Kore salutas,
M.G. (Glasgow)

[1] *'the man'*, i.e. *men in general.*
[2] lit. *'pre-judgments': prejudices.*
[3] *'speaking-out': pronunciation.*
[4] *turns-of-phrase.*
[5] *'of mother and father': mother tongue.*

Televido – kaj surduloj

Estimata Sinjoro!

Ĉiu blindulo rajtas posedi radioaparaton. Mi volas proponi, ke ĉiu surdulo devus posedi televidan aparaton. Mi mem ne estas surda, sed oni diras, ke la surduloj estas eĉ pli izolitaj ol la blinduloj. Televidaj dissendoj estas granda beno al ili. Publika monkolekto devus esti komencita por provizi niajn surdulojn per aparatoj.

Sincere via,
(F-ino) L.M. (Torquay)

Televido – kaj Shakespeare

Estimata Redaktisto!

Antaŭ kelkaj tagoj, dum mi estis foriganta amason da rubo el mia subtegmento, mi ekvidis ekzempleron de via ĵurnalo de antaŭ tridek jaroj! En ĝi estis artikolo de via tiama teatra kritikisto, kiu komentis, ke televidaj prezentaĵoj de Shakespeare ĉiam estos aĉaj, kaj ankaŭ, ke televido ruinigos la 'vivan' teatron. Sur alia paĝo aperis letero de iu leganto, kiu forte kontraŭis la kritikiston. Tiu leganto atentigis, ke kiam la radio estis elpensita[6], oni diris, ke tio estos mortobato al koncertejoj, sed laŭ li, la publika intereso pri muziko ege pligrandiĝis, kun la rezulto, ke 'nun' (t.e.[7] antaŭ 30 jaroj!) la koncertejoj estas ĉiam plenplenaj[8]. El tio via korespondanto evidente kredis, ke la televidaj prezentaĵoj simile stimulos publikan intereson pri Shakespeare, kaj simile plenigos la teatrojn. Mi ne scias, ĉu intertempe la televido fakte plenigis la teatrojn, sed ŝajnas al mi, ke ĝi tre sukcese malplenigis la kinejojn!

Via,
(S-ino) S.B. (Worcester)

[6] *'thought out': invented.*
[7] **t.e.: tio estas.**
[8] Emphasising by repetition, a trick borrowed from Italian (effective if not overdone). Two words at least have become firmly established: **plenplena** *chock full*, **finfine** *at long last*.

PRAKTIKO 13.4 Traduku anglen:

Ĉu vi opinias, ke virinoj regos la mondon pli saĝe ol viroj? Nenio indikis, ke ili amas pacon. Mia amiko opiniis, ke ĝi estas kukolo. Mi ne konsentas, ke edukado en du lingvoj kaŭzas nenian malutilon al infano. Mi volas proponi, ke ĉiu surdulo devus posedi televidan aparaton. Publika monkolekto devus esti komencita. Li diris, ke televidaj prezentaĵoj de Shakespeare ĉiam estos aĉaj. Li diris, ke televido ruinigos la 'vivan' teatron. Ĉu virino estas kreanto aŭ detruanto? Mi estis mirigita kiam mi rimarkis, kiel glate funkcias la instruado en du lingvoj. Mi estis edukita trilingve. Surduloj estas pli izolitaj ol blinduloj. La virino, kiu diris tion, loĝas en Torquay. La legantoj, kiuj skribis al la redaktisto, menciis diversajn aferojn. Mi ne konsentis kun ĉiuj leteroj, kiujn mi legis. La viro, kies domo estis detruita, estas mia amiko.

PRAKTIKO 13.5 Traduku esperanten:

Did you think that women were wiser than men? Who said they were sluts? The town has been destroyed. I was astonished to see you. A public collection should be started. When was radio invented? By whom was it invented? He was esteemed by everyone. She was loved by all. I was operated on by an Irish surgeon. The weather was rotten. Those children who are brought up in two languages speak both equally well. The two letters I received this morning were both from old friends. The lady whose handbag I found will have come for it before half past five.

PRAKTIKO 13.6 Respondu:

1 Ĉu la du personoj, kiuj skribis pri virinoj kiel registoj, konsentas pri la temo?
2 Kie loĝas la viro, kies rasaj antaŭjuĝoj estas detruitaj?
3 El kiu lando estis la ĥirurgo, kiu estas operaciinta tiun viron?
4 Kiel funkciis la instruado en la brazila lernejo por anglaj infanoj?
5 Kiomaĝaj estis la infanoj, kiuj lernis legi angle en la mateno kaj portugale en la posttagmezo?
6 Kial, laŭ f-ino L. M., ĉiu surdulo devus posedi televidan aparaton?
7 Por kio oni devus komenci publikan monkolekton?
8 De kiam estis la ĵurnalo, kiun trovis s-ino S. B.?
9 Kie ŝi estis trovinta ĝin?
10 Kian efikon, laŭ ŝi, la televido faris sur la kinejoj?

Dialogo

Universala Kongreso–La alveno

La komenco de aŭgusto. Rikardo kaj Klara Lang alvenis al la kongresejo de la Universala Kongreso, kaj ĵus vizitis la ĝiĉetojn, kie ili registris sian alvenon kaj ricevis ĉiujn necesajn dokumentojn.

Rikardo Do, nun ni jam estas kongresanoj! Ni sidu en tiu angulo de la vestiblo por rigardi niajn dokumentojn, kaj aparte la Kongresan Libron.

Klara Bona ideo! Tio utile okupos la tempon ĝis la kvara horo, kiam Chantal kaj Marteno esperas esti apud la giĉetoj.

* * *

Rikardo Mi vidas, ke hodiaŭ vespere je la oka okazos Interkona Vespero. Evidente ni devos ĉeesti tion.

Klara Certe. Ĝi okazos en la ĉambro Zamenhof. Ŝajnas, ke ĉiuj ĉambroj havas nomojn. Mi bone scias, ke d-ro (= doktoro) Zamenhof estis la kreinto de Esperanto, sed mi ne konas la aliajn nomojn.

Rikardo Ĉu vi ne rekonas la nomon de Edmond Privat? Li verkis la libron *La Vivo de Zamenhof*, kiun ni jam legis.

Klara Ho jes, mi memoras. Kaj la aliaj?

Rikardo Mi kredas, ke Hodler helpis fondi U.E.A.[1], kaj gvidi ĝin dum la fruaj jaroj. Grabowski kaj Kabe estis inter la unuaj verkistoj en Esperanto, kaj Kalocsay estis grava hungara poeto. La aliajn mi ne konas.

Klara Estas preskaŭ la kvara horo; eble ni devus alproksimiĝi al la giĉetoj . . . Ha! Jen, mi ĵus vidis Chantal . . . tie, en verda mantelo!

(Ili alproksimiĝas al la geamikoj.)

Rikardo Saluton, geamikoj!

Marteno (*turniĝas*) Ha! Saluton al vi! Mi ĝojas revidi vin!

Klara Kaj ni vin!

Chantal Niaj karuloj! Kia plezuro!

(Ili brakumas sin reciproke.[2])

Marteno Ĉu vi povas atendi, dum ni prenos niajn dokumentojn?

Rikardo Kompreneble! Ni sidos en tiu angulo por atendi vin.

(Ili disiĝas, kaj post iom da tempo la franca paro revenas al Rikardo kaj Klara.)

Marteno Jen, tio estas finita. Do! Estas vere bone ree esti kune. Kiel kaj kiam vi alvenis al Belurbo?

Rikardo Ni alvenis hieraŭ posttagmeze per aŭto, tranoktis en nia hotelo, kaj hodiaŭ matene ni veturigis la infanojn al la Infana Kongreseto kaj prezentis ilin al la ĉefgvidanto tie.

Chantal Kaj ĉu ĝi estas en bela loko? Ĉu la infanoj estis kontentaj?

Klara Laŭ tio, kion mi povis vidi, la kongresetejo estas tre bona; tre proksima al la maro, kun arbaro malantaŭe. Ni vidis la dormejojn, kaj Andreo kaj Maria estis prezentitaj al kelkaj infanoj.

Rikardo Kaj kompreneble, ili antaŭĝuas la alvenon de siaj geamikoj, Fulvio kaj Trudi, kiujn ili ekkonis en Grezijono. . . . Kaj vi, kiel vi veturis?

[1] **Universala Esperanto-Asocio** (**U.E.A.** is pronounced *oo-eh-ah*).

[2] *each other*.

Marteno Ni venis vagonare, kun kelkaj aliaj samideanoj. Ni multe babilis, kaj tio ŝajnis malplilongigi la veturon.

Chantal Mi rimarkis, kiam ni renkontis vin, ke vi havas la kongreslibron en la mano. Ĉu vi jam decidis ion ajn pri la programo?

Klara Nur pri hodiaŭ vespere. Je la oka horo okazos la interkona vespero, kiun ni certe devos ĉeesti, ĉu ne?

Marteno Ho, certe! Kaj kiu scias? – eble ni vidos iujn konatojn, kvankam inter tiom da homoj, tio estas iom neverŝajna!

Rikardo Nu, ni vidos! Intertempe, mi sugestas, ke ni iom esploru la kongresejon kaj eksciu, kie estas la diversaj ĉambroj, kaj post tio ni povos eliri por iom promeni dum la suno brilas, se vi ne estas tro lacaj.

Chantal Bona ideo! Kaj kompreneble necesos ankaŭ trovi restoracion por la vespermanĝo. Ni devos manĝi frue, se la Interkona Vespero komenciĝos je la oka!

Klara Fakte, ni kutime manĝas ĉirkaŭ la sesa horo hejme, kiam Rikardo revenas de la laborejo, sed mi scias, ke vi francoj vespermanĝas pli malfrue ol ni.

Rikardo Kaj okupas pli da tempo pri ĝi!

Marteno Ha, ĉe ni la manĝado estas serioza afero; ni traktas ĝin kun respekto!

Note: The events, etc., mentioned in this and the following dialogues, do not refer to any one specific Congress, but are all items which occur more or less regularly at such congresses. The name Belurbo is fictitious.

Demandoj

1 De kie ges-roj Lang ricevis siajn dokumentojn?
2 Kion ili aparte volas rigardi?
3 Kie okazos la Interkona Vespero?
4 Kiu verkis la libron *La Vivo de Zamenhof*?
5 Kian mantelon portas Chantal?
6 Kiel veturis Rikardo kaj Klara al Belurbo?
7 Kiel veturis Marteno kaj Chantal, kaj kun kiuj?
8 Kion antaŭĝuas la infanoj?
9 Kial la kvar geamikoj devos manĝi frue?
10 Je kioma horo Klara kaj Rikardo kutime vespermanĝas hejme?

antaŭĝui *to look forward to*
atentigi *to draw attention to, point out*
aŭto (= **aŭtomobilo**)
bati *to beat, strike*; **bato** *a blow*
bedaŭri *to regret*
beno *blessing*; **beni** *to bless*
brakumi *to embrace*
ĉagreno *grief, worry*; **ĉagreni sin** *to worry oneself*
ĉefgvidanto *leader, person in charge*
disko *disc, record*
doktoro *doctor (of science, philosophy, medicine, etc.)*
efiko *effect*
ekzemplero *copy (of a book, etc.)*
fidela *faithful*
flegi *to nurse (the sick)*; **flegistino** *nurse*
fondi *to found*
frapi *to knock*
fremda *foreign*
funkcii *to function, work*
gardi sin *to take care* (lit. *guard oneself*)
giĉeto *ticket-window, box-office, hatch*
glata *smooth*
ĥirurgo *surgeon* (now often seen as **kirurgo**)
indiki *to indicate*
interkona *'getting to know each other'*
intertempe *meanwhile*
juĝi *to judge*
kaŭzi *to cause*
krii *to shout, cry out*
kukolo *cuckoo*
kuraci *to treat medically*; **kuracisto** *doctor (med.)*
laca *tired, weary*
malgraŭ *in spite of*
malutilo *harm*; **malutila** *harmful*
mantelo *coat*
menso *mind*
operacio *operation (surg.)*; **operacii** *to operate on*
paco *peace* (pron. **pat-so**)
potenco *power*
provizi *to provide (someone with something)*
raso *race (of mankind)*
reciproke *reciprocally (each other)*
redakti *to edit*
registri *to register, record*
restoracio *restaurant*
rubo *rubbish*
serioza *serious, earnest*
stulta *stupid*
subtegmento *attic, loft*
verŝajna *probable, likely*; **neverŝajna** *unlikely*
vestiblo *vestibule, entrance hall*

Esprimoj:
antaŭ ol *before* (see Unit 14 note 2)
laŭ li *in his opinion*

14 Paĝo por la semajnfino

Past extending into present

1 As we saw in Dialogue 8 (footnote), an action or state having its origin in the past but extending into the present is expressed by the present tense (instead of by the perfect as in English):

Mi est**as** malsana jam de tri tagoj.
I have been ill for three days (and still am).

Li atend**as** jam de du horoj.
He has been waiting for two hours (and is still waiting).

Ŝi est**as** ĉi tie jam de kvar semajnoj.
She has (already) been here for four weeks (and is still here).

Ni sci**as** pri ĝi jam de longa tempo.
We have known about it for a long time.

Ili loĝ**as** en Londono jam de kvin jaroj.
They have been living in London for five years (and are still living there).

Note: **jam** is generally added to emphasise the connection with the past.

2 ***Antaŭ ol***

(*a*) When in English 'before' precedes a verb form (e.g. *before* eating; *before* I saw him) we use **antaŭ ol** in Esperanto, instead of **antaŭ** alone:

Li foriros **antaŭ ol** vi revenos.
He will leave (go away) before *you come back.*

Antaŭ ol li parolis, li tusis.
Before *he spoke, he coughed.*

(*b*) To translate the idiom 'before -ing,' we use **antaŭ ol** with an infinitive:

Mi laboros **antaŭ ol** ripoz**i**.
I shall work before *rest*ing.

Antaŭ ol manĝ**i**, li lavis siajn manojn.
Before *eating, he washed his hands.*

3 *Post kiam*

Similarly, when 'after' comes before a verb form, we use **post kiam**, instead of **post** alone:

> Li foriros **post kiam** vi revenos.
> *He will leave* after *you come back.*
>
> **Post kiam** mi finis la laboron, li eliris.
> After *I finished the work, he went out.*

Note, however, that **post kiam**, unlike **antaŭ ol**, is *not* used before an infinitive, when we prefer to use the adverbial participle, e.g. **fin**inte:

> After *work*ing *for two hours, he rested.*
> Labor**inte** dum du horoj, li ripozis.

(This construction is dealt with in more detail in Unit 15.)

Elliptical usage

4 This term refers to those cases in which, in ordinary speech, we do not use a complete sentence, the omitted words being understood. A common example is 'Good evening!', which actually means 'I wish you a good evening!'

Here are some more examples, with the missing (understood) words supplied in the right hand column:

Good day!	(I wish you a) good day!
One moment, please . . .	(Wait) one moment please.
Just a word of advice . . .	(I offer you) just a word of advice.
Who did that? Andrew.	Andrew (did that).
Whom did you see? Andrew.	(I saw) Andrew.

This, of course, happens in Esperanto too. However, the missing words often have an effect on the ending of the noun, which may, in fact, be the object of the omitted verb. Here are the Esperanto forms of the above examples:

Bona**n** tago**n**.	(Mi deziras al vi) bonan tagon.
Unu momento**n**, mi petas . . .	(Atendu) unu momenton, mi petas.
Nur unu vorto**n** da konsilo . . .	(Mi proponas al vi) nur unu vorton da konsilo.
Kiu faris tion? Andreo.	. . . Andreo (faris ĝin).
Kiun vi vidis? Andreo**n**.	. . . (Mi vidis) Andreon.

5 There are some cases in which the whole meaning of the sentence can be altered by the omission of the **-n**:

I love you more than John =
either (*a*) I love you more than John does.
or (*b*) I love you more than I love John.
I welcomed him as chairman =
either (*a*) I, as chairman, welcomed him.
or (*b*) I welcomed him (he was the chairman).

In Esperanto these become:

(*a*) Mi amas vin pli ol Johano.
(*b*) Mi amas vin pli ol Johano**n**.

(*a*) Mi bonvenigis lin kiel prezidanto.
(*b*) Mi bonvenigis lin kiel prezidanto**n**.

6 Another case of elliptical usage, but this time not involving the ending **-n**, occurs sometimes when answering the question 'Whose?'

Whose is that record?	(*It is*) Mary's (*record*).
Kies estas tiu disko?	(Ĝi estas la disko) **de Maria**.

7 ***-um-***

The suffix **-um-** has no defined meaning, but is used to show some act or object related to the root. It is sometimes used to coin words for the occasion where the meaning is clear, but it is mainly used with a few well-known roots. Here are the most common:

aero *air*	aer**umi** *to air, aerate*
akvo *water*	akv**umi** *to water (a garden)*
cerbo *brain*	cerb**umi** *to rack one's brains*
folio *leaf, page (of book)*	foli**umi** *to thumb one's way through (a book)*
kalkano *heel (of foot)*	kalkan**umo** *heel (of a boot or shoe)*
kolo *neck*	kol**umo** *collar*
malvarma *cold*	malvarm**umo** *a cold, chill*
okulo *eye*	okul**umi** *to make eyes at*
plena *full*	plen**umi** *to fulfil*
vento *wind*	vent**umi** *to fan*

PRAKTIKO 14.1 Traduku anglen:

Mi rigardis lin kiel bonan instruiston. Ŝi estas malsana jam de (unu) semajno. Mi multe cerbumis pri tio, sed ne sukcesis trovi solvon. Kiuj venis en la ĉambron? – Andreo kaj Maria. Nun kelkajn vortojn pri la Universala Kongreso. Ĉar mankas pluvo jam de kelkaj tagoj, mi devos akvumi la ĝardenon. Mi amas lin pli ol liaj fratoj (*Make your meaning quite clear!*) Mi promesis helpi ŝin, do mi nepre devas plenumi mian promeson. Mi estas instruisto jam de dudek jaroj. Kiujn vi renkontis en la urbo? – Andreon kaj Marian.

PRAKTIKO 14.2 Traduku esperanten:

Firstly, just a word about the meeting on Wednesday evening. It is necessary to aerate the soil from time to time. She has been waiting for an hour and a half. Who played in the garden? Mary. My sister has been living in London for ten years. I love her more than her sisters (i.e. than I love her sisters). I have been in bed for two days with (= because of) a cold. I have known about that for a long time. Whom did you see in (the) town? – Richard and Clare. These shoes need new heels. The meeting has already lasted two hours. I regard him as a very good friend.

PRAKTIKO 14.3 Parigu (*match*) la respondojn kun la demandoj:

1 Kiomlonge vi estas malsana?
2 Kiam vi foriros?
3 De kiu vi estis edukita?
4 Kiu ludas per la pupodomo?
5 Kun kiu ŝi ludas?
6 Kiun vi vidis en la ĝardeno?
7 Kies estas tiu pupo?
8 Kian malsanon li havas?
9 Kie oni lavas sin?
10 Kien iras Andreo?

(*a*) Post kiam vi revenos.
(*b*) La knabineto.
(*c*) En la banĉambro.
(*d*) Jam de du semajnoj.
(*e*) Malvarmumon.
(*f*) De la knabineto.
(*g*) En la banĉambron.
(*h*) S-ron Lang.
(*i*) De mia patro.
(*j*) Kun sia amikino.

Suffixes and prefixes

8 *-end-*

The suffix **-end-** denotes that which is to be done or has to be done:

pagi	*to pay*	pag**end**a	*payable, due, has to be paid*
lerni	*to learn*	lern**end**a	*has to be learned*
solvi	*to solve*	solv**end**a	*to be solved*
trovi	*to find*	trov**end**a	*has to be found*

9 *eks-*

The prefix **eks-** is used like the English 'ex' to denote *late*, *formerly*:

oficiro *officer*	**eks**-oficiro *ex-officer*
studento *student*	**eks**-studento *former student*
edzo *husband*	**eks**-edzo *ex-husband*
edzino *wife*	**eks**-edzino *ex-wife*
edziĝo *marriage*	**eks**-edziĝo *divorce*

eksigi *to put out of office, dismiss*
eksiĝi *to withdraw from office, resign*

Note: Although it is not absolutely necessary to use a hyphen with **eks**, it is perhaps clearer to do so with the longer words.

10 *pra-*

The prefix **pra-** has two uses: (*i*) to denote remoteness in time:

biciklo *bicycle*	**pra**biciklo *primitive bicycle*
arbaro *forest*	**pra**arbaro *primeval forest*
homo *man*	**pra**homo *primitive man*

and (*ii*) distant (in time) relationship:

avo *grandfather*	**pra**avo *great-grandfather*
nepo *grandson*	**pra**nepo *great-grandson*

11 *mis-*

The prefix **mis-** is used like the English 'mis-' to denote an error:

informi *to inform*	**mis**informi *to misinform*
kompreni *to understand*	**mis**kompreni *to misunderstand*
loko *place*	**mis**loki *to misplace, mislay*
paŝo *step*	**mis**paŝo *false step*
prononci *to pronounce*	**mis**prononci *to mispronounce*
uzi *to use*	**mis**uzi *ro misuse*

12 *-ing-*

The suffix **-ing-** is used to denote a holder for *one* of the objects named in the root. Often the object is held firmly by one end only.

kandelo *candle*	kandel**ingo** *candlestick*
plumo *pen*	plum**ingo** *penholder*
torĉo *torch*	torĉ**ingo** *torch-holder*
fingro *finger*	fingr**ingo** *thimble*
glavo *sword*	glav**ingo** *scabbard*

It is not greatly used other than in the above words, but **ingo** is useful as an independent word meaning *holder, socket* or *sheath*. Do not confuse it with **-uj-**, which denotes a container for a *quantity* of the objects named:

cigared**ingo** *cigarette-holder*
cigared**ujo** *cigarette box*

13 *-nj-*
The suffix **-nj-** is used after the first few letters of a feminine name to form a short affectionate name:

patrino *mother*	pa**nj**o *mummy*
onklino *aunt*	o**nj**o *aunty*
avino *grandmother*	avi**nj**o *granny*
Maria *Mary*	Ma**nj**o (*diminutive of Mary*)

14 *-ĉj-*
The suffix **-ĉj-** is used in the same way with masculine names:

patro *father*	pa**ĉj**o *daddy*
Johano *John*	Jo**ĉj**o *Johnny*
Vilhelmo *William*	Vil**ĉj**o *Bill, Billy*

PRAKTIKO 14.4 (This exercise should be done after working through the texts on the following two pages)

Traduku anglen:
Ĉu vi miskomprenis min? Li ĉiam miskomprenas spritaĵojn. Ŝi misprononcas ĉiujn vortojn. Ĉu la esploristo suferis pro* malvarmumo? Kio estas ventumilo? Ĉu vi cerbumis pri la krucvort-enigmo? La mezuro estas nur proksimuma. Ĉu la krucvort-enigmo estas solvenda? Ĉu la plej malalta loko estas nun trovenda? Kiam la konto estas pagenda? Kio estas la diferenco inter studento kaj eksstudento? Li volis esti eks-edzo, kaj ŝi volis esti eks-edzino; do ili aranĝis eks-edziĝon. Se li mem ne eksiĝos, ni eksigos lin. Ĉu ĝi estas prabiciklo? Kio estas prahomo? Ĉu via praavo ankoraŭ vivas? Ĉu vi havas pranepon? De kiu ajn flanko la vento blovas ni estas ŝirmataj. Mi volonte akceptos vin, kiam ajn vi venos. Per niaj aviadiloj vi facile atingos iun ajn parton de la mondo.

*Some esperantists say '**suferas pro**', others prefer '**suferas de**'.

Teksto

PAĜO POR LA SEMAJNFINO

Notu: Solvoj de la solvendaj problemoj staras en Apendico, p. xxx.

Krucvortenigmo

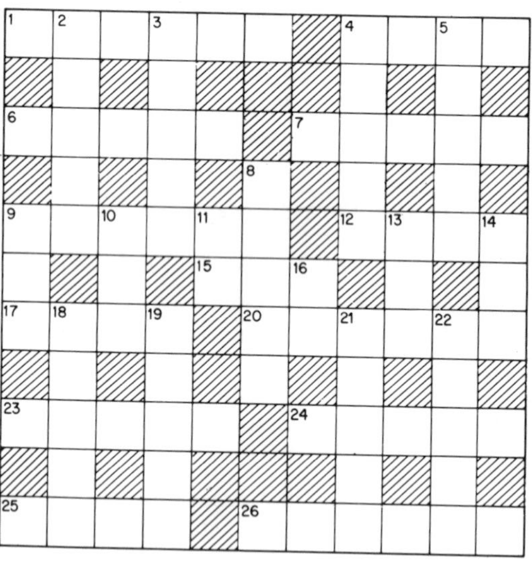

Horizontale: 1. Ĉefa ĉambro en domo. 4. Unua sezono de la jaro estas la— tempo. 6. Ronda plataĵo por gramofono. 7. Boligi malrapide. 9. La tuta loĝantaro de iu lando. 12. Plena de viveco kaj vigleco. 15. Nombro da jaroj, tra kiuj oni vivas. 17. Koloro de leterkesto. 20. Izolita peco de tero. 23. Akiri (*nur radiko*). 24. Laŭtaj, malplaĉaj sonoj. 25. Kuiri kukon. 26. La enloĝantoj de Britujo.

Vertikale: 2. Homo amata. 3. Frato de la patro aŭ patrino. 4. Demandas iun servon. 5. Ido de homo (*nur radiko*). 8. Vivis en certa loko. 9. Prepozicio kiu montras la *ilon*. 10. Presita paperfolio (*nur radiko*). 11. Difina artikolo. 13. Estu amika al! 14. Membro. 16. Sufikso kiu montras *frakcion*. 18. Uzinda. 19. Ricevi por mono. 21. Ĉirkaŭrigardi por io perdita. 22. Reĝo de la bestoj.

Spritaĵoj

La famega skulptisto Michelangelo Buonarroti, fininte sian belan statuon de Davido, staris apud la statuo kiam alvenis la urbestro de Florenco, kiu kredis sin spertulo pri la arto. Rigardinte* la statuon, tiu diris al la skulptisto, ke ĝi ja estas bela, sed ke al li ne plaĉas la nazo, kiu ŝajnas esti tro longa. Michelangelo pacience supreniris ŝtupetaron, tenante en la mano iomete da marmora polvo. Ŝajnigante, ke li laboras ĉe la nazo, li iom post iom faligis la polvon. Malsuprenirinte*, li demandis al la urbestro, ĉu tio plibeligis la statuon. 'Tio multe pli plaĉas al mi,' respondis tiu. 'Nun vi vere donis al ĝi la vivon!'

* See unit 15, note **2**.

La granda filozofo Hegel diris ĉe la fino de sia vivo: 'El ĉiuj miaj eks-studentoj, nur unu komprenis min – kaj li *mis*komprenis min!'

Sir Humphry Davy, la glora sciencisto, estis la protektanto de eĉ pli granda sciencisto, Faraday. Amiko demandis al la maljuna Davy: 'Laŭ via opinio, kiu estas la plej grava el ĉiuj viaj eltrovaĵoj?' Davy respondis: 'Mia plej grava eltrovaĵo estas tio – ke mi trovis Michael Faraday.'

Ĉi tie vi cerbumas!

Problemo 1

Smith: La plej alta loko en Britujo estas ja la pinto de Ben Nevis. Trovenda nun estas la plej *mal*alta loko.
Jones: Evidente! Ĉe la marbordo.

Ĉu li estas prava?

Problemo 2

Esploristo ĵus reveninta de la Norda Poluso diris:

'Mi multe suferis de malvarmumoj.'

Ĉu vi kredas lin?

Problemo 3

En Rejkjavik, Islando, estas tre malvarme dum la longa vintro. Tamen, la loĝantoj sentas sin tute varmaj en la hejmo. Kial?

Bild-Enigmoj

Tiu prabiciklo estis uzata jam en–kiu jaro? 1805? 1819? 1853?

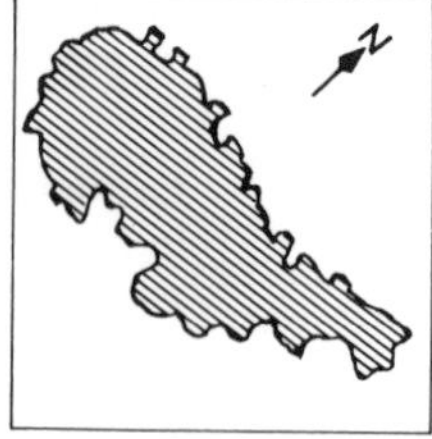

Jen silueto de konata lando. Kiu lando?

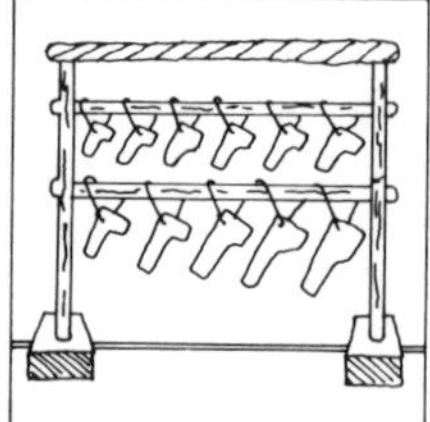

Ĉu la objekto estas
(*a*) ventumilo?
(*b*) muzika instrumento?
(*c*) fajr-avertilo?

La fraŭlino kiu okulumas vin portas popolkostumon el –
(*a*) Hispanujo?
(*b*) Jugoslavujo?
(*c*) Grekujo?

Tiu bovo estas desegnita de–
(*a*) infano?
(*b*) prahomo?
(*c*) Afrika nigrulo?

Ĉu la konstruaĵo estas
(*a*) teatro?
(*b*) fabriko?
(*c*) preĝejo?

PRAKTIKO 14.5 Traduku esperanten:

I have already fulfilled your orders. When is the bill payable? Here is one problem which has to be solved. He is now an ex-officer. My great-grandmother will soon be eighty. He often misuses the word. I shall love you whatever you do. I shall give it to him, whoever he is. I did not see anyone at all. I am ready to eat anything.

PRAKTIKO 14.6 Respondu:

1 Kiu estas la dua sezono de la jaro?
2 Se al plantoj mankas akvo, kion oni devus fari?
3 Kiom da studentoj, laŭ Hegel, komprenis lin?
4 Ĉu tiu studento bone komprenis lin?
5 Kio, laŭ Sir Humphry Davy, estis lia plej grava eltrovaĵo?
6 Kie troviĝas la plej malalta loko en Britujo?
7 Kial oni ne povas suferi de malvarmumo ĉe la Norda Poluso?
8 Kie la homoj utiligas varmegajn akvofontojn por varmigi la domojn?
9 Se via edzo aŭ edzino havas nur unu fraton, sed vi havas du bofratojn, kiu estas la alia?
10 Se ĉiuj viaj praavoj ankoraŭ vivus, kiom el ili vi havus?

Dialogo

Universala Kongreso – Infana Kongreseto

Iun tagon dum la kongresa semajno, la kvar geamikoj renkontas Roberton Chabot, kiun ili ekkonis en Grezijono.

Rikardo Roberto! Mi ĝojas renkonti vin denove! Mi vidis vian nomon sur la listo de kongresanoj, sed ne sciis, ĉu vi ĉeestas aŭ ne.

Roberto Jes, mi estas ĉi tie jam de sabato, sed inter tiom da homoj estas malfacile renkonti ĉiujn geamikojn kaj gekonatojn.

Klara Jes, ja! Kaj estas tiom da aferoj farendaj kaj kunvenoj ĉeestendaj, ke la tempo vere galopas!

Marteno Tio estas vera. Verdire, ni ne partoprenis en multaj kunvenoj ĝis nun, sed ni ĉeestis kelkajn distrajn aferojn.

Chantal Kaj pro la bela vetero ni kaptis plurajn okazojn eliri por vidi la urbon.

Roberto Jes, ankaŭ mi vagis en la urbo kelkfoje. Sed mi partoprenis en kelkaj kunvenoj: de fervojistoj kaj de filatelistoj, ĉar profesie mi estas fervojisto, kaj hobie mi estas filatelisto. Mi ĉeestis ankaŭ la kunvenon pri ekologio, pro ĝenerala intereso.

Rikardo Mi ĉeestis tiun por matematikistoj, kaj Klara tiun por instruistoj kaj ankaŭ tiun pri filologio.

Klara Kaj Chantal kaj mi ĉeestis tiun pri virina agado! Sed ni ĝuis ankaŭ la distrajn programojn.

Chantal Jes, la teatraĵoj estis bonegaj, kaj la geaktoroj vere brilaj.

Rikardo Estis tre strange al mi aŭskulti la tuton en Esperanto. Feliĉe, la geaktoroj tiel klare parolis, ke mi ĉion komprenis.

Marteno Mi aparte ĝuis la kabareton hieraŭ vespere.

Roberto Kaj kion vi intencas fari hodiaŭ posttagmeze?

Klara Hodiaŭ estas la tago kiam kongresanoj estas invititaj viziti la Infanan Kongreseton, kaj Rikardo kaj mi iros tien por vidi niajn gefilojn.

Chantal Se vi ne kontraŭas, Marteno kaj mi volonte akompanos vin kaj revidos la infanojn.

Rikardo Tio estos plezuro! Kaj vi, Roberto?

Roberto Dankon, ne. Mi partoprenos en la Internacia Kongresa Universitato[1].

* * *

(Kiam ili alvenas aŭtomobile antaŭ la kongresetejo, Rikardo, Klara kaj iliaj geamikoj vidas aron da infanoj atendantaj. Tuj Andreo kaj Maria venas antaŭen, kaj la pordeto de la aŭto estas apenaŭ malfermita kiam ili kune ekparolas.)

Andreo kaj Maria Saluton, saluton! Venu por vidi . . .

Rikardo He! momenton, mi petas! Lasu nin eliri el la aŭto! (*La kvar plenkreskuloj eliras.*) Vi memoras Chantalon kaj Martenon, ĉu ne?

Infanoj Jes. Saluton!

Chantal kaj Marteno Saluton, junuloj!

Marteno Ĉu vi ĝuas la kongreseton?

Maria Jes, tre multe! (*Ŝi mansvingas al iu en la infangrupo antaŭ la konstruaĵo*) Jen mia amikino Trudi, el Germanujo.

La adoltoj Saluton, Trudi!

Trudi Saluton!

Andreo Kaj jen Fulvio, el Italujo.

Adoltoj Saluton, Fulvio!

Fulvio Saluton, gesinjoroj!

[1] A series of lectures by university professors and lecturers.

Andreo Ni havas iom da tempo por montri al vi la ĉirkaŭaĵon, kaj poste ni devos eniri por montri al vi nian ekspozicion, kaj post tio ni faros koncerton por ĉiuj vizitantoj!

(Ili komencas promeni.)

Maria Estas bele ĉi tie! Ni naĝas en la maro ĉiutage, kaj ludas en la arbaro, kaj. . .

Klara Ĉu oni permesas al vi iri solaj en la maron?

Maria Ho, ne! Ĉiam devas esti plenkreskulo tie. Sed preskaŭ ĉiam estas plenkreskulo sur la strando,. . .

Andreo Kaj se ne, ni devas peti permeson iri en la maron, kaj se iu plenkreskulo estas libera, tiu elvenas, kaj ni rajtas iri en la akvon.

Rikardo Bone. Kaj kion alian vi faras?

Maria Ni jam ekskursis dufoje, al interesaj lokoj en la regiono, kaj ĉiutage ni promenas piede kun nia grupestro.

Chantal Kiom da infanoj estas en via grupo?

Andreo Ni ne estas en la sama grupo. En mia grupo ni estas sep, ĉiuj el malsamaj landoj!

Maria Mia grupo havas nur ses, el ses landoj. Sed Trudi estas en mia grupo, do ĉio estas bona!

(La infanoj montras diversajn lokojn, kaj poste ili ĉiuj eniras kaj rigardas la ekspozicion de faritaĵoj de la infanoj.)

Andreo Mi faris tiun pentraĵon!

Marteno Ĉu vere? Ĝi estas tre bona!

Maria Kaj mi faris tiun porketon el argilo!

Klara Ankaŭ tio estas tre bona. Mi ne sciis, ke vi ambaŭ estas tiel lertaj! Fakte, ĉiuj eroj estas bonaj. Certe vi ĉiuj estis okupitaj.

Andreo Ni faris tiajn laborojn vespere. Dum la tagoj ni ĉiam estis ekstere.

Gvidanto (*anoncas*) Atentu, mi petas, gesinjoroj kaj infanoj! Estas la horo por nia koncerto. Se la plenkreskuloj bonvolos sidiĝi, la infanoj scias kion fari.

(Oni disdonas multobligitan programon.)

Klara (*flustras*) Rigardu; Andreo kaj Maria aktoros kune! Ili faros skeĉon: 'Fajro, Fajro!'[2].

Rikardo (*flustras*) Ĉielo! Mia imago ne kapablas. . . ![3]

(La koncerto komenciĝas. Post la fino estas granda aplaŭdo.)

Marteno Brave! Ili ĉiuj bone faris, ĉu ne?
Chantal Kaj viaj du . . . tiu skeĉo estis tre amuza, kaj ili senerare faris ĝin!

(Andreo kaj Maria venas al ili.)

Klara Bonege! Vi du faris brave! Kiel vi sukcesis memori ĉion?
Maria Ni havis la libron antaŭ ni, Panjo! Ĉar ni ĉiam sidis kaj ŝajnigis paroli telefone, ni povis legi ĝin!
Klara Ho, mi komprenas! Tamen, necesis multe da praktikado por elparoli ĝin[4] tiel flue!
Infanoj Jes, Ja!

[2] Sketch by R. Mackay.
[3] *The mind boggles*! (lit. *My imagination can't . . .*)
[4] Lit. *speak it out*.

Demandoj

1 Kiam alvenis Roberto al la kongreso?
2 Kial la kvar geamikoj kaptis plurajn okazojn eliri?
3 Kio estas la profesio de Roberto?
4 Kaj de Klara?
5 Kial Roberto ne vizitas la Infanan Kongreseton?
6 Kion Andreo kaj Maria montras al la plenkreskuloj antaŭ la koncerto?
7 Kion la infanoj devas fari se ili volas naĝi, kaj ne estas plenkreskulo sur la strando?
8 Kiomofte la infanoj promenas piede?
9 El kiom da landoj venas la infanoj en la grupo de Andreo?
10 Kion faras Andreo kaj Maria por la ekspozicio?

akiri *to acquire, get*
apenaŭ *hardly, no sooner . . .*
argilo *clay*
averti *to warn*
bordo *bank, shore*
brave! *well done!*
brila *brilliant*
cerbo *brain*; **cerbumi** *rack one's brains*
ĉielo! *Heavens!*
desegni *to draw*
difini *to define*; **difina artikolo** *definite article*
distra *entertaining, of entertainment*
ekskursi *to go on a trip*
ekspozicio *exhibition*
eltrovaĵo *discovery*
enigmo *puzzle*
faritaĵo *something made*
flue *fluently*
flustri *to whisper*
folio *leaf, sheet (of paper)*
frakcio *fraction*
gramofono *record-player*
he! *hey! (exclamation)*
hobio *hobby*
Islando *Iceland*
kabareto *cabaret*
kesto *chest*; **leterkesto** *pillar box*
kruco *cross*
marmoro *marble*
multobligi *to duplicate*
nivelo *level*
okupita *busy*
paŝo *pace, step*
peco *piece*
piede *on foot*
pinto *summit*
plata *flat*
poluso *pole (North or South)*
profesio *profession*
rondo *circle, ring*
senerare *faultlessly*
silueto *silhouette*
skeĉo *sketch, short play*
sprito *wit*
strando *beach*
svingi *to wave*
ŝajnigi *to pretend*
ŝtupetaro *ladder*
ŝuo *shoe*
vagi *to ramble, wander*
verdire *telling the truth*
vigla *alert, brisk*
vorto *word*

Esprimoj:
de tempo al tempo *from time to time*
iun tagon *one day*
kapti la okazon *to take the opportunity*

15 Diversaĵoj el la tuta mondo

Adverbial participles

1 A common form in English is the sentence with a participial phrase tacked on (here in italics):

> *Wishing to speak to him*, I visited his house.
> *Seeing him in the garden*, I called to him.
> *Whistling tunefully*, he went upstairs.
> *Having a good brain*, he mastered everything.
> *Intending to stay*, we stood in the corridor.

The Esperanto form is similar, but the participle ends in **-e**:

> Dezirant**e** paroli al li, mi vizitis lian domon.
> Vidant**e** lin en la ĝardeno, mi vokis al li.
> Fajfant**e** melodie, li iris supren.
> Havant**e** bonan cerbon, li venkis ĉion.
> Intencant**e** resti, ni staris en la koridoro.

This participial phrase can be expanded into a complete sentence, whose subject is identical with that of the main clause (sentence):

Mi deziris paroli al li. *I wished to speak to him.*	Mi vizitis lian domon. *I visited his house.*
Mi vidis lin en la ĝardeno. *I saw him in the garden.*	Mi vokis al li. *I called to him.*
Li fajfis melodie. *He was whistling melodiously.*	Li iris supren. *He went upstairs.*
Li havis bonan cerbon. *He had a good brain.*	Li venkis ĉion. *He mastered everything.*
Ni intencis resti. *We intended to stay.*	Ni staris en la koridoro. *We stood in the corridor.*

The rule in Esperanto, then, is as in good English; i.e., the participial phrase must always relate to the subject of the main clause.

2 The past participle is likewise used as in English:

Mi estis skribinta la leteron. Mi eliris.
I had written the letter. I went out.

= Skribint**e** la leteron, mi eliris.
Having written (After writing) the letter, I went out.*

Li estis fininta la laboron. Li hejmeniris.
He had finished the work. He went home.

= Finint**e** la laboron, li hejmeniris.
Having finished (When he had finished) the work, he went home.*

3 The participle ending in **-onta** is similarly used:

Mi estis skribonta leteron. Mi serĉis plumon.
I was about to write a letter. I looked for a pen.

= Skribont**e** leteron, mi serĉis plumon.
(*Being*) *About to write a letter, I looked for a pen.*

Li estis enironta la ĉambron. Li tusis.
He was about to enter the room. He coughed.

= Eniront**e** la ĉambron, li tusis.
About to enter the room, he coughed.

Instead of simply saying 'writing', 'having finished', '(Being) About to enter', etc., we often use phrases such as 'While (he was) writing', 'After he had written', 'Just before entering', and so on. When such a phrase can be translated by an adverbial participle, it is generally best to use it.

4 The passive participles may also be used to form participle phrases, though this is rare with present and future participles:

Li ne estis rimarkita. Li forlasis la domon.
He was not noticed. He left the house.

= Ne-rimarkit**e**, li forlasis la domon.
Unnoticed, he left the house.

The object predicate

5 The word 'predicate' comes from the Latin *predico*, meaning 'preach', and is used in the sense of something said about the subject

* See Unit 14, note **3**.

or object. The *object predicate*, then, is something said about the object. It usually takes the form of a noun, adjective, or participle. The main point to remember is that **-n** is *not* added to the predicate, because **esti** (*to be*) can be understood.

A noun

La societo elektis min (esti) prezidanto.
The society elected me (to be) president.
Ni juĝis la viron (esti) fripono.
We judged the man (to be) a rascal.
Li nomis sian filon Petro.
He called his son Peter (gave him the name of Peter).

An adjective

Ili trovis lin (esti) sana kaj vigla.
They found him (to be) well and lively.
Li farbis la pordon bruna.*
He painted the door brown.
Ŝi montris sin (esti) preta kaj volonta.
She showed herself (to be) ready and willing.

A participle

Mi aŭdis la birdon (esti) kantanta.
I heard the bird (to be) singing.
Ŝi vidis lin (esti) kuranta.
She saw him (to be) running.
Li pentris ŝin sidanta.
He painted her sitting (while she was sitting).

PRAKTIKO 15.1 Traduku anglen:

Vidante lin sur la strato, mi sekvis lin. Fininte sian laboron, ŝi hejmeniris. Skribonte al mia korespondanto, mi serĉis lian adreson. Starante antaŭ sia domo li rigardis la montojn. Aŭdinte la hundon bojanta la knabo forkuris. Batite, li laŭte ploris. Helpate de mia

* Notice the difference between:

Li farbis la pordon bruna.
He painted the door brown (for it to become brown).
and Li farbis la pordon brunan.
He painted the brown door.

amiko, mi bone progresis. Estante kolera, ŝi rifuzis paroli al mi. Vidite de la policano, la ŝtelisto rapide forkuris. Mi trovis la bildon belan. Mi trovis la libron tre bona. Li montris sin saĝa. Ni trovis ŝin tre ŝanĝita. Ni aŭdis la birdon kantantan. Instruante oni lernas.

PRAKTIKO 15.2 Traduku esperanten:

Seeing her in the garden I called to her. While waiting for my friend I looked at the newspaper. Having decided to set off, I did not wait. While sitting in the garden I heard a noise. Not knowing the man, I asked who he was. As he was about to go out, he saw that it was raining. When about to be punished the boy ran away. Having been called, she came at once. Having met him, I found him very pleasant. I painted the door green. I painted the green door. The girl showed herself capable and willing.

Indirect commands

6 The ending **-u** is used in indirect speech after verbs like *want*, *wish*, or allied verbs like *order*, *tell*, *warn*, *advise*, *ask*, etc. where in English we use the infinitive after the object:

Ir**u** tien!
Go there!

Mi volas	**ke** vi ir**u** tien.
I want	*you to go there.*

Li kant**u**!
Let him sing!

Mi deziras	**ke** li kant**u**.
I wish	*him to sing.*

Rest**u**!
Stay!

Mi diris	**ke** li rest**u**.
I told	*him to stay.*
Mi petis	**ke** li rest**u**.
I asked	*him to stay.*
Mi ordonis	**ke** li rest**u**.
I ordered	*him to stay.*
Mi avertis	**ke** li rest**u**.
I warned	*him to stay.*
Mi konsilis	**ke** li rest**u**.
I advised	*him to stay.*

Various meanings of *de*

7 As you will see from the end vocabulary, the preposition **de** has at least five meanings: *of*, *from*, *off*, *by* and *since*, and as you will see in section (*e*) below, it can sometimes be translated as *for*. More often than not, when you are reading Esperanto the meanings will be obvious, though when writing or speaking you may find it necessary, for the sake of clarity, to use another word. Let us look at some examples of the various meanings.

(*a*) *of*

la centro **de** la urbo	*the centre of the town*
sumo **de** dek pundoj	*a sum of ten pounds*
la kreinto **de** Esperanto	*the creator of Esperanto*
la problemo **de** senarmiĝo	*the problem of disarmament*

and we may include the possessive use here:

la libro **de** Johano	*John's book*

(*b*) *from*

veturi **de** Londono ĝis Parizo	*to travel from London to Paris*
alveni **de** Germanujo	*to arrive from Germany*
kuri **de** la loko	*to run from the place*
suferi **de** febro	*to suffer from a fever*
distingi unu **de** alia	*to distinguish one from another*

(*c*) *off* (often has the sense of *from*)

fali **de** la tablo	*to fall off (from) the table*
plonĝi **de** la alta tabulo	*to dive off (from) the high board*
preni kukon **de** plado	*to take a cake off a dish*

(*d*) *since*

Ŝi laboras tie (jam) **de** januaro.	*She's been working there since January.*

(*e*) *for*

Mi estas tie (jam) **de** du monatoj.	*I've been there for two months.*

(*f*) *by*

	libro (verkita) **de** Dickens	*a book (written) by Dickens*
	ĉirkaŭita **de** la tuta familio	*surrounded by the whole family*
	ĉielo kovrita **de** nuboj	*a sky covered by (with) clouds*
but	ŝi kovris la tablon **per** tuko	*she covered the table with a cloth*

8 Confusion may be caused in such cases as:

(*a*) la amo **de** Dio *the love of God*

which may mean either

la amo **de** Dio **al** la homoj *the love of God towards people*
or la amo **al** Dio **de** la homoj *the love towards God by people*

In this case the appropriate use of **al** will make the meaning clear.

(*b*) la mono ŝtelita **de** li
which may mean '*the money stolen* ***from*** or ***by*** *him*'
We can overcome this problem by saying either

(*i*) la mono ŝtelita **for de** li
or (*ii*) la mono **kiun li ŝtelis**

(*c*) la venko **de** Anglujo **de** la Normandoj *the conquest of England by the Normans*

This one can be clarified by saying:
la venko **de** Anglujo **fare de (far)*** la Normandoj

9 Other doubtful meanings can be made clear by using an alternative preposition.

Instead of:	*We could say:*
la problemo **de** la senarmiĝo	la problemo **pri** la senarmiĝo
li venas **de** Germanujo	li venas **el** Germanujo
li kuris **de** la loko	li kuris **for de** la loko *or* li **forkuris de** la loko
la vazo falis **de** la tablo	la vazo falis **de sur** la tablo
li laboras tie **de** januaro	li laboras tie **ekde** januaro
li suferis **de** febro	li suferis **pro** febro
ni ne povas distingi liajn ŝafojn **de** la niaj	ni ne povas distingi liajn ŝafojn **disde** la niaj

In general, then, when using **de**, be especially careful to see that the meaning is clear. If in doubt, find some other way of expressing what you want to say.

PRAKTIKO 15.3 Traduku esperanten:

I must demand the return of the money stolen from me by that man. He disappeared from the house yesterday morning, and has not been seen since (then). He took a knife from the drawer to cut the bread.

* The word **far**, while not official, is sometimes used for *by* when it means *done by*.

The ground was entirely covered with snow. John can hardly walk, because he fell off a wall. The dying woman was surrounded by all her (= her whole) family. He wrote to tell (= say to) me that he was suffering from a cold. Those gloves were stolen from my brother. She has been working in that shop since January. Without saying a word she ran away from me.

Transitive and intransitive verbs

10 A *transitive* verb is one which expresses an action done to someone or something (the *object*):

La viro **batis** la hundo**n**.	*The man beat the dog.*
Mi **vidis** la domo**n**.	*I saw the house.*

An *intransitive* verb is one whose action is confined to the doer (the *subject*):

La knabo **dormis**.	*The boy slept (was asleep).*
La akvo **frostis**.	*The water froze.*

However, in English a number of verbs can be either transitive or intransitive, e.g.:

	Transitive	*Intransitive*
to boil	I boiled the milk.	The milk boiled.
to close	He closed the door.	The door closed.
to wake	She woke the child.	The child woke.

Since Esperanto follows international usage and makes all such verbs either transitive or intransitive, we must use a suffix if we want to change a verb from one to the other.

11 To make a transitive verb intransitive, we use the suffix **-iĝ-** (*to become, be -ed*):

Ŝi vekis la infanon. *She woke the child.*	La infano vek**iĝ**is. *The child woke (became awake).*
La instruisto komencis la lecionon. *The teacher began the lesson.*	La leciono komenc**iĝ**is. *The lesson began (was begun).*

Here is a list of common verbs which in English can be either transitive or intransitive, but which in Esperanto are all transitive, requiring **-iĝ-** to make them intransitive:

etendi *to extend, stretch*
fendi *to split*
fermi *to close, shut*
fini *to finish*
kolekti *to collect, gather*
komenci *to begin*
movi *to move*
renkonti *to meet*
rompi *to break*
ŝanĝi *to change*
turni *to turn*
veki *to wake*
vendi *to sell*

Example: Mi vendis mian aŭton. *I sold my car.* Tiu ero bone vend**iĝ**as. *That item sells well.*

12 To make an intransitive verb transitive, on the other hand, we add the suffix **-ig-** (*to make, cause*):

La akvo jam bolas. *The water is already boiling.*	Mi bol**ig**os la akvon. *I'll boil the water (cause it to boil).*
La balono krevis. *The balloon burst.*	La knabo krev**ig**is la balonon. *The boy burst the balloon (caused it to burst).*
La patrino sidis sur la seĝo. *The mother was sitting on the chair.*	Ŝi sid**ig**is la infanon apud si. *She sat the child by her (caused it to sit).*

Here is a list of common verbs which in English can be either transitive or intransitive, but which in Esperanto are all intransitive, requiring **-ig-** to make them transitive **(por transitiv**igi **ilin!)**:

boli *to boil*
bruli *to burn*
ĉesi *to stop, cease*
daŭri *to continue*
droni *to drown*
halti *to stop, halt*
kreski *to grow*
krevi *to burst*
pasi *to pass (by)*
pendi *to hang*
sidi *to sit, be sitting*
soni *to sound*
sonori *to ring*
stari *to stand*

Example:

La bildo pendis sur la muro.	Mi pend**ig**is la bildon en la salono.
The picture hung on the wall.	*I hung the picture in the lounge.*

Teksto

DIVERSAĴOJ
el la tuta mondo

Grupe Trinki

La konduto de alkoholtrinkantoj rilate al iliaj ĉirkaŭuloj povus esti konata per la sanga grupo, laŭ esploro farita de la firmao Asashi Breweries Ltd, la unua japana bierfabrikisto. La esploro, farita pri specimena grupo el 2464 personoj, montras, ke la A-sangaj personoj atentas pri siaj ĉirkaŭuloj. La B-sangaj personoj male, ignoras siajn ĉirkaŭulojn, kiam ili trinkas alkoholon. La O-sanguloj bone rilatas al la aliaj dum ili trinkas. La AB-sanguloj estas duvizaĝaj: ili povas bone rilati al iuj ĉirkaŭuloj kaj indiferenti al aliaj.

(el *Monato*)

Japana Rifuzo

Antaŭ multaj jaroj verkisto proponis novan verkon al japana eldonista firmo. La eldonistoj resendis la manuskripton, kun letero: 'Ni trovas vian verkon bonega. Sed se ni presus ĝin, Lia Imperia Moŝto legus ĝin kaj, leginte, li ordonus, ke ni neniam presu ion malpli bonan. Ĉar tio malhelpus, ke ni eldonu ion ajn dum almenaŭ dek mil jaroj, ni devas, kun profunda bedaŭro, resendi al vi la manuskripton.'

La Origino de la Bildkarto

Kvankam poŝtkartoj jam ekzistis de la jaro 1861, la bildkarto ŝajne ne 'naskiĝis' ĝis 1889. Kiam, en tiu jaro, oficiale malfermiĝis la mondkonata turo Eiffel dum la Ekspozicio de Parizo, poŝtkartoj eldoniĝis kun bildo de la turo, kaj oni povis enpoŝtigi ilin ĉe la supro. Ekde tiam bildkartoj estas popularaj, kaj la kolektado de ili baldaŭ disvastiĝis tra Eŭropo kaj poste tra la tuta mondo, aparte inter la esperantistaro. Ĝis 1902 oni rajtis skribi nur la adreson de la ricevonto sur la dorsflanko de bildkarto, kaj iun mesaĝon oni devis skribi sur la bildon mem. Sed en tiu jaro Britujo permesis la dividon de la dorsflanko per linio, kun unu duono por la adreso kaj la alia por la mesaĝo.

Kontraŭ Terorismo

En 1978 viro eniris bankon en Kalifornio, portante suspektindan pakon. La bankoficistoj, timante, ke en ĝi estas bombo, rifuzis tuŝi ĝin, kaj la supozata teroristo tuj fulme elkuris, je la granda trankviliĝo de la oficistoj. Ekster la konstruaĵo, tamen, apudstaranto vidis la fuĝanton kaj, kredante ke li estas rabisto, tuj postkuris kaj kaptis lin. Li reirigis lin en la bankon, sed kompreneble ne sciis, ke la pako ja enhavas larmigan gason, kaj post du minutoj ĝi eksplodis. Nur post tridek minutoj la aero estis denove klara.

Urbega Saltego

Du londonanoj estis la unuaj personoj paraŝutintaj de la supro de la 449 metrojn alta 'Empire State

Building' en Novjorko. Oni estis dirinta al ili, ke tia salto estas neebla pro la formo de la konstruaĵo, tamen unu el ili sukcesis surstratiĝi sendifekte, kaj rapide foriĝis, kun sia paraŝuto, en taksio. La alia (fakte la unue saltinto) preskaŭ atingis la straton, sed liaj paraŝutŝnuroj trafis trafiklumojn, kaj dum li senpove pendis tie la polico arestis lin kaj akuzis lin pri danĝera konduto. Post lia aresto li konfesis, ke la sperto estis timiga, sed li sentis, ke la vera danĝero estas la risko esti trafita de aŭto je la surteriĝo, aŭ eble eĉ rabatencita.

'Majstro de la Enciklopedio'

Ĉu iu persono legis la tutan *Encyclopaedia Britannica*? En la 19-a jarcento iu reĝo de Persujo (nun Irano) apenaŭ sukcesis plenumi tiun taskon; poste, li aldonis al siaj titoloj 'Majstro de la Encyclopaedia Britannica!' Sed legi la plej lastan eldonon, *kun plena kompreno*, estus preter la kapablo de unu homo. Ĝi ampleksas multajn volumojn, kun milionoj da vortoj!

Ejo por Perditaĵoj

Ĉiujare, la londona publiko postlasas proksimume cent kvindek mil objektojn en vagonaroj kaj aŭtobusoj. La ejo en Baker Street, en kiu dudek kvin oficistoj mastrumas tiun grandan, kaj strangan, kolekton, enhavas amasegon de la plej diversaj objektoj, ekde okulvitroj, ombreloj, globkrajonoj k.t.p. ĝis falsaj dentaroj, ĉemizoj kaj futbalŝuoj. Krome, oni raportas, ke en unu ekzempla jaro la oficistoj ricevis dudek kvar mil 'valorajn' objektojn, nome mansaketojn, monujojn kaj biletujojn. En tiu sama jaro la plej neatendita perditaĵo estis la supra tabulo de ĉevalsaltkonkursa obstaklo!

PRAKTIKO 15.4 Traduku anglen:

La turo Eiffel oficiale malfermiĝis dum la Ekspozicio de Parizo. La kolektado de bildkartoj jam disvastiĝis tra la tuta mondo. La unua japana bierfabrikista firmao faris esploron pri la konduto de alkoholtrinkantoj rilate al iliaj ĉirkaŭuloj. Leginte ĝin, li ordonus, ke ni neniam presu ion malpli bonan. Ni trovis vian verkon bonega. Oni certe opinios ilin pli kuriozaj. Tio malhelpus, ke ni eldonu ion ajn dum almenaŭ dek mil jaroj. La paraŝut-ŝnuroj de la unue saltinto trafis trafiklumojn, kaj la polico arestis lin dum li pendis senpove. Kiam la bankoficistoj rifuzis tuŝi la pakon, la teroristo fulme elkuris. La oficistoj mastrumas multajn diversajn objektojn, ekde globkrajonoj ĝis falsaj dentaroj.

PRAKTIKO 15.5 Traduku esperanten:

Having offered his manuscript to a publisher, he awaited (waited for) a reply. They call their son-in-law Peter. I found the place worth visiting. I want you to leave your hat behind. He ordered me to read the last edition. It is said that research by a Japanese brewery showed something about the conduct of alcohol-drinkers. The first picture-postcard was apparently published during the Paris Exhibition of 1889, and bore (carried) a picture of the Eiffel Tower. The arrested man had feared being hit by a car or even mugged. The boy refused to touch the food. Twenty-five officials look after a hundred and fifty thousand objects.

PRAKTIKO 15.6 In each of the following sentences, the verb has been given in English. Write down the correct Esperanto form of each *before* looking at the key; then make sure you understand why the particular form is used in each case:

1 La laca infano (*closed*) siajn okulojn.
2 Trovinte la domon, mia amiko (*will ring*) ĉe la pordo.
3 Bedaŭrinde, la multekosta vazo (*broke*) kiam ĝi falis de la tablo.
4 La konstruaĵo ankoraŭ (*is burning*), sed oni esperas baldaŭ regi la flamojn.
5 Granda homamaso (*gathered*) ĉe la sceno de la akcidento.
6 La lignopeco (*split*) sub la bato de la hakilo.
7 Mi devas tuj (*change*) mian bibliotekan libron.
8 Bonvolu (*pass*) la salon!
9 Tiu viro (*is drowning*)! Helpu lin tuj!
10 La policano (*stopped*) la trafikon por ke ambulanco pasu laŭ la strato.

Dialogo

Universala Kongreso – Ĝis revido!

Estas la fina tago de la kongreso, kaj la kvar geamikoj ĉeestas la oficialan fermon. Dum ili atendas la komencon ili diskutas la okazojn de la antaŭaj tagoj.

Chantal Mi opinias, ke tiu koncerto hieraŭ vespere estis bonega, ĉu vi ne konsentas?

Rikardo Jes, mi ĝuis la tuton.

Klara La nivelo de ĉiuj distraj programoj estis tre alta, laŭ mi. Kompreneble, el preskaŭ tri mil partoprenantoj en la kongreso, devas esti multaj talentaj homoj.

Rikardo La tuta kongreso ja estis vera festeno de kulturo kaj de distraĵoj!

Chantal Kiun, el ĉiuj eroj, vi plej memoros?

Rikardo Ho, kia demando! Mi kredas, ke mi neniam forgesos ion ajn pri la kongreso!

Klara Tio ja estas malfacile respondebla demando; oni pensas pri la teatraĵoj, la pupteatro, la muziko . . .
Marteno . . . la bankedo, la balo . . .
Chantal Ŝŝ! Jen la prezidanto kaj eminentuloj venas sur la podion!

(Sekvas la ferma ceremonio. Kiam nia kvaropo elvenas, ili ree babilas.)

Marteno Tre kontentiga fino al bona kongreso, ĉu ne?
Klara Jes, vere! Mi trovis la paroladon de la prezidanto bonega, kaj tre sprita. Sed tio, kion mi trovis plej impona, estis la transdono de la standardo al la reprezentanto de la venontjara kongreso.
Chantal Jes, tio estas tradicia ĉe la Universalaj Kongresoj.
Rikardo Nu, mi devos tuj iri por Andreo kaj Maria ĉe la Infana Kongreseto, sed tio ne okupos longan tempon. Mi sugestas, ke vi tri iru al nia kutima restoracio por la tagmanĝo, kaj rezervu sidlokojn por mi kaj la infanoj. Mi revenos rekte tien. Ĉu bone?
Marteno Tute bone. Ni certe povos okupi nin per babilado dum vi estos for.
Rikardo Do, ĝis baldaŭa revido!
Ĉiuj Ĝis!

(Rikardo foriras rapide al la vesto-deponejo, kaj la aliaj iras malpli rapide, babilante.)

Marteno Mi scivolas, ĉu ni revidos nin[1] en la venonta kongreso . . .
Klara Ho, tio bezonos multe da pripensado. Grava afero estas la kosto! Sed ekzistas ankaŭ aliaj eblecoj, eĉ se la U.K.[2] ne eblos al ni: Grezijono denove, aŭ vi povus viziti nin, – eble je la tempo de la Brita Kongreso, tiel, ke ni denove estus inter esperantistoj.
Chantal Tio estus bela! Aŭ vi povus veni al ni, aŭ ni ĉiuj povus viziti la Kulturan Centron Esperantistan en Svislando.
Klara Mi ne aŭdis pri tio.
Marteno Ĝi situas apud la urbo La Chaux-de-Fonds, en bela montara regiono de Svislando. Ĝi kuŝas, se mi bone memoras la ciferojn, je 1100 metroj super la marnivelo, meze de la Ĵurasaj Montoj.[3]
Chantal Kaj ĝi havas gastejon konsistantan el sep domoj, kie esperantistoj povas loĝi, ĉu por ferii aŭ por studi, aŭ ambaŭ.

[1] *will see each other* (see Dialogue 13).
[2] **Universala Kongreso.**
[3] *Jura Mountains* (stretching through France, Germany and Switzerland).

Marteno Oni ja parolas pri la 'Esperanto-kvartalo' de la urbo La Chaux-de-Fonds, ĉar la domoj estas sufiĉe grandaj, kaj situas en vastaj ĝardenoj!
Klara Kaj kiam oni povas viziti la Centron?
Marteno Ĝi estas malfermita dum la tuta jaro.
Klara Do, tio certe meritas pripensadon.

(Fine ili atingas la restoracion, kie Rikardo kaj la infanoj baldaŭ alvenas, kaj ĉiuj ĝuas bonan tagmanĝon. Fininte la manĝon kaj paginte la kalkulon ili eliras.)

Marteno Do, jam venis la horo por adiaŭi[4] nin! Vi volas foriri preskaŭ tuj, ĉu ne?
Rikardo Jes, ni havas kajuton rezervitan sur la nokta pramŝipo, kie ni esperas dormi sufiĉe por povi veturigi la aŭton hejmen morgaŭ!
Marteno Ni ne foriros ĝis morgaŭ matene, sed ni devos ellitiĝi sufiĉe frue por trafi la unuan trajnon.
Klara Do, ĝis revido, karaj geamikoj, ĝis iam en la venonta jaro. Bonan vojaĝon, kaj alvenu sekure hejmen!
Ĉiuj Ĝis revido! Bonan Vojaĝon! Ĝis la venonta jaro! Ĝis!

Demandoj

1 Kiom da homoj partoprenas en la kongreso?
2 Kion la geamikoj ĉeestis hieraŭ vespere?
3 Kion opinias Klara pri la distraj programoj?
4 Kion Rikardo kredas, ke li longe memoros?
5 Kion Klara trovis plej impona en la ferma kunveno?
6 Kion faros la aliaj tri dum Rikardo iros por revenigi Andreon kaj Marian?
7 Kie en Svislando situas la Kultura Centro Esperantista?
8 Kiam la centro estas malfermita?
9 Sur kio Rikardo kaj Klara rezervis kajuton?
10 Kiam la kvar geamikoj esperas ree renkontiĝi?

Note: There are **Esperanto-Domoj** and Cultural Centres in a number of countries, which Esperanto-speakers can visit for holidays and/or study. Information about an English one at Morecambe, Lancashire, may be obtained from the Esperanto Centre.

[4] Although **adiaŭi** is fairly common, **adiaŭ**! is not very often used, esperantists preferring to use **Ĝis revido** as indicating the hope of another meeting! This expression varies, in fact, from **Ĝis la revido!** through **Ĝis revido!** and **Ĝis la!** to **Ĝis!**

akuzi *to accuse, charge*
alkoholo *alcohol*
ampleksa *extensive*; **ampleksi** *to comprise, cover*
aresti *to arrest*
atenti *to pay attention*
balo *ball, dance*
bankedo *banquet*
banko *bank (financial)*
bildkarto *picture-postcard*
bileto *(bank) note*; **biletujo** *wallet*
boji *to bark*
cifero *figure, digit*
ĉapelo *hat*
ĉemizo *shirt*
ĉevalo *horse*; **ĉevalsalt-konkursa obstaklo** *show-jumping fence*
difekti *to damage*; **sendifekta** *undamaged, unharmed*
disvastiĝi *to spread (widely)*
dorsflanko *reverse (side)*
duvizaĝa *two-faced*
eldoni *to publish*; **eldono** *edition*
enpoŝtigi *to post*
esplori *to explore, investigate*; **esploro** *research*
falsa *false*
festeno *feast*
finfine *eventually*
firmo[1] *a firm (commercial)*
fojo *a time, occasion*; **trifoje** *three times*
foriĝi *to get away*
fuĝi *to flee*
fulme *like lightning*
futbalo *football*
gaso *gas*
ignori *to ignore*
impona *imposing, impressive*
indiferenta *indifferent*; **indiferenti** *to be indifferent*
jarcento *century*
kalkulo *bill*
kajuto *cabin*
Kalifornio *California*
kolekto *collection*
kolera *angry*
konkurso *competition, contest*
konstruaĵo *building*
krome *in addition*
kvaropo *quartet*
kvartalo *district (of a city)*
larmo *tear (drop)*; **larmiga gaso** *tear gas*
lasi *to leave*; **postlasi** *to leave behind*
ligno *wood*
majstro *master (craftsman)*; *maestro*
male *on the contrary*
malhelpi *to hinder, prevent*
mansaketo *handbag*
mastrumi *to look after*
meriti *to deserve*
mesaĝo *message*
moŝto[2] *(general title)*
neatendita *unexpected*
nome *namely*
Novjorko *New York*
objekto *object, article*
obstaklo *obstacle*
oficisto *official*
okulvitroj *glasses*
ombrelo *umbrella*
ordoni *to (give an) order*
paraŝuti, paraŝuto *parachute*; **paraŝut-ŝnuroj** *parachute lines*
perditaĵoj *lost property*
Persujo *Persia*

[1] **firmo**: Since this also means *firmness*, **firmao** is often used for a business firm.
[2] **moŝto** is a general honorific title: **Via moŝto**. The rank can be indicated by an adjective: **Via reĝa moŝto** *Your Majesty*; **Ŝia princina moŝto** *Her Royal Highness*, etc.

plenumi *to fulfil*
plori *to weep, cry*
po *at the rate of,* @
podio *podium, platform*
polico *police*;
polican(in)o *police(wo)man*
populara *popular*
postlasi *to leave behind*
poŝtkarto *postcard*
pramŝipo *ferry*
preter *beyond, past*
proksimume *approximately*
pupteatro *puppet theatre*
rabi *to steal by force or threat*;
rabisto *robber*
rabatencita *mugged*
reirigi (re-ir-igi) *to take back*
rilati *to relate, refer*; **rilate** *in relation to*
risko *risk*
scivoli *to wonder (want to know)*
senpove *helplessly*
situi *to be situated*
solena *solemn, formal*
specimeno *specimen*
standardo *(official) flag*
streĉiga *causing strain, stressful*
supro, supra *top*
surstratiĝi, surteriĝi *to land*
ŝnuro *rope, line, cord*
ŝŝ! *hush!, sh!*
ŝteli *to steal*; **ŝtelisto** *thief*
tabulo *board, plank*
taksio *taxi*
talenta *talented*
terorismo *terrorism*;
teroristo *terrorist*
timiga *frightening*
tradicia *traditional*
trafi *to hit (the mark), catch (train etc.)*
trafiklumoj *traffic lights*
trajno *train* (= **vagonaro)**
tuko *cloth for particular purpose* (see end vocabulary)
tuŝi *to touch*
vagonaro *train (railway)*
vestodeponejo *cloakroom*

Further Study

Having worked through this book, you will be ready to conquer new worlds; in particular you will wish to do some reading. There are many books in and on Esperanto, and a complete list of those normally stocked may be obtained from:

The British Esperanto Association,
140 Holland Park Avenue,
London W11 4UF (Tel. 01–727 7821)

The first acquisition will no doubt be a dictionary. *The Concise Esperanto and English Dictionary* (Teach Yourself Books) should meet all the needs of the beginner, and for the more advanced student, *Plena Vortaro de Esperanto* (in Esperanto) is invaluable, while the *Esperanto–English Dictionary* (Butler) is a mine of information.

There are many excellent readers for beginners, but the following may be particularly recommended: *Gerda malaperis!* (Piron), a short mystery novel, with a parallel book of separate texts; *Lasu min paroli plu*, by the same author; *Ili kaptis Elzan* (Valano), a humorous story; *Kumeŭaŭa, la filo de la ĝangalo* (Sekelj), an adventure story set in the Amazon jungle; *La Nekonata konato* (Boatman), a mystery novel; and *Japanaj fabeloj* (Mikami), five fables from Japan.

The following are the addresses of other national Esperanto Associations in the English-speaking countries:

Australian Esperanto Association, P.O. Box 48, Jamison Centre ACT 2614

Canadian Esperanto Association, C.P. 126, Succursale Beaubien, Montréal, Qué H2G 3C8

New Zealand Esperanto Association, P.O. Box 330, Wellington 1

Esperanto Federation Bharat, c/o B. R. Tulsyani, 41-B Kutub Enclave, New Delhi 110016

South African Esperanto Association, 75 Bronkhurst Street, Groenkloof 0181

Esperanto League for North America, P.O. Box 1129, El Cerrito, CA. 94530, USA

Universal Esperanto Association, Nieuwe Binnenweg 176, 3015 BJ Rotterdam, Netherlands

Appendix

1 Table of correlatives

	which, what	that
one	**kiu** *which (one), who*	**tiu** *that (one)*
thing	**kio** *what (thing), what*	**tio** *that (thing)*
kind	**kia** *what kind of what a . . .*	**tia** *that kind of, such a . . .*
place	**kie** *where*	**tie** *there*
way	**kiel** *in what way, how*	**tiel** *in that way, thus*
reason	**kial** *for what reason, why*	**tial** *for that reason, so*
time	**kiam** *at what time, when*	**tiam** *at that time, then*
quantity	**kiom** *what quantity, how much, how many,*	**tiom** *that much/many, so much/many*
one's	**kies** *which one's, whose*	**ties** *that one's*

some	no	each, every
iu *someone* *somebody*	**neniu** *no-one,* *nobody*	**ĉiu** *each (one),* *everybody*
io *something*	**nenio** *nothing*	**ĉio** *everything*
ia *some kind of*	**nenia** *no kind of*	**ĉia** *every kind of*
ie *somewhere*	**nenie** *nowhere*	**ĉie** *everywhere*
iel *in some way,* *somehow*	**neniel** *in no way,* *nohow*	**ĉiel** *in every way*
ial *for some reason*	**nenial** *for no reason*	**ĉial** *for every reason*
iam *at some time*	**neniam** *at no time,* *never*	**ĉiam** *every time,* *always*
iom *some (quantity)*	**neniom** *no quantity,* *none*	**ĉiom** *the whole* *quantity,* *all of it*
ies *someone's,* *somebody's*	**nenies** *no-one's,* *nobody's*	**ĉies** *everyone's,* *everybody's*

2 List of affixes

bo- relation by marriage. **Bopatrino** mother-in-law. (Unit 12.)

dis- separation, scattering. **Disĵeti** to scatter about. **Dissendi** to broadcast. (Unit 12.)

ek- sudden or momentary action. **Ekbrili** to flash. **Ekkrii** to shout out. (Unit 11.)

eks- former, ex-. **Eksreĝo** ex-king. (Unit 14.)

fi- shameful, nasty. **Figazeto** 'smutty' magazine. (Unit 13.)

ge- both sexes together. **Gepatroj** father and mother. (Unit 1.)

mal- opposite. **Granda** big, **malgranda** small. **Aperi** appear, **malaperi** vanish. (Unit 2.)

mis- mis-, wrongly. **Miskompreni** to misunderstand. (Unit 14.)

pra- of great antiquity; great (in relationships). **Pratempo** the ancient past. **Pranepo** great-grandson. (Unit 14.)

re- over again, back again. **Resendi** to send back. **Reverki** to re-write (a book, etc.). (Unit 4.)

-aĉ contemptible, disgusting. **Veteraĉo** filthy weather. **Virinaĉo** hag. (Unit 13.)

-ad frequent or continuous action. **Kuirado** cooking. (Unit 8.)

-aĵ substance. **Pakaĵo** package, thing packed. **Sendaĵo** transmission (thing sent). (Unit 7.)

-an inhabitant, member, adherent. **Nederlandano** Dutchman. **Kristano** Christian. **Londonano** Londoner. (Unit 5.)

-ar collection, set of. **Libraro** library. **Arbaro** forest. **Homaro** mankind. (Unit 8.)

-ebl possibility. **Videbla** visible. **Kredebla** believable, probable. (Unit 8.)

-ec abstract quality. **Amikeco** friendship. **Boneco** goodness. (Unit 10.)

-eg great size, intense degree. **Domego** a mansion. **Ridegi** to guffaw. **Varmega** intensely hot. (Unit 3.)

-ej place. **Lernejo** school. **Hundejo** dog kennel. (Unit 1.)

-em propensity, tendency. **Parolema** talkative. **Ludema** playful. (Unit 12.)

-end 'which must be done'. **Solvenda problemo** problem which must be solved. (Unit 14.)

-er single unit, item. **Pluvero** raindrop. (Unit 6.)

-estr leader, manager. **Lernejestro** headmaster. **Hotelestro** hotel manager. (Unit 12.)

-et smallness, small degree. **Dometo** cottage. **Varmeta** tepid. **Blueta** bluish. (Unit 3.)

-id offspring. **Katido** kitten. (Unit 8.)

-ig causing something to be. **Blankigi** to make white, whiten. (Unit 10.)

-iĝ becoming something. **Blankiĝi** to become white. (Unit 10.)

-il tool, instrument. **Tranĉilo** knife. (Unit 11.)

-ind worthy of. **Memorinda** memorable. (Unit 8.)

-ing: holder for one object. **Kandelingo** candlestick. (Unit 14.)

-in feminine. **Onklino** aunt. **Porkino** sow. (Unit 1.)

-ism, -ist as in English. **Dentisto, socialismo,** etc. (Unit 10.)

-obl, -op, -on occur with numerals. **Trioble** triply, **triope** three together, **triono** a third. (Unit 7.)

-uj container. **Inkujo** ink-well. Also in sense of country: **Anglo** an Englishman, **Anglujo** England. (Unit 5.)

-ul person possessing a certain quality. **Riĉulo** a rich man. **Maljunul(in)o** an old man (woman). (Unit 3.)

-um 'stop-gap' suffix with no definite meaning. **Plena** full, **plenumi** to fulfil. **Okulumi** to ogle. (Unit 14.)

-ĉjo and **-njo** are affectionate endings for males and females respectively. **Patro** father, **Paĉjo** daddy, **Panjo** mummy. (Unit 14.)

3 The sixteen rules: Zamenhof's summary of the grammar of Esperanto

1 There is no indefinite *article*; there is only a definite article (**la**), alike for all sexes, cases, and numbers.

2 *Substantives* end in **-o**. To form the plural, **-j** is added. There are only two cases: nominative and accusative; the latter is obtained from the nominative by adding **-n**. Other cases are expressed by prepositions (genitive **de**, dative **al**, ablative **per**, etc.).

3 The *adjective* ends in **-a**. Case and number as for substantives. The comparative is made by means of the word **pli**, the superlative by **plej**; with the comparative the conjunction **ol** is used.

4 The cardinal *numerals* (not declined) are: **unu, du, tri, kvar, kvin, ses, sep, ok, naŭ, dek, cent, mil**. Tens and hundreds are formed by simple junction of the numerals. To mark the ordinal numerals, **-a** is added; for the multiple, **obl**; for the fractional, **on**; for the collective, **op**; for the distributive, the preposition **po**. Substantival and adverbial numerals can also be used.

5 *Personal pronouns*: **mi, vi, li, ŝi, ĝi** (thing or animal), **si, ni, vi, ili, oni**; possessives are formed by adding **-a**. Declension as for substantives.

6 The *verb* undergoes no change with regard to person or number. Forms of the verb: time *being* (present) takes the termination **-as**; time *been* (past), **-is**; time *about to be* (future) **-os**; conditional mood **-us**; imperative mood **-u**; infinitive **-i**. Participles (with adjectival or adverbial sense): active present **-ant**; active past **-int**; active future **-ont**; passive present **-at**; passive past **-it**; passive future **-ot**. The passive is rendered by a corresponding form of the verb **esti** and a passive participle of the required verb; the preposition with the passive is **de**.

7 *Adverbs* end in **-e**; comparison as for adjectives.

8 All *prepositions* govern the nominative.

9 Every word is *pronounced* as it is *spelt*.

10 The *accent* is always on the second-to-last syllable.

11 *Compound words* are formed by simple junction of the words (the chief word stands at the end). Grammatical terminations are also regarded as independent words.

12 When another *negative* word is present, the word **ne** is left out.

13 In order to show *direction* towards, words take the termination of the accusative.

14 Each *preposition* has a definite and constant meaning; but if the direct sense does not indicate which it should be, we use the preposition **je**, which has no meaning of its own. Instead of **je** we may use the accusative without a preposition.

15 The so-called *foreign words*, that is, those which the majority of languages have taken from one source, undergo no change in Esperanto, beyond conforming to its orthography; but with various words from one root, it is better to use unchanged only the fundamental word and to form the rest from this latter in accordance with the rules of the Esperanto language.

16 The *final vowel* of the substantive and of the article may sometimes be dropped and be replaced by an apostrophe.

Key to the Exercises

Introduction (2)
1066: mil sesdek ses
1789: mil sepcent okdek naŭ
1815: mil okcent dek kvin
1666: mil sescent sesdek ses
1588: mil kvincent okdek ok
1415: mil kvarcent dek kvin
1564: mil kvincent sesdek kvar
1887: mil okcent okdek sep
1905: mil naŭcent kvin*
1969: mil naŭcent sesdek naŭ
1953: mil naŭcent kvindek tri
2061: dumil sesdek unu

* Remember that **naŭcent** is pronounced as **nowt-sent!**

PRAKTIKO 1.1 The father and the son. A table is a piece of furniture. The father is a man. The son is a boy. The two sons are boys. The father and the son are standing. That man is the father. That piece of furniture is a table. Those three animals are dogs. That man is standing. The son is sitting and reading. Who are those men? Which man is sitting and reading? Which men are sitting and reading?

PRAKTIKO 1.2 La patro kaj la filo. La patroj kaj la filoj. La patro estas viro. La viro staras. La viro staras. La patro kaj la filo sidas. La patro sidas kaj legas. Hundoj estas bestoj. Tiuj kvar bestoj estas hundoj. Kiu viro estas la patro? Kiuj knaboj estas la filoj? Kiu legas? Tiu viro legas. Tablo estas meblo. Tabloj estas mebloj.

PRAKTIKO 1.3 The father is Mr Lang, and the mother is Mrs Lang. Andrew and Mary are the children. Andrew and Mary are the son and daughter of Mr and Mrs Lang. Who is Mr Lang? Who is Mrs Lang? Who is Andrew? Who is Mary? Here is the house of the Lang family. In which room does the family eat? In which room do Mr and Mrs Lang sleep? In which room do the children play? In which room do the children sleep? In which room does Mr Lang read? In which room do Mrs Lang and Andrew cook? The dog is in the kennel, and the car is in the garage.

PRAKTIKO 1.4 Kiu estas sinjoro Lang? Kiu estas sinjorino Lang? Kiuj estas la infanoj? Kiu estas la domo de gesinjoroj Lang? Kiu estas la manĝoĉambro? Kiu estas la kuirejo? Kiu estas la dormoĉambro? Kiu estas la infanĉambro? Kiu estas la banĉambro? Kiu estas la salono? En kiu ĉambro la infanoj ludas? En kiu ĉambro la infanoj dormas? En kiu ĉambro sinjoro Lang legas?

Demandoj 1 1 Maria estas en la infanejo. 2 Ŝi legas. 3 Andreo estas en la kuirejo. 4 Sinjorino Lang (*or* La patrino) kaj Andreo kuiras. 5 Ili kuiras en la kuirejo.

PRAKTIKO 2.1 Is Mary the daughter of Mr and Mrs Lang? Is Andrew the daughter of Mr and Mrs Lang? Is Mrs Lang the father? Is Andrew a boy? Is Mary a dog? Does the family eat (Is the family eating) in the kitchen? Do Mr and Mrs Lang sleep (Are . . . sleeping) in the bedroom? Does the dog sleep (Is . . . sleeping) in the bedroom? Is Mr Lang reading in the bathroom? Are the children playing in the children's room?

PRAKTIKO 2.2 Ĉu sinjoro Lang estas la patro? Kiu estas la patrino? Ĉu Andreo estas knabo? Ĉu li estas la filo de gesinjoroj Lang? Ĉu la familio manĝas en la manĝoĉambro? Sinjoro Lang ne estas la patrino. Maria ne dormas en la hundejo. La geknaboj ne dormas en la dormoĉambro, ili dormas en la infanejo. Ĉu la hundo estas en la aŭtomobilejo? Ne, ĝi ne estas en la aŭtomobilejo, ĝi estas en la hundejo. La gefratoj lernas en la lernejo. Ili ludas en la infanejo kaj ekster la domo.

PRAKTIKO 2.3 Jes, Maria estas la filino de gesinjoroj Lang. Ne, Andreo ne estas la filino (de gesinjoroj Lang), li estas la filo. Ne, sinjorino Lang ne estas la patro, ŝi estas la patrino. Jes, Andreo estas knabo. Ne, Maria ne estas hundo, ŝi estas knabino. Ne, la familio ne manĝas en la kuirejo, ili manĝas en la manĝoĉambro. Jes, gesinjoroj Lang dormas en la dormoĉambro. Ne, la hundo ne dormas en la dormoĉambro, ĝi dormas en la hundejo. Ne, sinjoro Lang ne legas en la banĉambro, li legas en la salono. Jes, la infanoj ludas en la infanejo.

PRAKTIKO 2.4 Here is the house. Here is the room. The room is modern and comfortable. Is the room modern and comfortable? Are the pieces of furniture new? Mr Lang and Mary are sitting in the room. Are they working? Who is sitting in a comfortable chair? Who is reading? Who is sitting at the table? Are there two toys (standing) in front of her? Are the toys new or old? Are they clean or dirty? Is Mary pleased (satisfied)? Are you pleased (satisfied)? Are the cupboards (standing) in front of Mary or behind her? Are they big or little? Which cupboard is big? Which cupboard is small? Is the cupboard wide or narrow? Is the garden beautiful or ugly?

PRAKTIKO 2.5 Kiu estas la domo? Kiu estas la ĉambro? Ĉu la ĉambro estas moderna? Ĉu ĝi estas komforta? Ĉu la mebloj estas novaj aŭ malnovaj? Ĉu la seĝo estas komforta? Kiu sidas en la seĝo? Kiu laboras? Kiu legas? Kiu sidas ĉe la tablo? Ĉu ŝi estas kontenta? Ĉu vi estas kontenta? Unu ludilo estas nova, kaj unu estas malnova. Unu ludilo estas pura, kaj unu estas malpura. Kiu ludilo estas pura? Ĉu la ĝardeno estas bela? Ĉu ĝi estas granda aŭ malgranda? Ĉu ĝi estas larĝa aŭ mallarĝa? Malantaŭ Maria estas du ŝrankoj. Unu ŝranko estas granda, kaj la alia estas malgranda. Unu ŝranko estas larĝa, kaj la alia estas mallarĝa.

PRAKTIKO 2.6 Sinjoro Lang sidas antaŭ la kameno (*or* antaŭ la fajro). Maria sidas ĉe la tablo. Antaŭ ŝi sur la tablo estas aŭtomobilo kaj pupo (*or* Aŭtomobilo kaj pupo estas antaŭ ŝi sur la tablo). En la kameno estas fajro. Ne, sinjoro Lang ne sidas sur la tablo, sed en brakseĝo. Jes, la granda ŝranko estas por libroj. Jes, ĝi estas larĝa. Ne, ĝi ne pendas sur la muro. Malgranda, mallarĝa ŝranko pendas sur la muro. Ĝi estas por la ludiloj de Maria. Ne, la ĝardeno ne estas antaŭ la kameno, sed ekster la domo. Ne, la ludiloj ne estas sur la planko, sed sur la tablo. La aŭtomobilo estas nova, sed la pupo estas malnova. La brakseĝo estas komforta. Jes, la libroŝranko estas granda. La elektra lumo pendas super Maria.

Demandoj 2 1 Jes, la seĝo de sinjorino Brown estas tre komforta. 2 Jes, la kafo estas tre bona. 3 Ne, la infanoj ne estas en la ĝardeno, sed en la lernejo. 4 Maria estas kontenta pri tio. 5 La tago estas bela. 6 Gesinjoroj Lang laboras en la ĝardeno. 7 Jes, ili estas kontentaj pri ĝi. 8 Ne, sinjorino, Brown ne estas kontenta. 9 Ne, sinjoro Brown ne laboras en la ĝardeno. 10 Li sidas kaj legas.

PRAKTIKO 3.1 Where are Mary's toys? They are on the table in front of her. What is the father doing? He is sitting and reading a book. What kind of book is he reading? He is reading a good book. He is sitting comfortably and reading quickly. Mary is very pleased because she goes (is going) to school*. She goes quickly. But Andrew is not pleased. He goes slowly to school. Mary loves school, but Andrew hates it.

* For 'goes to school' we say **iras al** la **lernejo**, because **iras al lernejo** would mean 'goes to *a* school'.

PRAKTIKO 3.2 1 (*i*); 2 (*f*); 3 (*j*); 4 (*g*); 5 (*b*); 6 (*h*); 7 (*d*); 8 (*a*); 9 (*e*); 10 (*c*).

PRAKTIKO 3.3 Ne, urbego ne estas malgranda urbo, sed granda urbo. Sinjoro Lang legas libron. Maria sidas ĉe la tablo. La ŝranko de Maria (*or* Ĝi) estas malgranda kaj mallarĝa. Ĝi pendas super Maria. Ne, mi ne loĝas kun gesinjoroj Lang. Ne, aŭtomobilo ne estas tiel granda kiel trajno. Ne, ŝi ne estas maljuna, ŝi estas juna. Ĝi estas bela. Ne, ĝi ne estas malkomforta, ĝi estas komforta. Ne, fajro ne estas malvarma, ĝi estas tre varma. La pupo estas malpura. Maria/Andreo/La patrino amas la patron. La patro amas la patrinon/Marian/Andreon. Ne, ĝi (la familio Lang) konsistas el kvar personoj.

PRAKTIKO 3.4 The town is small. It is not a big city like London. Are the streets wide or narrow? In the middle of the square stands a statue, and behind that is the town hall. In the square (there) is also a large church. Where is the art gallery? It is in the public park. And where is the park? It is on the left of the main street. At the other side of the street is the hospital. A path leads from the main street to the hospital. Where do the people (men and women) of the town walk? Where do the children play? The men and women walk in the public park, and the children play there. In the main street cars and buses travel. How does the car go (travel)? It goes fast (quickly). Trains do not run in the street; they run on the railway.

Note: In Esperanto, we say **sur la strato** (not **en**).

PRAKTIKO 3.5 Kie vi loĝas? Mi loĝas en urbego. Ĝi ne estas tiel granda kiel Londono. Ĝi havas du stacidomojn. Trajnoj veturas sur la fervojo, sed aŭtomobiloj veturas sur la vojoj. Ĉu vi havas aŭtomobilon? Jes, mi havas malgrandan aŭtomobilon, sed ĝi ne veturas tre rapide. La ĉefstratoj en la urbo estas larĝaj, sed la aliaj stratoj estas mallarĝaj. Kia estas la urbo? Ĝi estas moderna kaj pura.

PRAKTIKO 3.6 1 Kie veturas la aŭtobuso? 2 Kio staras en la parko? 3 Ĉu la granda strato (ĉefstrato) iras rekte al la ĉefplaco? 4 Kiu(j) promenas kaj ripozas en la parko? 5 Ĉu trajno veturas sur la strato? 6 Kie staras la urbo? (*or* Kie la urbo staras?) 7 Kiel veturas trajno? 8 Kio staras en la mezo de la placo? 9 Kion vi vidas sub la ponto? 10 Kie vi vidas la dometojn?

Demandoj 3 1 La vetero estas bela kaj varma. 2 La du sinjorinoj sidas en la publika parko. 3 La floroj estas belaj. 4 La familio Lang fartas tre bone. 5 Sinjoro Brown laboras en la ĝardeno. 6 Tio estas surprizo al sinjorino Brown. 7 La sinjorinoj vidas hundojn. 8 La hundoj ludas sur la vojeto kaj sub la arboj (antaŭ la artgalerio). 9 Ne, la sinjorinoj ne ludas, ili sidas kaj ripozas. 10 Jes, tio plaĉas al ili.

PRAKTIKO 4.1 The mother gave (has given) two beautiful toys to Mary. A friend (has) sent me a letter. The tree was in front of the house. The cat was sitting under the table. Did you see it (*or* Have you seen it?) No, I did not see it (have not seen it). Have you read that book? Yes, I have already read it. Who sent her the letter? The house was full yesterday.
1 I did not speak to him; I have not spoken to him; I was not speaking to him. 2 Did you write to her? Have you written to her? Were you writing to her? 3 He travelled in a bus; He has travelled in a bus; He was travelling in a bus.

PRAKTIKO 4.2 En la domo estis ses grandaj ĉambroj. Mi vidis Andreon en la ĝardeno. Ĉu vi vidis lin? Mi vidis Marian en la infanejo. Mi jam vidis ŝin. Ŝi ludis. Mi ne vidis sinjoron Lang hieraŭ. Li ne estis en la domo. Ĉu vi vidis sinjorinon Lang? Jes, mi vidis ŝin hieraŭ. Kie ŝi estis? Ŝi sidis en la parko. Ĉu vi vidis tiun aŭtomobilon? Ĝi veturis tre rapide (*or* rapidege). Mi sendis leteron al sinjorino Brown. Mi sendis al ŝi leteron hieraŭ. Ŝi legis ĝin je la tria horo. La malgrandaj katoj sidis sur la novaj tabloj. La hundo sidis apud la fenestro.

PRAKTIKO 4.3 1 (*j*); 2 (*i*); 3 (*d*); 4 (*c*); 5 (*g*); 6 (*h*); 7 (*b*); 8 (*e*); 9 (*a*); 10 (*f*).

PRAKTIKO 4.4 I have already learnt the elements of Esperanto. Now I am corresponding with a friend abroad. I have just received a letter and I shall soon write a reply. In that way (thus) I shall use Esperanto. A Norwegian friend, Edvard, wrote (has written) a letter to Mr Lang. He wrote about the small town of Voss, in which he lives. This little town stands on the railway from Bergen to Oslo. Mr Lang is the husband of Mrs Clare Lang. Mr and Mrs Lang are husband and wife. I received many letters and postcards from abroad. I have friends in many countries. My friend is a youngster (young man/youth), but he is not a sportsman. Are there many Youth Hostels in Norway? I don't know. What do the old people do? They catch fish in the lake. They also look at the many historical houses. Here in my town I don't catch fish. Do you know why? Because this town is not (does not stand) near a lake.

PRAKTIKO 4.5 Ĉu vi korespondas kun amikino en eksterlando? Ĉu vi jam ricevis leteron? Kion ŝi skribis? Kie ŝi loĝas? Ĉu ŝi loĝas en Norvegujo? Kie la amiko de S-ro Lang vidis la anoncon? Kion li skribis? Ĉu li skribis en Esperanto? Ĉu S-ro Lang baldaŭ respondos? Pri kio li skribos? Kion li sendos? Kio estas viaj ĉefaj interesoj? Ĉu vi estas sportulo? Kio vi estas? Ĉu vi ofte relegas leterojn? Ĉu S-ro Lang ofte relegas la leteron? Ĉu vi konas s-ron Lang? Ĉu vi scias, kie li loĝas? Ĉu vi scias, ĉu li ricevis leteron?

PRAKTIKO 4.6 1 vera. 2 malvera. 3 malvera. 4 vera. 5 malvera. 6 vera. 7 malvera. 8 vera. 9 vera. 10 vera.

Demandoj 4 1 S-ro Lang renkontas la norvegan amikon ĉe la stacidomo. 2 La aŭtomobilo de s-ro Lang staras ekster la stacidomo. 3 Edvard estas bonvena. 4 Jes, li tre komforte veturis. 5 Dum Edvard iros al la dormoĉambro, s-ino Lang finos la vespermanĝon. 6 La vespermanĝo estos preta baldaŭ (*or* baldaŭ estos preta). 7 Li esperas, ke Edvard trovos la ĉambron komforta.* 8 Ne, nur du tirkestoj estas je lia dispono. 9 Kiam li estos preta, Edvard iros al la salono. 10 Se la vespermanĝo ne estos preta, Edvard sidos komforte kaj atendos, dum Rikardo helpos Klaran en la kuirejo.

* Not **komfort**an, because the phrase really means *will find the room* to be *comfortable*. **trovos la ĉambron komfortan** would mean *will find the comfortable room* (see Unit 2, note **3**).

PRAKTIKO 5.1 Where are you going (to)? Where is Andrew going? Mary runs (is running) into the dining-room. Andrew is not playing in the children's room. Go forward, please, as far as the bridge over the railway. Let's go to the park. Let's look at these pictures. I am now at your disposal; where shall we go? Shall we go to the station? How shall we go? Let's go by bus! I like that cat very much. Look at it; it's playing in front of the house. Who is Andrew's sister? Don't you know that Mary is his sister, and he is her brother? Speak to his father about him, please. I am not going to him; let him come to me! What shall we do? Don't do that please! I am going home now; goodbye!

PRAKTIKO 5.2 Iru al la pordo, mi petas! Iru en la salonon, mi petas! Ĉu ni iru al kinejo? Ni legu ĉi tiun libron! Ne iru en la aŭtomobilejon. Kie estas la kato? Kien ĝi iris? Ĝi iris el la domo en la ĝardenon. Iru supren al la dormoĉambro, mi petas. Miaj fratinoj iris al la kinejo, sed mi restis hejme. La kato venis en (envenis) la ĉambron, kaj la muso kuris sub la liton. Ĉi tiu ĉambro estas je via dispono. Prenu la pupon de sur la tablo, mi petas. Kion ni faru nun? Venu ĉi tien! Ĉu vi iras hejmen nun? Ĝis revido!

PRAKTIKO 5.3 According to my reckoning there are 148 possible meaningful sentences to be made from this list. (Make sure you haven't used any **-n** words after **al** or **el**.)

PRAKTIKO 5.4 Do you speak Esperanto? Where do you come from? Are you an Englishwoman? No, I am a Scot. I live in Glasgow. And where do *you* live? I am a Frenchman and live in Paris. I am a Parisian, and my wife is a Parisienne. The French (people) speak the French language, and the Italians speak Italian. Is Esperanto similar to (Does Esperanto resemble) the Italian language? Do you go north from Germany to Italy? No, I go south, because Italy lies to the south of Germany. Where shall we go for our holiday? I am thinking about Switzerland. What kind of country is it? It's a beautiful country with many mountains, and the air is very pure. Because of that, many sick people go there. How shall we go there? Let's travel by rail(way) to (as far as) the sea, then by ship to France, and from there by rail into Switzerland. What are we going to do* while we are there? We'll visit various interesting towns, and we will see the Alps.

* Note the difference between **Kion ni faru?** and **Kion ni far**os? The **-u** ending implies a decision, whereas **-os** simply implies something that is going to happen. **Kion ni faros?** could also be expressed as *What shall we be doing?*

PRAKTIKO 5.5 Ĉu vi jam pensis pri via ferio? Ĉu vi jam pensis pri Svislando? Ĉu vi scias, ke en Svislando vi trovos kvar oficialajn lingvojn? Ĉu vi parolas la germanan? la francan? la italan? la romanĉan? la nederlandan? la rusan? Ĉu vi estas Londonanino? Manĉestrano? Glasgovano?Kiel ni iru al Svislando? Ĉu ni veturu per aŭtomobilo, biciklo, aŭtobuso, aŭ fervojo? Ĉu ni veturu trans Svislandon al aliaj landoj? Kien ni iru? Norden, suden, orienten aŭ okcidenten?

PRAKTIKO 5.6 1 malvera. 2 vera. 3 malvera. 4 malvera. 5 malvera. 6 vera. 7 malvera. 8 vera. 9 vera. 10 vera.

Demandoj 5 1 S-ro Lang renkontas unue la prezidanton de la grupo. 2 Ne, li ne nur vizitas la urbon; li loĝas tie. 3 Li lernas Esperanton hejme. 4 Li ne vizitis la grupon ĝis nun ĉar li ne estis libera je la vesperoj de la kunvenoj. 5 La nomo de la prezidanto estas John Danby. 6 S-ro Lang poste parolas kun fraŭlino (f-ino) Jones. 7 La grupo komencas la kunvenojn per mallongaj lecionoj en klasoj. 8 Hodiaŭ s-ro Franks parolos pri Norvegujo kaj Svedujo. 9 Tio estos interesa al s-ro Lang (Rikardo). 10 Ĝi estos interesa al li ĉar li korespondas kun norvego.

PRAKTIKO 6.1 Is it snowing today? Did it rain (was it raining) yesterday? No, yesterday it didn't rain, but perhaps it will rain today. What is the weather like now? It is sunny, and the sky is blue, but it isn't warm. They say (it is said) that Esperanto is like (resembles) the Italian language. If you have (one has) holidays you want (wish) to have fine weather. Everyone knows that Switzerland is a mountainous country. Did you receive (have you received) a letter today? No, no one in the family received a letter today, but I received (got) one yesterday from my brother. What is in this drawer? There is nothing in it; it is empty. I (have) just looked into it, but I didn't see anything. What is in the coal-scuttle? That is not empty; there is (some) coal in it.

PRAKTIKO 6.2 Ĉi tiu (tiu ĉi) ŝranko estas plena de ĉiaj libroj. Kien vi iris hieraŭ? Mi iris nenien; mi restis hejme. Mi ĵus ricevis leteron de mia fratino. Ŝi diras, ke estas tre malvarme tie. Estas malvarme ĉie hodiaŭ. Frostas. Oni diras, ke neĝos. Kie pluvis hieraŭ? Ĉie! Se estas sune, ĉiu estas kontenta. Ĉu vi havas monujon? Kio estas en ĝi? Estas nenio en ĝi; ĝi estas malplena. Ĉiu ĉambro en la domo estas je via dispono. Dankon! Vi estas bona amiko.

PRAKTIKO 6.3 Kio? Kie? Kiel? Tiu. Tie. Tial. Ĉiu, Ĉia. Neniu. Nenial. Kia? Tie. Ĉie. Neniel! Kiu? Kial? Tia. Tiel. Tial. Nenie. Tiel. Tia . . . Kiu? Kiel? Kia . . .! Tiu. Ĉiu. Nenio. Kial? Tiel. Ĉiu. Ĉiel. Neniu. Ĉio. Ĉial.

PRAKTIKO 6.4 What is the weather like in your town? Does it often rain? In Spain it doesn't often rain. What is the summer like in Italy? Usually during the summer it is warm (hot) there. In Scotland there is often snow during the winter, and from time to time it isolates several villages. I will (shall; am going to) visit you on Wednesday. I waited three weeks, but didn't receive a reply. That wall is two metres high. On Monday I'll go into (the) town. The (railway) station is one kilometre away from my house. What is the weather like today? It is sunny, with a gentle wind. Do you work on Saturdays? No, I work from Monday to Friday every week.

PRAKTIKO 6.5 En Italujo dum la somero kutime estas varme. Kia estas la vetero en Parizo dum la somero? Cu estas varme, aŭ ĉu estas malvarme? Ne ofte neĝas en mia urbo. Ĉu vi legas la veter-prognozon? Kutime estas varme ĉi tie tage (dum la tago), kaj malvarme nokte. Oni diras, ke estas sune en Italujo dum marto. Ĉu vi (oni) ofte vidas neĝon en Hispanujo? Februaro venas post januaro. Kiu monato venas antaŭ junio? Ĉu oni kutime laboras dimanĉe? Ne, oni kutime laboras dum kvin tagoj de la semajno, sed ne sabate aŭ dimanĉe.

PRAKTIKO 6.6 1 La ludiloj de Maria estas nov**aj** kaj bel**aj**. 2 Ili kuŝ**as** sur la grand**a** tabl**o**. 3 Hieraŭ mi vid**is** mi**an** amik**on**. 4 S-ro Lang ricev**is** leter**on** el Norveg**ujo** hieraŭ. 5 La kato saltis de la plank**o** sur la tabl**on**. 6 Morgaŭ mi ir**os** en la urb**on** kaj sid**os** en la park**o**. 7 Trajno oft**e** ir**as** tre rapid**e**. 8 Mi ĵus leg**is** ti**un** libr**on**. Fakte, mi leg**is** ĉi**ujn** el ili. (How many of the 25 blanks did you fill in correctly?)

Demandoj 6 1 Rikardo revenis de kunveno de la Esperantogrupo. 2 La kunveno estis tre interesa. 3 La membroj estis tre afablaj al li. 4 Rikardo estis en la altgrada klaso. 5 Poste s-ro Franks parolis pri Norvegujo kaj Svedujo. 6 S-ro Franks veturis de Bergen ĝis Oslo. 7 La fervoja muzeo en Hamar uzas Esperanton en klarigaj tekstoj. 8 La kastelo Grezijono apartenas al la francaj esperantistoj. 9 Ĝi situas apud la urbeto Baugé, sude de Le Mans. 10 Ili ne diskutas la aferon nun ĉar estas malfrue.

PRAKTIKO 7.1 What time is it? Is it seven o'clock? Not yet, it is only quarter to seven (6.45). What are you going to (will you) do today? This morning I am going (will go) into town. First(ly) I'll go to the post and (will) buy stamps. Then (afterwards) I'll go to the station for information about trains to London. Didn't you go there yesterday afternoon? Yes, but I forgot about the stamps. Yesterday morning I met an old friend. I first (lit. firstly) met him three years ago in France. In thirty minutes it will be ten o'clock. Then (so) it is now half past nine (nine thirty).

PRAKTIKO 7.2 Mi iras (ir**os** *if you have not yet started!*) al la stacidomo hodiaŭ matene. Kiam vi revenos? Mi ne revenos ĝis la dek-dua (horo). Mi renkontis gesinjorojn Lang hieraŭ vespere. Hieraŭ estis la dudek-unua de januaro. Kio estos la dato morgaŭ? Mi estis tie trifoje. Mi estis tie antaŭ kvar jaroj. Mi estos tie denove post tri monatoj. Kie estas la kunvenejo de la Esperantogrupo? Ĝi estas apud la urbodomo. La grupo kunvenas lundon vespere (*note*: lund**e** vespere *if you mean every Monday*) je la sepa kaj duono. Kiel longe* daŭras la kunvenoj? Kutime ili daŭras du horojn.

* Some esperantists use **Kiomlonge**, on the grounds that the expression is quantitative, and there is some justification for this.

PRAKTIKO 7.3 1 Estas la tria horo. 2 Estas la kvara (kaj) dek. 3 Estas la sesa (kaj) kvindek. 4 Estas la unua kaj duono (tridek). 5 Estas la kvara (kaj) kvardek kvin. 6 Estas la dek-unua (kaj) kvin. 7 Estas la dek-dua horo. 8 Estas la oka (kaj) dudek. 9 Estas la oka (kaj) tridek kvin. 10 Estas la deka (kaj) kvindek kvin.

PRAKTIKO 7.4 What time is it? It is half past seven. In an hour and a half it will be nine o'clock. Two hours ago he was in school. In two months I shall be in Sweden. Do you like tea? Yes, I like it very much. How much coffee do you want? One kilo(gramme) please. Yesterday was the first of May. When shall I visit you? Come on Monday or Tuesday; I shall be free at seven (o'clock). Yesterday I received a piece of news from my friend in France. Do you prefer pork or veal? Did you hear (have you heard) the news this morning? (At) what time shall we see the film *The Green Fire*? We shall see it at half past nine, after the news. I like the programme 'Study Places'. Usually it is about universities and colleges, but today it will be about a château in France.

PRAKTIKO 7.5 Je kioma horo vi aŭdas la veterprognozon? Kiam vi aŭdis la novaĵojn? Ĉu vi venos lundon aŭ vendredon? Ni aŭdis orkestron je la tria horo. Ni venos je la kvara kaj duono aŭ la kvara (kaj) kvardek kvin. Kio estas duono de ses? Kio estas kvarono de dek-duo? Antaŭ tri tagoj mi vidis teatraĵon. Post sep semajnoj mi ricevos permeson. Kiom da horloĝoj vi havas? Ni aŭdis unu horon da muziko per diskoj.

PRAKTIKO 7.6 1 La novaĵoj je la televido estas je la sesa kaj la naŭa horoj. 2 Oni diskutos ideojn el la mondo de la sciencoj je la kvina kaj duono (tridek). 3 Oni vidos pop-grupojn en (la programo) 'La Supraj Dek'. 4 John Russell prezentos la programon 'Loka Gazeto'. 5 Je la naŭa kaj duono (tridek) okazos filmo *La Verda Fajro*. 6 La stelino en tio estos Francine Marmont. 7 Je la kvara kaj duono (tridek) okazos la teatraĵo *La Tridek Naŭ Ŝtupoj*. 8 Flora Lloyd raportos el Vieno je la sesa kaj duono. 9 Ni aŭdos pri 'La Urbega Ĝangalo' je la naŭa (kaj) kvardek kvin. 10 La Kastelo Grésillon apartenas al la francaj esperantistoj.

Demandoj 7 1 La familio veturos de Newtown ĝis Grezijono per aŭtomobilo kaj ŝipo (*or* aŭtomobile kaj ŝipe). 2 Ili ekveturos sabaton frumatene. 3 Ili suriros la ŝipon en Dovro. 4 Ili manĝos surŝipe (sur la ŝipo). 5 Ili eble tranoktos en Neufchâtel. 6 De Bulonjo ĝis Neufchâtel estas inter cent kaj cent dek mejloj. 7 Kaj de Neufchâtel ĝis Grezijono estas ĉirkaŭ cent naŭdek mejloj. 8 En Le Mans okazas dudek-kvar-hora vetkurado ĉiun jaron. 9 Jes, Rikardo opinias, ke ili veturos ĉirkaŭ kvin mejlojn laŭ la vetkurejo. 10 Kiam ili alvenos en Grezijono la familio unue trovos la dormoĉambron, kaj poste ĉirkaŭrigardos la lokon.

PRAKTIKO 8.1 He is kinder than she. I have a better dog than you. My brother is taller than I. He is the tallest in the family. Andrew goes to bed earlier than Mary. A tiger is more dangerous than a cat. That book is most interesting. Stephen is the most intelligent of those three boys. A train goes (travels) faster than a bus. I hope (that) you are better now. Which is the most direct way to the town centre? She sings the most beautifully of all the girls. With whom did you visit London? In which room do you eat? I don't know what you are talking about.

PRAKTIKO 8.2 1 (*d*); 2 (*f*); 3 (*i*); 4 (*e*); 5 (*j*); 6 (*b*); 7 (*h*); 8 (*a*); 9 (*c*); 10 (*g*).

PRAKTIKO 8.3 Nia domo estas pli malgranda (malpli granda) ol (la) via. Tiu knabino estas la plej bela en la klaso, sed ŝi ne estas la plej feliĉa. Mi estas pli forta ol mia frato ĉar li estas pli juna ol mi. Tiu strato estas pli larĝa ol ĉi tiu (tiu ĉi). Ĝi estas la plej larĝa strato en la urbo. Kiu estas la plej rekta vojo al la urbodomo? Andreo estis malsana hieraŭ, sed li estas pli sana (li fartas pli bone) nun. Kiu estis la plej fama angla poeto? Pri kio vi parolas? Al kiu urbo vi iras? (veturas, *if in a vehicle*) Kun kiu vi venis? Mi venis kun mia pli juna frato.

PRAKTIKO 8.4 Is a calf bigger than a lamb? You see more lambs and calves (more lambs and calves are seen) in spring than in autumn. You often see flowers (flowers are often seen) in the country during summer. In our national parks you don't (one doesn't) see lions, giraffes and elephants. A young lion is a lion cub. Which flowers can be seen (are visible) early in spring? What is remarkable (noteworthy) about the migration of swallows? In autumn the swallows fly from Britain to (as far as) South Africa. Do you like walking (strolling, etc.) through a wood? Yes, woods are often worth visiting. I don't like dancing very much; I prefer singing. National parks are always worth seeing. They give incalculable pleasure to all who visit them. Our national parks give pleasure not only to the British people, but also to those foreigners who visit us. The use of Esperanto is easier than the use of other languages.

PRAKTIKO 8.5 Kion vi scias pri la birdmigrado? Kiu estas pli alta, hundido aŭ katido? Oni ne vidas elefantarojn en tiu ĉi (ĉi tiu) lando. Hirundaroj migras en aŭtuno. La ŝtatparko estas laŭdinda ideo. Kio estas rimarkinda pri la ŝtatparko en Wyoming? Ĉu la ŝtatparko Kruger* estas la plej granda en la mondo? Mi ne scias, sed mi scias, ke du el la plej grandaj en Britujo estas tiuj de Norda Kimrujo kaj la Laga Regiono. La Arkta marhirundo migras de la Arkto ĝis la Antarkto.

PRAKTIKO 8.6 1 malvera. 2 vera. 3 vera. 4 malvera. 5 malvera. 6 vera. 7 malvera. 8 vera. 9 malvera. 10 vera.

*(cf. 'la familio Lang')

Demandoj 8 1 Klara sentas sin kvazaŭ hejme ĉar ili jam ekkonis tiom da homoj. 2 Andreo ĉeestos la kurson por geknaboj ĉar liaj du amikoj Petro kaj Fulvio ĉeestos ĝin. 3 La geamikoj de Andreo kaj Maria venas el Francujo, Italujo kaj Germanujo. 4 Klara provos la kurson pri makramo ĉar la ekzemploj, kiujn la instruistino alportis, estis belaj. 5 Rikardo kaj Klara (Ges-roj Lang) akompanas Roberton al Baugé. 6 Ili promenas tra la arbaro. 7 Ili unue vizitas la muzeon de la Kastelo de Baugé. 8 La kuratoro de la muzeo rekomendas viziton al la farmaciejo. 9 La farmaciejo ne vendas medikamentojn ĉar ĝi estas de la dek-sepa jarcento, kaj oni konservas ĝin en ĝia tiama stato. 10 Roberto jam vizitis ĝin.

PRAKTIKO 9.1 I must (have to) go to (the) town this morning. Do you want to buy a necklace? Close the door please. If I had a car I could go more quickly than by bicycle. Thank you for your letter. I haven't time now to reply fully, but I shall soon be able to do so. Instead of working in the garden he sits and reads (is sitting and reading). That skirt is very nice (beautiful), isn't it? I would like to buy it, if I had the money. I like it too. If I were rich I would buy so many things! Yes, if one were rich one could buy many (a lot of) things without thinking about the cost, couldn't one?

PRAKTIKO 9.2 Anstataŭ komenci hieraŭ li atendis ĝis hodiaŭ. Mi vidos vin hodiaŭ posttagmeze por helpi vin. Se mi estus vi, mi irus sen atendi lin. Krom lerni Esperanton ŝi lernas ankaŭ la francan. Ĉu vi povus helpi min porti ĉi tion, mi petas? Se mi havus la tempon mi povus piediri al via domo. Mi iras al la preĝejo nur dimanĉe. Mi iris al la kinejo sabaton, kaj ankaŭ Andreo venis. Plaĉas al mi iri al kinejo kiam mi estas libera.

PRAKTIKO 9.3
Nur mi rigardos la gazeton hodiaŭ vespere (*I, but nobody else*).
Mi nur rigardos la gazeton hodiaŭ vespere (*but I won't read it*).
Mi rigardos nur la gazeton hodiaŭ vespere (*the magazine, but nothing else*).
Mi rigardos la gazeton nur hodiaŭ vespere (*but not tomorrow*).
Mi rigardos la gazeton hodiaŭ nur vespere (*but not in the morning*).
Ankaŭ mi rigardos la gazeton hodiaŭ nur vespere (*I too, as well as others*).
Mi ankaŭ rigardos gazeton hodiaŭ nur vespere (*as well as paying for it*).
Mi rigardos ankaŭ gazeton hodiaŭ nur vespere (*as well as the letters*).
Mi rigardos gazeton ankaŭ hodiaŭ vespere (*as well as on other evenings*).
Mi rigardos gazeton hodiaŭ ankaŭ vespere (*as well as in the afternoon*).

PRAKTIKO 9.4 If I received £50 000, I would buy a new house. If Richard received so much money, he would go (travel) round the world. What would you do? Would you devote money to your children's education, or help some 'worthy' society? Clare wishes to be, and remain, fit. She does physical exercises every day. I've lost my ball-point (pen): it must be somewhere, but I don't know where. Perhaps someone will find it and give it back (return it) to me. Something unusual happened to me yesterday. For some reason he ran away. Why is the door closed? The task was already done (had already been done). Instead of closing the door, he did the opposite. That man is a member of our group. The art of the Chinese cooks is very subtle. Two thousand five hundred years ago, Confucius proposed rules which are still obeyed. In China they eat chiefly vegetables, because meat is expensive. Do you prefer roast beef or roast pork? Do you like salad? You need much longer to prepare a meal than to eat it!

PRAKTIKO 9.5 Kion vi farus se vi estus riĉa? Mi esperas, ke mi uzus mian monon saĝe (ke mi saĝe uzus . . .). Ĉiutage mi faras korpajn ekzercojn antaŭ malfermita fenestro. Ĉi tiu (tiu ĉi) salato estas preparita el freŝaj legomoj. La legomoj devas esti zorge lavitaj (oni devas zorge lavi . . .). Ĉu plaĉus al vi taso de teo* ? Ĉu mi povas iri tien kaj reen en unu tago? Tio povus esti la kialo. Ĉu mi povas fari ion por helpi? Tiu rivero fluas tre rapide (rapidege). Mi esperas, ke la infanoj bone kondutos.

PRAKTIKO 9.6 La celo de la korpaj ekzercoj estas helpi la homojn esti kaj resti sanaj. La salato en la recepto estas por ĉiuj sezonoj (ne havas sezonon). Unue oni devas purigi la freŝajn legomojn. Oni devas kuiri ilin en salita akvo. Oni kuiras ilin ĝis ili estas preskaŭ molaj. Se oni uzas konservitajn legomojn el skatolo, oni devas forverŝi la likvaĵon. Konfucio proponis la regulojn laŭ kiuj la kuiristinoj en Ĉinujo ankoraŭ kuiras. Li proponis ilin antaŭ dumil kvincent jaroj. Oni manĝas ĉefe legomojn ĉar la viando estas altekosta (multekosta). Oni spicas la manĝaĵojn por forpreni malagrablajn odorojn. La ĉinaj kuiristinoj stufas grasan porkaĵon. Ili fritas malgrasan porkaĵon.

Demandoj 9 1 Ges-roj Lang dankas la francajn geamikojn pro ilia afabla zorgo pri Andreo kaj Maria dum la posttagmezo. 2 Ambaŭ infanoj amis la ĉimpanzojn. 3 Rikardo kaj Klara vizitis la urbon Angers. 4 Plej plaĉis al Klara la grandiozaj tapetoj faritaj inter la dek-kvara kaj la dek-oka jarcentoj. 5 Klara kaj Rikardo rigardis multajn skulptaĵojn kaj pentraĵojn de francaj artistoj de la dek-oka jarcento. 6 Marteno sugestas, ke ili vizitu la kastelon de Le Lude dum la vespero. 7 Nokte okazas unika spektaklo per 'Sono kaj Lumo'. 8 Oni komencas la spektaklon je la naŭa kaj tridek. 9 Ĝi daŭras du horojn (dum du horoj). 10 Oni devas tuj ekveturi por havi bonajn sidlokojn.

PRAKTIKO 10.1 That man is talking to himself. I get washed (wash myself) before my breakfast. I saw him yesterday. I saw myself in the mirror. He did not flatter (was not flattering) me, but he flattered (was flattering) himself. The children were reading to themselves when I saw them. Andrew is not pleased because his father drank his (Andrew's) milk. The mother did not know whether Mary was drinking her (the mother's) milk or her own. But Mary told her that she was drinking her own milk. That pleased her mother (caused her mother to be pleased). I explained to my brother how I did the work. I did it like that (in that way) to make it easy. The boy lay down (laid himself) on the bed. The girls were playing with their toys.

* Not ***da* teo,** as we are asking about the beverage, not the quantity.

PRAKTIKO 10.2 La instruisto parolis al la klaso, sed li ne amuzis ilin. Ili amuzis sin. Johano diras, ke lia amiko trinkas sian bieron. Johano diras, ke lia amiko trinkas lian bieron. Mi vidis, ke la infanoj finis sian laboron. La infano ludis per ruĝa inko, kaj ruĝigis siajn manojn. Li ruĝigis ankaŭ siajn vestojn. Ĉu vi povas klarigi al mi ĉi tion? Ĉu vi purigis la plankon? Sekigu viajn vestojn kaj poste vestu vin.

PRAKTIKO 10.3 1 resanigi. 2 plibonigi. 3 faciligi. 4 devigi. 5 diversigi. 6 egaligi. 7 rejunigi. 8 liberigi. 9 necesigi. 10 enpoŝtigi.

PRAKTIKO 10.4 What did you say to yourself? They get washed (wash themselves) every morning, don't they? Einstein was the most famous mathematician. His genius in (*lit.* about) mathematics became evident in early youth. He was also a good pianist and violinist, wasn't he? Perhaps somewhere, some time, there will be an even more wonderful mathematician, whose name we don't yet (still don't) know. Do you think (that) mankind (the human race) will destroy itself with atom(ic) bombs? Einstein feared (was afraid) that that could happen. Nobody can know everything, but everyone can learn, and so (thus) know more than before. Please continue your work. The cat went into the garden and frightened the birds. Yesterday I got rid of (*lit.* caused to be away) a large pile of papers from my desk (writing-table) and burned them all.

PRAKTIKO 10.5 Maria legas sian libron. La infanoj amas siajn lecionojn, ĉu ne? La suno baldaŭ sekigis la vestojn. Vi devas ĉiam purigi viajn dentojn. Li kompletigis sian taskon hieraŭ matene, ĉu ne? Ĉu vi boligis la akvon? Do, bonvolu fari la teon. Mi eliris en la pluvon, kaj malsekiĝis. Mia frato edziĝis en marto, kaj mia fratino edziniĝos en septembro. Johano kaj Maria geedziĝis en junio. Mi estas ano (membro) de la societo, kaj mia amiko aniĝos morgaŭ. Kiam li naskiĝis?

PRAKTIKO 10.6 1 malvera. 2 vera. 3 malvera. 4 vera. 5 malvera. 6 vera. 7 vera. 8 vera. 9 malvera. 10 malvera.

Demandoj 10 1 La tuta familio ĝuis siajn feriojn. 2 La ferioj faris bonon al la infanoj ĉar ili kutimigis ilin al la kunesto de alilandanoj. 3 La gepatroj instigos la infanojn skribi al siaj novaj geamikoj. (NB **siaj** because **la infanoj** is the subject of the verb **skribi**.) 4 Rikardo devos skribi al la geamikoj de la gepatroj ĉar estas li, kiu ĉiam faras la korespondadon. 5 Klara devos skribi al Chantal ĉar Chantal donis al ŝi belan kolĉenon kiel memorigilon. 6 En la kunveno de la Esperantogrupo oni petis Rikardon fari paroladon pri siaj ferioj. 7 Li timas ĉar li neniam antaŭe faris publikan paroladon. 8 Kiam ges-roj Smith promenis sole en Francujo, ili vojeraris. 9 S-ino Smith demandis al Klara ĉu ŝi kaj Rikardo parolis Esperanton la tutan tempon dum la ferioj. 10 Mirigis ŝin, ke en Grezijono (Grésillon) ili parolis Esperantlingve kun homoj el almenaŭ ses landoj.

PRAKTIKO 11.1 I saw the running boy (the boy who was running). The old man sat and looked (was sitting and looking) at the people passing (by). The girl looked at the fallen tree. The politician addressed the people present. The children who were going to bed said 'good night' to their parents. The men went away from the tree that was about to (going to) fall. I hope the weather is going to get warmer. I had heard the news. At two o'clock Arthur will have finished his lunch (midday meal). I have learnt a lot from (out of) this book. They had enjoyed the holidays. Mary has grown a lot during the year. When you come, I shall have prepared the lunch. My parents had visited me the previous day.

PRAKTIKO 11.2 Mi estas aĉetinta novan jakon. Je la tria horo li estos fininta la taskon. Je la sepa kaj duono (tridek) mi estis pakonta miajn vestojn. Mi estis longe admirinta tiun verkiston. Mi estis informonta lin pri tio, sed mi forgesis. Ŝi estos decidinta tion antaŭ morgaŭ. Mi estis anoncinta ĝin kiam li envenis. La spektaklo estas daŭronta du horojn.

PRAKTIKO 11.3 (You may have these in a different order)

Ŝi estis ludinta.	*She had played.*
Ŝi estas ludinta.	*She has played.*
Ŝi estos ludinta.	*She will have played.*
Ŝi estis ludanta.	*She was playing.*
Ŝi estas ludanta.	*She is playing.*
Ŝi estos ludanta.	*She will be playing.*
Ŝi estis ludonta.	*She was about to play.*
Ŝi estas ludonta.	*She is about to play.*
Ŝi estos ludonta.	*She will be about to play.*

PRAKTIKO 11.4 By means of our 'flying buses' you will reach any part of the world. We will arrange your holidays abroad in the coming (next) summer. Are you about to buy furniture? The more you look at any piece of furniture from our factory, the more you will like it. Have you got an electric iron? Have you got an electric washing machine? In which room is your cooker? Is your cooker electric? Our business has grown from (out of) one simple shop. We shall always be at your service in years to come, as in the past. The more you use our services, the more money you will save. The quicker you travel, the better. Soon we shall have (take possession of) a new house. We set off (started) early to reach the shop.

PRAKTIKO 11.5 La aviadilo estas fluginta norden. Nia komerco estas kreskanta tre rapide. Ĝi estas kreskinta el malgranda butiko. Ni estas je via servo kiel en pasintaj jaroj. Mi estas vidinta vian magazenon. Ni estis jam aĉetintaj niajn meblojn. Li estis vojaĝonta al Germanujo. Ŝi ekiris frue. Kion vi faros en la venonta vintro? Ju pli mi rigardas ĝin, des malpli ĝi plaĉas al mi. Kie estas la ŝlosilo? Ĉu vi posedas tranĉilon? Mi ne havas kombilon. Li pasis antaŭ la virino sen ekrigardo.

PRAKTIKO 11.6 1 Hieraŭ ni ekvetur**is** al Italujo por ni**aj** ferioj. 2 Mi vizitis butik**on** por aĉe**ti** jup**on**, sed vid**is** bel**an** rob**on** kiu tre plaĉ**is** al mi. 3 Help**u** mi**n**, mi petas. Bonvol**u** ne forir**i**. 4 Kiam mi iris en la kuirej**on** mi vid**is** mi**ajn** du fratin**ojn**. 5 Rigardu ti**un** falint**an** arb**on**!

Demandoj 11 1 Rikardo ne tuj legas la leteron ĉar li vespermanĝas. 2 Chantal kaj Marteno demandas, ĉu Klara kaj Rikardo intencas partopreni en la Universala Kongreso de Esperanto venontjare. 3 La Universala Kongreso de Esperanto okazas ĉiujare, en diversaj landoj. 4 Ne, ili ne konsistas nur el kunvenoj. 5 Klara kaj Rikardo dubas, ĉu la kongresoj taŭgos por la infanoj. 6 Ili ne iras kune al la Esperantogrupo ĉar unu el ili devas prizorgi la infanojn. 7 La infanoj povos partopreni en Infana Kongreseto. 8 La Infanaj Kongresetoj kutime okazas ne tro malproksime de la Universala Kongreso. 9 La infanoj dividiĝas en malgrandajn grupojn, ĉiu kun sia plenkreska gvidanto. 10 Ne, oni organizas ilin tiel, ke ĉiu grupo konsistas, laŭeble, el infanoj el diversaj landoj.

PRAKTIKO 12.1 It is true that our business is growing rapidly (quickly, fast). We must (It is necessary that we) go there at once (immediately). It is possible that he is deaf. Only he himself knows that. It is true that Esperanto is simpler than other languages. But even Esperanto will not learn itself; you must work in order to learn it. It seems to me that that is obvious (self-evident). It is dangerous to cross the road without looking to both sides. It is easier to advise than to accept advice. It is not convenient to me to do that job now; you will have to do it yourself.

PRAKTIKO 12.2 Estas multaj arboj en la parko. Estis mi, kiu diris tion. Mi mem renkontis la reĝinon. Mi renkontis la reĝinon mem. Estas tute eble, ke li ne povos veni. Estis malfrue: mi ellitiĝis rapide kaj vestis min. Ju pli rapide li kuris, des pli baldaŭ li alvenis. Estas memevidente, ke li mem ne povas iri. Estas du bildoj sur la muro de mia ĉambro. Ju pli mi vidas ilin, des malpli ili plaĉas al mi.

PRAKTIKO 12.3 1 alveni 2 banĉambro 3 ĉarmo 4 manĝoĉambro 5 eraro 6 patrolando 7 ĉevalido 8 erari 9 manĝaĵo 10 novaĵo 11 malnova 12 reveni 13 trovaĵo (trovitaĵo) 14 ĉevalejo 15 ĉambraro 16 trovinda 17 ĉarme 18 banejo 19 ĉevalino 20 novul(in)o

PRAKTIKO 12.4 To photograph birds, you need neither expensive apparatus nor professional skill. Neither the quantity nor the quality is satisfactory. The nest must be either on land or on water. He is either too sensible or too timid. You can put them either in pots or in the garden. It is both necessary and useful. Birds are both suspicious and timid. The hide-out (hiding-place) is both simple and cheap. You can stand them sometimes in a porch, sometimes in a window. You will succeed whether you are a professional photographer or a bungling photographer. Are birds very suspicious and timid? Are you very diligent? Are rock plants apt to creep? Are you a headmistress? or a postmistress? Did the head gardener invite the members of our gardening club?

PRAKTIKO 12.5 Li estas nek bona nek malbona. Nek proksima nek malproksima. Ĝi estas nek la pordo nek la fenestro. Vi povas elekti aŭ unu aŭ la alian. La rezultoj estas bonaj, kaj laŭ kvanto kaj laŭ kvalito. Jen ŝi kuras, jen ŝi marŝas. Mi ne scias, ĉu iri aŭ resti. Kiu estas la urbestro? Ĉu vi konas la lernejestron? La katido estas tre ludema. Li estas tre kverelema. Li fuŝas ĉion.

PRAKTIKO 12.6 1 Ne, ne necesas profesia lerteco por sukcese fotografi birdojn. 2 Prudenta komencanto elektos birdon kies nesto ne kuŝas en alta arbo. (*Did you notice how the* **-n** *in the question indicated the object of the verb* **elektos**?) 3 Oni devus havi multe da filmo ĉar oni certe fuŝos kelkajn bildojn. 4 La birdo ne suspektas, ke alia homo restas en la kaŝejo. 5 Se oni havas malgrandan ĝardenon, rokĝardeno havas la avantaĝon, ke ĝi utiligas negrandan spacon. 6 Ne, oni ne bezonas multe da rokoj. 7 Oni apartigu la rokojn per roketoj aŭ brikoj. 8 Necesas severe regi la kreskadon de la rokplantoj ĉar ili estas tre rampemaj. 9 La anoj (membroj) de la ĝardenista klubo faros viziton al Kew venontan sabaton. 10 Ili iros tien laŭ invito de la Ĝardenestro.

Demandoj 12 1 Dorina estas la bofratino de Rikardo, kaj li estas ŝia bofrato. 2 La avino estas la bopatrino de Rikardo, kaj li estas ŝia bofilo. 3 La avino estas la avino de Andreo, kaj li estas ŝia nepo. 4 Oni manĝis meleagraĵon je la Kristnaska tagmanĝo. 5 Oni trinkis vinon. 6 Rikardo elektis tion. 7 Marko proponas lavi la manĝilaron kun Stefano. 8 Dum la adoltoj trinkas, la infanoj ŝanĝas la etikedojn sur la Kristnaskdonacoj. 9 Klara unue suspektas ke estas io stranga. 10 La patrino ne sendas la infanojn al la litoj ĉar estas Kristnasko, kaj ankaŭ ĉar la ŝanĝado estis amuza ŝerco.

PRAKTIKO 13.1 He said (that) he would go that afternoon. She thought (that) her brother was intelligent. I wondered whether he had said anything (something) to her. I imagined (that) my brother would go there. My cousin asked whether I had written the letter. I replied that I would write it later. They sent me a printed letter. My new house is going to be built next year. Is that job done yet (already done)? No, it is being done now. Have you sent the letter yet (already sent the letter)? No, it is still to be written.

PRAKTIKO 13.2 Mi demandis ŝin kien ŝi iras, kaj ŝi respondis, ke ŝi iras al la butikoj. Mia frato diris, ke li forgesis sian libron. Li esperis, ke li memoros ĝin hodiaŭ. Mi esperis, ke ŝi finis ĝin. Andreo diris, ke li lernas Esperanton. Mi demandis Marian, ĉu ŝi alportos sian novan diskon, sed ŝi diris, ke ŝi perdis ĝin. Andreo opiniis, ke ĝi estas en la ŝranko, kaj diris, ke li serĉos ĝin.

PRAKTIKO 13.3 1 Non-smokers only. 2 Road Closed. 3 Road under Repair. 4 House For Sale. 5 Construction Site for Church. 6 One-Way Street: No Entry. 7 Table Reserved. 8 Danger! Workmen on the Road. 9 Beware of the dog! 10 Worker wanted in this shop. 11 Keep left. 12 P.T.O. (please turn the page). 13 R.S.V.P. 14 Please knock and enter.

PRAKTIKO 13.4 Do you think that women will rule the world more wisely than men? Nothing indicated that they loved peace. My friend thought that it was a cuckoo. I do not agree that education in two languages causes no sort of harm to a child. I wish to propose that every deaf person should have (possess) a television set. A public fund should be started. He said that television productions of Shakespeare would always be rotten. He said that television would ruin the 'live' theatre. Is a woman a creator or destroyer? I was astonished when I noticed how smoothly the teaching in two languages worked. I was educated in three languages. Deaf people are more isolated than blind people. The woman who said that lives in Torquay. The readers who wrote to the editor mentioned various matters. I did not agree with all (the) letters (which) I read. The man whose house was destroyed is my friend.

PRAKTIKO 13.5 Ĉu vi opiniis, ke virinoj estas pli saĝaj ol viroj? Kiu diris, ke ili estas fivirinoj? La urbo estas detruita. Mi estis mirigita vidi vin. Publika kolekto devus esti komencita. Kiam la radio estis elpensita? De kiu ĝi estis elpensita? Li estis estimata de ĉiu. Ŝi estis amata de ĉiuj. Mi estis operaciita de Irlanda ĥirurgo. La vetero estis aĉa. Tiuj infanoj, kiuj estas edukitaj en du lingvoj, parolas ambaŭ egale bone. La du leteroj, kiujn mi ricevis hodiaŭ matene, estis ambaŭ de malnovaj amikoj. La sinjorino, kies mansakon mi trovis, estos veninta por ĝi antaŭ la kvina kaj duono.

PRAKTIKO 13.6 1 Ne, la du personoj, kiuj skribis pri virinoj kiel registoj, ne konsentas pri la temo. 2 La viro, kies rasaj antaŭjuĝoj estas detruitaj, loĝas en Derby. 3 La ĥirurgo, kiu estas operaciinta tiun viron, estis el Irlando. 4 La instruado en la Brazila lernejo por anglaj infanoj funkciis glate. 5 La infanoj, kiuj lernis legi angle en la mateno kaj portugale en la posttagmezo, estis kvinjaraj. 6 Laŭ f-ino L. M., ĉiu surdulo devus posedi televidan aparaton ĉar la surduloj estas eĉ pli izolitaj ol la blinduloj, kiuj rajtas posedi radioaparaton. 7 Oni devus komenci publikan monokolekton por provizi niajn surdulojn per aparatoj. 8 La ĵurnalo, kiun trovis s-ino S. B., estis de antaŭ tridek jaroj. 9 Ŝi estis trovinta ĝin en la subtegmento. 10 Laŭ ŝi, la televido sukcesis malplenigi la kinejojn.

Demandoj 13 1 Ges-roj Lang ricevis siajn dokumentojn de unu el la giĉetoj. 2 Ili aparte volas rigardi la kongresan libron. 3 La Interkona Vespero okazos en la ĉambro Zamenhof. 4 Edmond Privat verkis la libron *La Vivo de Zamenhof*. 5 Chantal portas verdan mantelon. 6 Rikardo kaj Klara veturis al Belurbo aŭtomobile. 7 Marteno kaj Chantal veturis vagonare kun kelkaj samideanoj. 8 La infanoj antaŭĝuas la alvenon de

Fulvio kaj Trudi. 9 La kvar geamikoj devos manĝi frue ĉar la Interkona Vespero komenciĝos je la oka horo. 10 Klara kaj Rikardo kutime vespermanĝas hejme je la sesa horo, kiam Rikardo revenas de la laborejo.

PRAKTIKO 14.1 I regarded him as a good teacher. She has been ill for a week. I racked my brains a lot about that, but did not manage to find (succeed in finding) a solution. Who came into the room? – Andrew and Mary. Now a few words about the World (Universal) Congress. Since (because) there has been no rain for several days, I shall have to water the garden. I love him more than his brothers do. I (have) promised to help her, so I must without fail keep (fulfil) my promise. I have been a teacher for twenty years. Whom did you meet in (the) town? – Andrew and Mary.

PRAKTIKO 14.2 Unue, nur unu vorton pri la kunveno merkredon vespere. Necesas aerumi la grundon de tempo al tempo. Ŝi atendas jam de horo kaj duono. Kiu ludis en la ĝardeno? Maria. Mia fratino loĝas en Londono jam de dek jaroj. Mi amas ŝin pli ol ŝiajn fratinojn. Mi estas en la lito jam de du tagoj pro malvarmumo. Mi scias pri tio jam de longa tempo. Kiun vi vidis en la urbo? – Rikardon kaj Klaran. Ĉi tiuj ŝuoj bezonas novajn kalkanumojn. La kunveno daŭras jam de du horoj. Mi rigardas lin kiel tre bonan amikon.

PRAKTIKO 14.3 1 (*d*); 2 (*a*); 3 (*i*); 4 (*b*); 5 (*j*); 6 (*h*); 7 (*f*); 8 (*e*); 9 (*c*); 10 (*g*).

Unit 14: Crossword puzzle

1 S	2 A	L	3 O	N	O		4 P	R	5 I	N
	M		N				E		N	
6 D	I	S	K	O		7 S	T	U	F	I
	K		L		8 L		A		A	
9 P	O	10 P	O	11 L	O		12 S	13 A	N	14 A
E		A		15 A	Ĝ	16 O		M		N
17 R	18 U	Ĝ	19 A		20 I	N	21 S	U	22 L	O
	T		Ĉ		S		E		E	
23 R	I	C	E	V		24 B	R	U	O	J
	L		T				Ĉ		N	
25 B	A	K	I		26 B	R	I	T	O	J

Ĉi tie vi cerbumas!
Problemo 1: Ne. La plej malalta loko en Britujo estas apud Holme en Cambridgeshire. Ĝi staras 2.5 metrojn *sub* mar-nivelo.
Problemo 2: Bedaŭrinde ne! Ĉe la Poluso estas tiel malvarmege, ke mikroboj de malvarmumo ne povas vivi.
Problemo 3: En Islando ekzistas multaj varmegaj akvofontoj. Oni uzas ilin por varmigi la domojn.

Picture puzzles 1 En 1819. 2. Ĉeĥoslovakujo. 3 'Ĉang': Ĉina muzika instrumento. 4 Jugoslavujo. 5 Prahomo; proksimume 13 000 jarojn antaŭ Kristo. 6 Preĝejo: en Frankfurt-am-Main, Germanujo.

PRAKTIKO 14.4 Did you misunderstand me? He always misunderstands witticisms. She mispronounces all the words. Did the explorer suffer from a cold? What is a fan? Did you rack your brains over the crossword puzzle? The measure is only approximate. Has the crossword puzzle to be solved? Has the lowest point now to be found? When is the account payable? What is the difference between a student and an ex-student? He wanted to be an ex-husband, and she wanted to be an ex-wife; therefore they arranged a divorce. If he himself will not resign, we shall dismiss him. Is it a primitive bicycle? What is a primitive man? Is your great grand-father still alive (still living)? Have you a great-grandson? From whichever side the wind blows we are sheltered. I shall willingly receive you whenever you come. By means of our planes, you will easily reach any part of the world.

PRAKTIKO 14.5 Mi jam plenumis viajn ordonojn. Kiam la konto estas pagenda? Jen unu problemo, kiu estas solvenda. Li nun estas eks-oficiro. Mia praavino baldaŭ havos okdek jarojn. Li ofte misuzas la vorton. Mi amos vin, kion ajn vi faros. Mi donos ĝin al li, kiu ajn li estas. Mi ne vidis iun ajn. Mi estas preta manĝi ion ajn.

PRAKTIKO 14.6 1 La dua sezono de la jaro estas somero. 2 Se al plantoj mankas akvo, oni devus akvumi ilin. 3 Laŭ Hegel, nur unu studento komprenis lin. 4 Ne, tiu studento miskomprenis lin. 5 Laŭ Sir Humphry Davy, lia plej grava eltrovaĵo estis Michael Faraday. 6 La plej malalta loko en Britujo, oni diras, estas apud Holme, en Cambridgeshire. 7 Oni ne povas suferi de malvarmumo ĉe la Norda Poluso ĉar tie estas tiel malvarmege, ke mikroboj de malvarmumo ne povas vivi. 8 La homoj utiligas varmegajn akvofontojn por varmigi la domojn en Islando. 9 La alia bofrato estus la edzo de via fratino. 10 Se ĉiuj viaj praavoj ankoraŭ vivus, vi havus kvar el ili.

Demandoj 14 1 Roberto alvenis al la kongreso sabaton. 2 La geamikoj kaptis plurajn okazojn eliri pro la bela vetero. 3 Roberto estas fervojisto. 4 Klara estas instruistino. 5 Roberto ne vizitas la Infanan Kongreseton ĉar li partoprenas en la Internacia Kongresa Universitato.

6 Andreo kaj Maria montras al la plenkreskuloj la ĉirkaŭaĵon kaj poste ekspozicion de faritaĵoj de la infanoj. 7 Se la infanoj volas naĝi, kaj ne estas plenkreskulo sur la strando, ili devas peti permeson. 8 La infanoj promenas piede ĉiutage. 9 La infanoj en la grupo de Andreo venas el sep landoj. 10 Por la ekspozicio Andreo faras pentraĵon, kaj Maria faras porketon el argilo.

PRAKTIKO 15.1 Seeing him in (*lit.* on) the street, I followed him. Having finished (after finishing) her work, she went home. Being (when I was) about to write to my correspondent, I looked for his address. Standing in front of his house, he looked (was looking) at the mountains. Having heard the dog barking, the boy ran away. Having been (after being) beaten, he cried loudly. (Being) Helped by my friend, I progressed well (made good progress). Being angry, she refused to speak to me. Having been seen by the policeman, the thief ran away quickly (fast). I found the beautiful picture. I found the book very good. He showed himself wise. We found her very (much) changed. We heard the singing bird. (By) Teaching, one learns.

PRAKTIKO 15.2 Vidante ŝin en la ĝardeno, mi vokis al ŝi. Atendante mian amikon, mi rigardis la ĵurnalon. Decidinte ekiri (ekveturi), mi ne atendis. Sidante en la ĝardeno, mi aŭdis bruon. Ne konante la viron, mi demandis, kiu li estas. (*Note tense*!) Elironte, li vidis, ke pluvas. Punote, la knabo kuris for (forkuris). Vokite, ŝi tuj venis. Renkontinte lin, mi trovis lin tre agrabla. Mi farbis la pordon verda. Mi farbis la verdan pordon (*or* la pordon verdan, *though this is less usual*). La knabino montris sin kapabla kaj volonta.

PRAKTIKO 15.3 Mi devas postuli la redonon (resendon) de la mono ŝtelita for de mi de tiu homo (kiun tiu homo ŝtelis de mi). Li malaperis de la domo hieraŭ matene, kaj ne estas vidita (oni ne vidis lin) de (ekde) tiam. Li prenis tranĉilon el la tirkesto por tranĉi la panon. La tero estis tute kovrita de neĝo. Johano apenaŭ povas piediri (marŝi), ĉar li falis de (de sur) muro. La mortantino (mortanta virino) estis ĉirkaŭita de sia (*not* ŝia!) tuta familio. Li skribis por diri al mi, ke li suferas de (pro) malvarmumo. Tiuj gantoj estis ŝtelitaj for de mia frato. Ŝi laboras en tiu butiko ekde (jam de) januaro. Sen diri vorton, ŝi kuris (for) de mi.

PRAKTIKO 15.4 The Eiffel Tower was officially opened during the Paris Exhibition. The collecting of picture-postcards has already spread through the whole world. The first Japanese brewery did (carried out) research about the conduct of alcohol-drinkers in relation to those about them. Having read it, he would order us never to print anything less good. We found your work excellent. They will certainly be thought more curious. That would prevent us from publishing anything at all for at least ten thousand years. The parachute-lines of the one who jumped first (the first to have jumped) hit traffic lights, and the police arrested him as he hung helplessly. When the bank officials refused to touch the parcel, the terrorist ran out like lightning. The officials look after many different objects, from ball-point pens to false teeth.

PRAKTIKO **15.5** Proponinte sian manuskripton al eldonisto, li atendis respondon. Ili nomas sian bofilon Petro. Mi trovis la lokon vizitinda. Mi deziras, ke vi postlasu vian ĉapelon. Li ordonis, ke mi legu la lastan eldonon. Oni diras, ke esploro (fare) de japana bierfabrikisto montris ion pri la konduto de alkoholtrinkantoj. La unua bildkarto ŝajne publikiĝis dum la Ekspozicio de Parizo de 1889, kaj portis bildon de la turo Eiffel. La arestito estis timinta esti trafita de aŭto, aŭ eĉ rabatencita. La knabo rifuzis tuŝi la manĝaĵon. Dudek kvin oficistoj mastrumas cent kvindek mil objektojn.

PRAKTIKO **15.6** 1 fermis. 2 sonorigos. 3 rompiĝis. 4 brulas. 5 kolektiĝis. 6 fendiĝis. 7 ŝanĝi. 8 pasigi. 9 dronas. 10 haltigis.

Demandoj 15 1 Preskaŭ tri mil (3000) homoj partoprenas en la Kongreso. 2 Hieraŭ vespere la geamikoj ĉeestis koncerton. 3 Klara opinias, ke la nivelo de la distraj programoj estas tre alta. 4 Rikardo kredas, ke li longe memoros ĉion pri la Kongreso. 5 Klara trovis plej impona la transdonon de la standardo al la reprezentanto de la venontjara kongreso. 6 Dum Rikardo iros por revenigi Andreon kaj Marian, la aliaj tri iros al restoracio, kaj rezervos sidlokojn por li kaj la infanoj. 7 La Kultura Centro Esperantista situas apud La Chaux-de-Fonds. 8 La Centro estas malfermita dum la tuta jaro. 9 Rikardo kaj Klara rezervis kajuton sur la nokta aŭtomobila pramŝipo. 10 La kvar geamikoj esperas ree renkontiĝi iam en la venonta jaro.

Esperanto–English Vocabulary

Note: (tr.) = transitive, (intr.) = intransitive (see Unit 15).

abomeni *abhor, loathe*
aboni *subscribe to (magazine, etc.)*
absoluta *absolute*
acida *sour, acid*
-aĉ- *(see Appendix)*; aĉa *bad, rotten, etc.*
aĉeti *buy*
-ad- *(see Appendix)*
adiaŭ *good-bye*; adiaŭi *say good-bye to*
admiri *admire*
adolta *adult*
adori *adore, worship*
adreso *address*
aero *air*; aerumi *air, aerate*
afabla *kind, affable*
afero *matter, affair, thing*
agariko *species of mushroom*
agi *act*; agado *activity*
agiti *agitate*
agrabla *pleasant*
aĝo *age*
ajn *-ever, whatever (used after* ki- *and* i- *words)*
-aĵ- *(see Appendix)*; aĵo *substance, thing*
akceli *accelerate*
akcepti *accept*
akcidento *accident*
akiri *acquire, get*
akompani *accompany*
akra *sharp*
akrobato *acrobat*
aktoro *actor*; aktori *act (a role)*
aktuala *topical, present* (not *actual*)
akurata *punctual, prompt* (not *accurate*)
akuzi *accuse, charge*
akvo *water*
al *to, towards*
alfabeto *alphabet*
algebro *algebra*
alia *other, another*
alkoholo *alcohol*
allogi *attract*
almenaŭ *at least*
alta *high, tall*
amaso *pile, heap, mass, crowd*
amatoro *amateur*
ambasadoro *ambassador*
ambaŭ *both, the two*
ambulanco *ambulance*
ami, amo *love*
Ameriko *America (continent)*
amiko *friend*
ampleksa *extensive*; ampleksi *comprise, cover*
amuzi *amuse*; amuzo *amusement, fun*
-an- *(see Appendix)*; ano *member*
anglo *Englishman*
angulo *angle, corner*
animo *soul*; unuanima *unanimous*
ankaŭ *also, too*
ankoraŭ *still, yet*; — ne *not yet*
anonci *announce*
anstataŭ *instead of*
antarkta *antarctic*

antaŭ *before, in front of*;
antaŭa *previous*
aparato *apparatus*
aparta *separate, particular*;
aparte *especially*
apartamento *flat, apartment*
aparteni *belong*
apenaŭ *hardly, scarcely*
aperi *appear*
aplaŭdi *applaud, clap*
apokalipso *apocalypse*
aprilo *April*
aprobi *approve*
apud *beside, near to*
-ar- *(see Appendix)*; aro *set, flock, group, etc.*
aranĝi *arrange*
arbo *tree*; arbaro *wood, forest*
aresti *to arrest*
argilo *clay*
arĝento *silver*
aritimetiko *arithmetic*
arkta *arctic*
armi *arm*; armilo *weapon*
artikolo *article (gram., magazine, etc.)*
artiŝoko *artichoke*
arto *art*
aspekto *appearance*; aspekti *look, seem*
ataki *attack*
atenci *assault*
atendi *wait (for), await, expect*
atenti *pay attention*
atesti *testify*
atingi *reach, attain*
atomo *atom*
aŭ *or*; — . . . — *either . . . or*
aŭdi *hear*
aŭgusto *August*
aŭskulti *listen (to)*
aŭstra *Austrian*
Aŭstralio *Australia*;
aŭstraliano *Australian*
aŭto(mobilo) *car*
aŭtobuso *bus, coach*
aŭtomata *automatic*
aŭtuno *autumn*
avantaĝo *advantage*
avara *miserly, mean*;
malavara *generous*
aventuro *adventure*
averti *warn*
aviado *aviation*; aviadilo *aircraft*
avo *grandfather*
azeno *donkey, ass*
Azio *Asia*

babili *chat, chatter*
baki *bake*; bakujo *oven*
balai *sweep*; balailo *broom*
baldaŭ *soon*
baleto *ballet*
balo *ball, dance*
bani *bath(e)*; bantuko *(bath) towel*
bankedo *banquet*
banko *bank (financial)*
bari *bar, block, dam*; barilo *barrier*
bastono *stick*
batali *fight*; batalo *battle*
bati *beat, strike*
bazo *base, basis*
bedaŭri *regret*;
bedaŭrinde *unfortunately*
bela *beautiful, lovely, fine*
belga *Belgian*
beni *bless*; malbeni *curse*
benko *bench*
benzino *petrol*
besto *animal*; bestĝardeno *zoo*
bezoni *need, require*
biblio *bible*
biblioteko *library*
biciklo *bicycle*
bido *bead*
biero *beer*
bildo *picture*
bildkarto *picture postcard*
bileto *ticket, (bank)note*;
biletujo *notecase, wallet*
birdo *bird*
Birmo *Burma*
biskvito *biscuit*
blanka *white, blank*
blinda *blind*
blovi *blow*
blua *blue*
bo- *(see Appendix)*; bopatro *father-in-law*
boji *to bark*
boli *boil* (intr.)
bona *good*
bonvena *welcome*

bonvolu *please*
bordo *bank (of river etc.), shore*
botelo *bottle*
bovo *ox*; bovino *cow*; virbovo *bull*
brako *arm*; brakumi *embrace*
branĉo *branch (of tree etc.)*
brasiko *cabbage*;
florbrasiko *cauliflower*
brava *worthy, valiant*; brave! *bravo! well done!*
Brazilo *Brazil*
breto *shelf*
briko *brick*
brili *shine*; brila *brilliant*
brito *Briton*; brita *British*
brodi *embroider*
brokolo *broccoli*
broso *brush*
brui *make a noise*; bruo *noise*
bruli *burn, be on fire*
bruna *brown*
brusto *chest*
bulgara *Bulgarian*
Bulonjo *Boulogne*
buŝo *mouth*
butero *butter*
butiko *shop*; butikumi *go shopping*
butono *button*

celi *aim at*; celo *aim, purpose, destination*
cent *hundred*
centrifuga *centrifugal*
centro *centre*
cepo *onion*
cerbo *brain*; cerbumi *rack one's brains*
certa *certain, sure*
cetera *remaining*; cetere *moreover*
cifero *figure, digit*
cigno *swan*
Cipro *Cyprus*
cirklo *circle*
citrono *lemon*

ĉagreni *annoy, vex, distress*
ĉambro *room*
ĉapelo *hat*
ĉapo *cap*
ĉar *because*
ĉarma *charming*;
ĉarmo *charm*

ĉaro *cart, trolley*
ĉasi *hunt*
ĉe *at*; ĉeesti *be present, attend*
ĉefa *chief, main*
ĉeĥa *Czech*
ĉemizo *shirt*
ĉeno *chain*
ĉesi *cease* (intr.)
ĉevalo *horse*
ĉi *used with* ti- *words to denote nearness*
ĉia *every kind of*
ĉial *for every reason*
ĉiam *always*
ĉie *everywhere*
ĉiel *in every way*
ĉielo *sky, heaven*
ĉies *everyone's*
Ĉilio *Chile*
ĉimpanzo *chimpanzee*
ĉina *Chinese*
ĉio *everything*
ĉiom *all, the whole quantity*
ĉirkaŭ *about, around*;
ĉirkaŭi *surround*
ĉiu *each, every, everyone*
ĉokolado *chocolate*
ĉu (interrogative particle) *whether, is it true that*

da *of (after expressions of quantity)*
danci, danco *dance*
danĝero *danger*
danki *thank*; dankon! *thanks, thank you!*
dano *Dane*; Danlando *Denmark*
dato *date*
daŭri *last, continue*
de *of, from, off, by, since*
decembro *December*
decidi *decide*
dediĉi *dedicate, devote*
defendi *defend*
dek *ten*
dekstra *right (hand)*
delikata *delicate, fine, dainty*
demandi *ask (a question)* (not *demand*)
denove *again*
densa *dense*
dento *tooth*
dependi *depend*

deponi *deposit*; deponejo *depot*
des *so much the*; — pli bone *so much the better*
desegni *draw, design*
detrui *destroy*
devi *must, have to, be obliged to*
deziri *wish, desire, want*
dialekto *dialect*
dialogo *dialogue, conversation*
difekti *spoil, damage*
diferenci *differ, be different*
difini *define*
dika *thick, stout, fat*
diligenta *diligent, hard-working*
dimanĉo *Sunday*
dio *god*; dia *divine*; diino *goddess*
direkto *direction*
diri *say, tell*
dis- *(see Appendix)*; disdoni *distribute*
disko *disc, record, dial (of phone)*
diskuti *discuss*
distanco *distance*
distingi *distinguish*
distri *entertain, distract*
distrikto *district (administrative area)*
disvastigi *to spread (widely)*
diveni *guess*
diversa *varied*; diversaj *various, different*
dividi *divide, share*
do *so, then, therefore*
doktoro *doctor (of law, science, medicine etc.)*
dokumento *document*
dolaro *dollar*
dolĉa *sweet, soft, gentle*
dolori *hurt, be painful*
domo *house*
donaco *gift, present*
doni *give*
dormi *to sleep*
dorso *back*
droni *drown* (intr.)
du *two*
dubi *to doubt*
dum *during, while*

ebena *even, level*
ebla *possible*; eble *perhaps*
-ec- *(see Appendix)*; eco *quality*
eĉ *even;* — ne unu *not even one*
eduki *educate, bring up*
edzo *husband*; edzino *wife*
efektiva *actual*; efektive *in fact*
-eg- *(see Appendix)*; ege *extremely*
egala *equal*
-ej- *(see Appendix)*; ejo *place, locale*
ek- *(see Appendix)*; ekiri *set off*; ekrigardi *glance*
ekipaĵo *equipment*
ekologio *ecology*
ekrano *screen*
ekskurso *excursion*
ekspluati *exploit*
ekspozicio *exhibition*
ekster *outside*
ekstrema *extreme*
ekzameni *examine*; ekzameno *examination*
ekzemplero *copy (of book etc.)*
ekzemplo *example*; ekzemple *for example*
ekzerco *exercise*
ekzisti *exist*
el *out of, (made) of*
elasta *elastic*
eldoni *to publish*; eldono *edition*
elefanto *elephant*
eleganta *elegant*
elekti *choose*
elektro *electricity*
elemento *element*
-em- *(see Appendix)*; emo *inclination*
emajlo *enamel*
emfazo *emphasis*
eminenta *eminent, distinguished*
en *in, at*
-end- *(see Appendix)*; endi *be compulsory*
energio *energy*
enigmo *puzzle*
entrepreni *undertake*
entuziasmo *enthusiasm*
enui *be bored*
epoko *epoch, age, period*
-er- *(see Appendix)*; ero *element, item*
erari *make a mistake*; eraro *error, mistake*
esenco *essence*; esenca *essential*
esperi, espero *hope*; malesperi, malespero *despair*

esplori *explore, investigate*;
  esploro *research*
esprimo *expression*
esti *be*; kio estas (al vi)? *what's the matter?*
estimi, estimo *esteem*
estingi *extinguish*
estro *leader, head*
-et- *(see Appendix)*; eta *tiny*
etaĝo *floor, storey*
etendi *spread, extend* (tr.)
etikedo *label*
Eŭropo *Europe*
evento *event*
evidenta *evident, obvious*
eviti *avoid*
evolui *develop*

fabriko *factory*; fabriki *manufacture*
facila *easy*
fadeno *thread*
fajfi *whistle*
fajro *fire*
fako *compartment, department*
fakto *fact*; fakte *in fact*
faldi *fold*
fali *fall*
falsa *false*
fama *famous*
familio *family*
fantomo *ghost, phantom*
farbi *to paint, colour*; farbo *paint*
fari *do, make*; far, fare de *by*
farmacio *(science of) pharmacy*
farmi *to farm*; farmbieno *farm*;
  farmdomo *farmhouse*
farti *fare, be (health)*
fazeolo *bean (kidney-, haricot-)*
febro *fever*
februaro *February*
feliĉa *happy, fortunate*
fendi *split*
fenestro *window*
fenomeno *phenomenon*
ferio *holiday*; ferioj *holidays, vacation*
fermi *close, shut*
fero *iron*; fervojo *railway*
festeno *feast, banquet*
festi *celebrate*; festo *celebration, party*

fi! *shame! (as prefix, see Appendix)*
fidi *trust*
fiera *proud*
figuro *figure, form*
fiksi *fix*
filatel(i)o *philately*
filmo *film*
filo *son*; filino *daughter*
filologio *philology*
filozofo *philosopher*;
  filozofio *philosophy*
fingro *finger*
fini *finish, end* (tr.); fina *final*
finno *Finn*
firma *firm*; firmo, firmao *(business) firm*
fiŝo *fish*
flago *flag*
flanko *side*; flankokupo *hobby*
flari *to smell (something)* (*see* odori)
flati *flatter*
flava *yellow*
flegi *to nurse*; flegist(in)o *a nurse*
floro *flower*; florbrasiko *cauliflower*
flosi *float*
flugi *fly*; flugilo *wing*
flui *flow*; flua *fluent*
flustri *whisper*
fojo *time, occasion*; trifoje *three times*
folio *leaf, sheet (of paper)*
fondi *found, set up*;
  fondaĵo *foundation*
fonto *source, spring*;
  fontplumo *fountain pen*
for *away*; fora *distant*
forgesi *forget*
forko *fork*
formo *form, shape*
forno *furnace, stove*;
  kuirforno *cooker*
forta *strong*
fosi *dig*; fosilo *spade*
foti *to photograph*; fotilo *camera*
fotografaĵo *a photograph*
frakcio *fraction*
franco *Frenchman*
fraŭlino *Miss, young lady*
frazo *sentence*
fremda *foreign*
freŝa *fresh*
fridujo *refrigerator*

fripono *rogue, rascal, crook*
friti *fry*
fromaĝo *cheese*
frosto *frost*; frosti *freeze*; frostigilo *freezer*
froti *rub*
frua/frue *early*; malfrua/e *late*
frukto *fruit*
fuĝi *to flee*
fulmo *lightning*
fumo *smoke*
fundamento *foundation, basis*; fundamenta *fundamental*
fungo *mushroom, fungus*
funkcio *function*; funkcii *function, work*
fuŝi *bungle, mess up, botch*
futbalo *football (soccer)*

gaja *cheerful, merry*
gajni *to gain, win*
galerio *gallery*
galinolo *moorhen*
galopi *gallop*
ganto *glove*
garantii, garantio *guarantee*
gardi *guard*
gaso *gas*
gasto *guest*
gazeto *magazine, periodical, paper*
ge- *(see Appendix)*; geknaboj *boys and girls*
genio *genius*
germana *German*
giĉeto *hatch, box-office, ticket window*
gimnazio *grammar school, high school*
glacio *ice*; glaciaĵo *ice-cream*
gladi *iron (clothes)*
glaso *drinking glass, tumbler, wine glass*
glata *smooth*
glavo *sword*: glavingo *scabbard*
gliti *to slip, slide*
globo *globe*; globkrajono *ball-point pen*
gloro *glory*; glora *glorious*
glui *to stick, glue*; glumarko *sticker*
gorĝo *throat*
grado *degree, grade*
gramofono *record-player*
granda *large, big, great*
grandioza *splendid, magnificent, grand*
graso *fat, grease*
gratuli *congratulate*
grava *important, serious*
greka *Greek*
grimpi *climb*
griza *grey*
Groenlando *Greenland*
grundo *soil, earth*
grupo *group*
gusto *taste*; gusti *to taste (of, like)*; gustumi *to taste (something)*
guto *drop (liquid)*
gvidi *to guide, lead*

ĝangalo *jungle*
ĝardeno *garden*
ĝemelo *twin*
ĝenerala *general*
ĝeni *worry, disturb*
ĝentila *polite, courteous*
ĝi *it*; ĝia *its*
ĝirafo *giraffe*
ĝis *until, up to, as far as*
ĝoji *be glad*
ĝui *enjoy*
ĝusta *right, correct, exact*

ha! *ah!*
hajlo *hail (weather)*
haki *to chop*; hakilo *axe*
halti *to stop, halt*
haro *a hair*; haroj, hararo *hair*
haveno *harbour*; flughaveno *airport*
havi *have*; havebla *available*
he! *hey! (exclamation)*
hejmo *home*; hejme *at home*
hela *bright, clear, light (-coloured)*
helpi *to help*
herbo *grass*
heroo *hero*; heroino *heroine*
heziti *hesitate*
hieraŭ *yesterday*
hinda *Indian (of India)*
hirundo *swallow*
hispana *Spanish*
historio *history, story*
ho! *oh!*; ho, ve! *oh dear!*
hobio *hobby*
hodiaŭ *today*
hoko *hook*

homo *person*; la homaro *mankind*
honori, honoro *honour*
honti *be ashamed*; honto *shame*
horizontala *horizontal*
horloĝo *clock, watch*
horo *hour, time (of day)*
hotelo *hotel*
humila *humble*
humo *humus*
humoro *temper, mood, humour*
humuro *humour, wit*
hundo *dog*
hungara *Hungarian*

ĥirurgo *surgeon*
ĥoro *choir, chorus*

ia *some (any) kind of*
ial *for some (any) reason*
iam *once, some time*
-id- *(see Appendix)*; ido *offspring, young*
idealo *ideal*
ideo *idea*
idioto *idiot*
ie *somewhere*
iel *somehow*
ies *someone's*
-ig- *(see Appendix)*: igi *make, cause to be*
ignori *to ignore*
-iĝ- *(see Appendix)*; iĝi *become*
-il- *(see Appendix)*; ilo *tool, instrument*
ili *they, them*; ilia *their*
ilustri *illustrate*; ilustraĵo *illustration*
imagi *imagine*
imiti *imitate*
imperio *empire*; imperiestro *emperor*
imponi *impress*; impona *impressive*
-in- *(see Appendix)*; ino *female*
-ind- *(see Appendix)*: inda *worthy*
indiferenta *indifferent*
indiki *indicate*
industrio *industry*
infano *child*; infanĉareto *pram*
informi *inform*; informo *(a piece of) information*
-ing- *(see Appendix)*; ingo *socket*
inkluziva *inclusive*; inkluzivi *to include*
inko *ink*
insigno *badge*
insisti *insist*
instigi *urge, prompt, spur on*
instrui *teach*
instrumento *instrument*
insulo *island*
inteligenta *intelligent*
intenci *intend*
intensa *intense, intensive*
inter *between, among*
interesa *interesting*; interesi *interest*
interna *internal*
internacia *international*
intuicio *intuition*
inventi *to invent*
inviti *invite*
io *something, anything*
iom *some, somewhat*; iomete *a little*
Irano *Iran*
iri *to go*; ekiri *set off*
Irlando *Ireland*
Islando *Iceland*
-ism- *(see Appendix)*
Israelo *Israel (modern state)*
-ist- *(see Appendix)*
itala *Italian*
iu *some, someone, a certain*
izoli *isolate, insulate*

ja *(emphatic particle) indeed*
jako *jacket*
jam *already*; — ne *no longer*
januaro *January*
japana *Japanese*
jaro *year*
je *(indefinite preposition) at*; — la dua *at two o' clock*
jen *here is (are), there is (are)*; jene *as follows*
jes *yes*
Jesuo *Jesus*
jeto *jet (plane)*
ju. . . des. . . *the. . . the. . .* ; — pli multe, — pli bone *the more the better*
judo *Jew*
jugoslava *Yugoslav*
juĝi *judge*
julio *July*
juna *young*
junio *June*

jupo *skirt*
Juraso *Jura (mountains)*
justa *just, fair*

ĵaŭdo *Thursday*
ĵeti *throw*
ĵurnalo *newspaper*
ĵus *just (a moment ago)*

kabareto *cabaret*
kafo *coffee*; kafejo *café*
kaj *and*; — . . . — *both . . . and . . .*
kajuto *cabin (ship or plane)*
kaĵoli *cajole, coax*
kalendaro *calendar*
kalkano *heel (foot)*; kalkanumo *heel (shoe)*
kalkuli *calculate*; kalkulo *bill*
kalsono *(under)pants, knickers, panties*
kameno *hearth, fireplace*
kampo *field*; kamparo *country(side)*
Kanado *Canada*
kandelo *candle*
kanibalo *cannibal*
kanti *sing*; kanto *song*
kapabla *capable*
kapo *head*
kapti *catch, capture*
kara *dear*; karul(in)o *dear, darling*
karbo *coal*
kariero *career*
karoto *carrot*
karto *card*
kaso *till, cash-box, fund*; kasisto *treasurer*
kastelo *castle, château*
kaŝi *hide* (tr.)
kato *cat*
katedralo *cathedral*
katoliko, katolika *catholic*
kaŭzo *cause*
kazo *case (gram., med., law)*
ke *that* (conj.)
kelkaj *several, a few*
kesto *chest, large box*; poŝtkesto *postbox*
kia *what kind of, what a*
kial *why*; kialo *reason*
kiam *when*
kie *where*; kien *where (to)*
kiel *how, as, like*; — eble plej . . . *as . . . as possible*
kies *whose*
kilogramo *kilogram*
kilometro *kilometre*
kimro *Welshman*
kinejo *cinema*
kio *what*
kiom *how much, how many*
kirurgo *surgeon*
kisi *to kiss*
kiu *who, which (one)*
klara *clear*; klarigi *explain*
klaso *class*
klini *to tilt, incline*
klopodi *endeavour, take steps (to)*
klubo *club (society)*
knabo *boy*; knabino *girl*
koko *cock, rooster*; kokino *hen*
kolaziono *tea, light meal in afternoon*
kolegio *college*
kolekti *collect, gather* (tr.)
koleri *be angry*; kolero *anger*
kolo *neck*; kolumo *collar*; kolĉeno *necklace*
kolonelo *colonel*
koloro *colour*
kombi *to comb*; kombilo *a comb*
komenci *begin* (tr.)
komenti *comment, remark*
komerco *commerce, business*
komforto *comfort*
komika *comic(al)*
komitato *committee*
kompanio *company*
kompari *compare* (tr.)
kompati *pity*; kompatinda *poor*
kompleta *complete*; kompleto *set, suit (of clothes)*
komplezo *favour, kindness*
komplika *complicated*
kompreni *understand*; kompreneble *of course*
komputi *compute, meter*; komputilo *computer*
komuna *common*
koncepto *concept*
koncerto *concert*
kondiĉo *condition*
konduki *lead, drive (vehicle)*
konduti *behave (well or badly)*

konfesi *confess, admit*
kongreso *congress*
koni *know (be acquainted with)*; rekoni *recognise*
konkurso *competition, contest*
konsenti *agree, consent*
konservi *keep, preserve*
konsili *advise*
konsisti (el) *consist (of)*
konstanta *constant, permanent*
konstrui *build, construct*; konstruaĵo *building*
konsulti *consult*
kontenta *content, satisfied, pleased*
kontrasto *contrast*
kontraŭ *against, opposite*; kontraŭi *be opposed (to)*
kontroli *check* (not *control*)
konversacio *conversation*
kopii *copy*
korbo *basket*
korespondi *correspond*
koridoro *corridor*
koro *heart*; kora *cordial*
korpo *body*
kosti *cost*; multekosta, altekosta *expensive*
kostumo *costume (for a special purpose)*
koverto *envelope*
kovri *to cover*; kovrilo *lid, cover*
krajono *pencil*
krei *create*
kredi *believe*; kredeble *probably*
kreski *grow* (intr.)
krevi *burst* (intr.)
krii *to cry, shout*; ekkrii *exclaim*
krimo *crime*; krimulo *criminal*
Kristo *Christ*; Kristano *Christian*
kritiki *criticise*
krom *besides, apart from*
krono *crown*
kruco *cross*
kruĉo *jug, (coffee-, tea-) pot*
kruela *cruel*
kruro *leg*
kudri *sew*; kudrilo *needle*
kuiri *cook*; kuirejo *kitchen*; kuirforno *cooker*
kuko *cake*
kukolo *cuckoo*
kulero *spoon*
kulpa *guilty*; mia kulpo *my fault*
kulturo *culture*
kun *with*; kune *together*
kupro *copper*
kuri *to run*
kuraci *give medical treatment*; kuracisto *doctor*
kuraĝo *courage*; kuraĝa *brave*; kuraĝi *to dare*
kuratoro *curator*
kurioza *curious, quaint*
kurso *course (of lessons)*
kurteno *curtain*
kuŝi *to lie, recline*; kuŝiĝi *lie down*
kutimo *custom, habit*
kuvo *tub*; bankuvo *bath (tub)*
kuzo *cousin*
kvadrato *square*; kvadratmejlo *square mile*
kvalito *quality*
kvankam *although*
kvanto *quantity*
kvar *four*; kvarono *quarter*; kvaropo *quartet*
kvartalo *quarter, district (of a city)*
kvazaŭ *as if, as it were*
kvereli *quarrel*
kvin *five*
kvitanco *receipt*

la *the*
labori *work*; laboristo *worker*
laca *tired*
lago *lake*
lakto *milk*
lampo *lamp*
lano *wool*
lando *country*
larĝa *broad, wide*
larmo *tear (drop)*; larmiga gaso *tear gas*
lasi *leave, let*
lasta *last, most recent*
latva *Latvian*
laŭ *along, according to*
laŭdi *praise*
laŭta *loud*
lavi *wash* (tr.)
leciono *lesson*
legi *read*; legebla *legible*
legomo *vegetable*

leĝera *light, slight*
leĝo *law*
leki *lick*
leono *lion*
lerni *learn*; lernanto *pupil*; lernejo *school*
lerta *clever, skilful*
letero *letter (correspondence)*
li *he, him*; lia *his*
Libano *Lebanon*
libera *free*; malliberejo *prison*
Libio *Libya*
libro *book*
ligno *wood, timber*
likvaĵo *liquid*; (*as adjective*, likva)
lingvo *language*
linio *line*
listo *list*
lito *bed*; litkovrilo *blanket*; littuko *sheet*
litero *letter (of alphabet)*
literaturo *literature*
litovo *Lithuanian*
litro *litre*
liveri *to deliver, dispense*
loĝi *live, dwell*; loĝantaro *population*
loko *place*; loka *local*
longa *long*
ludi *to play*; ludo *game*; ludilo *toy*
lukso *luxury*
Luksemburgo *Luxemburg*
lukti *wrestle, struggle*
lumi *shine*; lumo *light*
luno *moon*
lundo *Monday*

magazeno *large shop, store*
magazino *(illustrated) magazine*
magneto *magnet*
magnetofono *tape- (cassette-) recorder*
majo *May*
majonezo *mayonnaise*
majstro *master (-craftsman), maestro*
makramo *macramé (knotted thread work)*
makulo *spot, stain*
mal- *(see Appendix)*; male *on the contrary*
malgraŭ *in spite of*
manĝi *eat*; manĝo *meal*; manĝaĵo *food*
maniero *way, manner*
manki *be lacking, be absent*
mankso *Manxman*; Manksinsulo *Isle of Man*
mano *hand*; mansaketo *handbag*; mantuko *towel*
mantelo *coat, cloak*; pluvmantelo *raincoat*
manuskripto *manuscript*
mapo *map*
mardo *Tuesday*
marmoro *marble*
maro *sea*; marbordo *shore, coast*
marŝi *march, walk*
martelo *hammer*
marto *March*
mastro *master (of house, servants, etc.)*
maŝino *machine*
matematiko *mathematics*
mateno *morning*
materialo *material*
matura *ripe, mature*
meblo *piece of furniture*; meblaro *furniture*
medikamento *medicine*
mejlo *mile*
meleagro *turkey*
melodio *melody, tune*
mem *self, selves*
membro *member, limb*
memori *remember*; memoro *memory*
mencii *mention*
mendi, mendo *order, book(ing)*
menso *mind*
mensogi, mensogo *(tell a) lie*
merito *merit*; meriti *deserve*
merkredo *Wednesday*
mesaĝo *message*
metalo *metal*
meti *put, place*
metodo *method*
metro *metre*
mezo *middle*
mezuri, mezuro *measure(ment)*
mi *I, me*; mia *my*
migri *migrate*; migrado *migration*
mikro-onda *microwave* (adj.)
mikrofono *microphone*
miksi *mix* (tr.)
mil *thousand*

milda *mild, gentle*
miliono *million*
milito *war*; militisto *soldier*
minaci, minaco *threat(en), menace*
minimumo *minimum*
minuto *minute (time)*
miraklo *miracle*
miri *be amazed, wonder*;
mirinda *wonderful*
mis- *(see Appendix)*
mistero *mystery*
moderna *modern*
modo *fashion, vogue*
mola *soft*
momento *moment*
monato *month*
mondo *world*
mono *money*; monero *coin*
monto *mountain*; monteto *hill*
montri *to show*
morgaŭ *tomorrow*
morti *die*; morto *death*;
mortinta *dead*
moŝto *general honorific title*: Ŝia Reĝina Moŝto *Her Majesty*
motoro *motor, engine*
movi *move* (tr.); movado *movement*
multa *much*; multaj *many, a lot (of)*
muro *wall*
muso *mouse*
muŝo *fly (insect)*
muzeo *museum*
muziko *music*

nacio *nation*; nacia *national*
naĝi *swim*
najbaro *neighbour*
najlo *nail (metal)*
naski *give birth to*; naskiĝi *be born*
naturo *nature*
naŭ *nine*
nazo *nose*; naztuko *handkerchief*
ne *no, not*
nebulo *fog*; nebuleto *mist*
necesa *necessary*; necesejo *toilet, loo*
Nederlando *the Netherlands*;
nederlanda *Dutch*
neĝo, neĝi *snow*; neĝero *snowflake*
nek *neither, nor*
nenia *no, no kind of*
nenial *for no reason*
neniam *never*
nenie *nowhere*
neniel *in no way*
nenies *nobody's*
nenio *nothing*
neniom *none (at all)*
neniu *no, no one, nobody*
nepo *grandson*;
nepino *granddaughter*
nepre *without fail*
nevo *nephew*; nevino *niece*
ni *we, us*; nia *our(s)*
nigra *black*
nivela, nivelo *level*
nokto *night*
nombro *number*; nombri *to count*
nomo *name*; nomiĝi *be called*
nordo, norda *north(ern)*
normanda *Norman*
norvega *Norwegian*
nova *new*; novaĵoj *news*;
Novzelando *New Zealand*
novembro *November*
nu *well, now*
nubo *cloud*
nul *zero*; nulo *nought*
numero *number (of house, etc.)*
nun *now*
nur *only, merely*
nutri *feed* (tr.), *nourish*

obei *obey*
objekto *object; subject (of study, etc.)*
-obl- *(see Appendix)*
obstaklo *obstacle*
odori *to smell (have a smell)*
oferi, ofero *sacrifice* (not *offer*)
ofico *office (held), function, post*;
oficejo *office, bureau*
oficiala *official*
oficiro *officer (in forces)*
oficisto *official*
ofta *frequent*; ofte *often, frequently*
ok *eight*
okazi *happen, occur*;
okazo *occurrence*
okcidento, okcidenta *west(ern)*
oktobro *October*
okulo *eye*
okupi *occupy*; okupita *busy*
ol *than*
oleo *oil*
olimpikoj *Olympic Games*

ombrelo *umbrella*
ombro *shadow*
-on- *(see Appendix)*; ono *fraction*
ondo *wave*
oni *one, people, they, etc*; oni diras *they say*
onklo *uncle*; onklino *aunt*
-op- *(see Appendix)*
operacio *operation*
opero *opera*
opinii *think (have an opinion)*
oportuna *convenient, opportune*
oranĝo *orange*
ordinara *ordinary*
ordo *order*; ordigi *put in order*
ordoni, ordono *order, command*
orelo *ear*
organizi *organise*
oriento, orienta *east(ern)*
originala, originalo *original (not a copy)*
orkestro *orchestra*
ornami *decorate, adorn*; ornamaĵo *ornament*
oro *gold*
osto *bone*
ovo *egg*

pacienco *patience*
pacifismo *pacifism*; pacifisto *pacifist*
paco *peace*
paĉjo *Dad(dy)* (**pa**tro + -ĉj-)
pafi *shoot*; pafilo *gun*
pagi *pay*
paĝo *page*
paki *pack*; pako *packet, parcel*
pala *pale*
panelo *panel*
panjo *Mum(my)* (**pa**trino + -nj-)
pano *bread*
pantalono *(pair of) trousers, pants*
papero *paper*
paraŝuto, paraŝuti *parachute*
parfumo *perfume*
paro *pair, couple*
pardoni *pardon, excuse, forgive*
parenco *relative, relation* (not *parent*)
Parizo *Paris*
parko, parki *park*
paroli *speak, talk*; parolado *speech*
parto *part*
pasi *pass (by)*; pasigi *pass (something)*
pasinta, pasinteco *past*
Pasko *Easter, Passover*
pastro *priest, clergyman, minister*
paŝi, paŝo *pace, step, stride*
patento *patent*
patro *father*; patrino *mother*
paŭzo *break, pause, interval*
peco *piece*; peceto *a bit*
pejzaĝo *landscape, scenery*
peki *to sin*; peko *sin*
peli *drive, propel*
penco *penny*
pendi *hang* (intr.); pendigi *hang* (tr.)
peni *try, endeavour*
pensi *think*
pentri *to paint (a picture)*; pentraĵo *painting*
per *with, by means of*
perdi *lose*
perfekta *perfect*
periodo *period*
permesi *allow, permit*; permeso *permission*
persono *person*
Persujo *Persia (Iran)*
Peruo *Peru*
pesi *weigh (find weight of)*; pesilo *scales*
peti *ask, request*; mi petas *please*
petroselo *parsley*
pezi *weigh (have weight)*; peza *heavy*
piano *piano*
piedo *foot*; piede *on foot*; piediri *to walk*
piki *prick, sting*
pilko *ball (to play with)*
pinglo *pin*
pinto *tip, point, summit*
pioniro *pioneer*
pipo *pipe (tobacco-)*
pipro *pepper*
pitoreska *picturesque*
pizo *pea*
placo *square (in town)*
plaĉi *be pleasing*; plaĉas al mi *I like*
plado *dish*
plafono *ceiling*
planko *floor*
plano *plan*

planto *plant*
plasto *plastic (material)*
plata *flat*
plej *most, -est*
plena *full*; plenumi *fulfil*
plendi *complain*
pleto *tray*
plezuro *pleasure*
pli *more, -er*; — -malpli *more or less*
plonĝi *to dive, plunge*
plori *weep, cry*
plu *further*; ne — *no longer*; kaj tiel — *and so on*
plumbo *lead*; plumbisto *plumber*
plumo *feather, pen*; fontplumo *fountain pen*
pluraj *several*
pluvo *rain*; pluvas *it is raining*
po *at the rate of*
podio *podium, platform*
poemo *poem*
poento *point, mark (in scoring)*
poeto *poet*
polo, pola *Pole, Polish*
polico *police*; policano *policeman*
politiko *politics, policy*
poluri *polish*
poluso *pole (north or south)*
polvo *dust*; polvosuĉilo *vacuum-cleaner*
pomo *apple*
ponto *bridge*
popgrupo *pop-group*, popstelo *pop-star*
popolo *people (race)*
populara *popular*
por *for, in order to*; — ke *in order that*
pordo *door, gate*; pordego *(town) gate*
porko *pig*; porkaĵo *pork*
porti *carry, wear*; alporti *bring*
portugala *Portuguese*
posedi *possess*
post *after*; poste *then, afterwards*
postuli *demand, require*
poŝo *pocket*; poŝtuko *handkerchief*
poŝto *post, mail*; poŝtmarko *postage stamp*
potenco *power*; potenca *powerful*
povi *be able*; povas *can*
pra- *(see Appendix)*; prapatroj *ancestors*
praktiko *practice*; praktiki *to practise*
pramo *ferry*; pramŝipo *seagoing ferry*
prava *right (in opinion)*
precipa *chief, principal*
preciza *precise*
preferi *prefer*; preferata *favourite*
preĝi *pray*; preĝo *prayer*
premi *to press*
premio *prize*
preni *take, pick up*
prepari *prepare*
presi *to print*; presaĵo *printed matter*
preskaŭ *almost, nearly*
preta *ready*
preter *beyond, past*
prezenti *present, introduce*
prezidi *preside*; prezidanto *chairman, president*
prezo *price*
pri *about, concerning*
principo *principle*
printempo *spring(time)*
pro *for, because of, on account of*
problemo *problem*
procedi *proceed*
profesio *profession*
profunda *deep, profound*
prognozo *prognosis, forecast*
programo *programme*
progresi, progreso *progress*
proksima *near*; proksimuma *approximate*
promeni *go for a walk, ride, drive, etc.*
promesi, promeso *promise*
pronunci *pronounce*
proponi *propose, offer*
propra *one's own*
protekti *protect*
provi *try out, try on*
provizi *provide, supply*
prudenta *sensible, reasonable*
prunti, prunto *loan*; pruntedoni *lend*; pruntepreni *borrow*
pruvi *prove*; pruvo *proof*
publika, publiko *public*
pundo *pound, £*

puni *punish*
punkto *point, dot, full stop*
pupo *doll, puppet*
pura *clean, pure*
puŝi *push*

rabi *steal by force or threat*; rabisto *robber*
rado *wheel*
radaro *radar*
radikala *radical*
radiko *root*
radio *ray, radio*; radiofono, radioaparato *radio set*
rajdi *ride (horse, cycle, etc.)*
rajti *be entitled to*; Ĉu mi rajtas? *May I?*
rakonto *story*; rakonti *tell (a story)*
rampi *crawl, creep*
rando *edge, rim*
rapida *rapid, quick, fast*
raporti, raporto *report*
raso *race, breed*; rasismo *racism*
ravi, ravo *delight*; rava *delightful*
razeno *lawn*
razi *to shave* (tr.)
re- *(see Appendix)*; ree *again*; reen *back(wards)*
reala *real*
recepto *recipe*
reciproke *reciprocally, each other*
redakti *edit*; redaktisto *editor*
regi *rule, control*
regiono *region*
registri, registro *register, record*
regno *realm, kingdom*
regulo *rule*; regula *regular*
reĝo *king*; reĝino *queen*; reĝa *royal*
rekomendi *recommend*
rekordo *record (best performance)*
rekta *straight, direct*
relativa *relative*
religio *religion*
remizo *garage*
renkonti *meet, encounter* (tr.)
reprezenti *represent*
respekti, respekto *respect*
respondi, respondo *reply, answer*
respubliko *republic*
resti *remain, stay*; rest(aĵ)o *remainder, rest*
restoracio *restaurant*
reto *net, network*
revi, revo *daydream*
revolucio *revolution (political)*
revuo *revue, journal, magazine*
rezervi *reserve*
rezulti, rezulto *result*
ricevi *receive, obtain, get*
riĉa *rich*
ridi, rido *laugh*; rideti, rideto *smile*
rifuzi *refuse*; rifuzo *refusal*
rigardi *look at, regard*
rikolti *harvest, reap*; rikolto *harvest*
rilati (al) *refer to, relate to*
rimarki *notice* (not *remark*)
ripari *repair, mend*
ripeti *repeat*
ripozi, ripozo *rest, repose*
riproĉi *reproach; scold*
riveli *develop (a photograph)*
rivero *river*
rizo *rice*
robo *dress, robe, gown*
roboto *robot*
roko *rock*
rolo *rôle, part (in play, etc.)*
romanĉa *Romanche*
rompi *break* (tr.)
ronda *round*; rondo *round, ring, circle*
rosti *roast, toast (bread)*
rozo *rose*; rozkolora *pink*
rubo *rubbish, rubble*
rugbeo *rugby, rugger*
ruĝa *red*; ruĝiĝi *blush, flush*
ruli *roll* (tr.); ruldomo *caravan*
rumana *Romanian*
rusa *Russian*
ruza *cunning, crafty*

sabato *Saturday*
sablo *sand*
sago *arrow*; sageto *dart*
saĝa *wise*; saĝo *wisdom*
sako *bag, sack*; mansaketo *handbag*
salajro *wages, salary*
salato *salad*
salo *salt*
salono *drawing room, lounge, salon*
salti, salto *jump*
saluti *greet*; saluton! *hello, hi!*

sama *same*; samideano *fellow thinker (esperantist)*
sana *well, healthy*; malsanulejo *hospital*
sango *blood*; sangi *bleed*
sankta *holy, sacred*; Sankta Paŭlo *St Paul*
sapo *soap*
sata *full, satiated*; malsata *hungry*
savi *save, rescue*
sceno *scene*; scenejo *stage*
scienco *science*
scii *know (a fact)*; sciigi *inform, notify*
scivoli *wonder*
se *if*
sed *but*
seĝo *chair*; brakseĝo *armchair*
seka *dry*
sekreto, sekreta *secret*
sekretario *secretary*
sekura *safe, secure*
sekvi *follow*; sekvo *consequence*
semajno *week*
sen *without*; (*as prefix, -less*); sensignifa *meaningless*
senco *sense*; sensencaĵo *nonsense*
sendi *send*; dissendi *broadcast*
senti *feel* (tr.); sento *feeling*
sep *seven*
septembro *September*
serĉi *look for, seek*; priserĉi *search* (tr.)
serio *series*
serioza *serious, earnest*
serpento *snake, serpent*
seruro *lock*
servi *serve*; servo, servado *service*
ses *six*
severa *severe, strict*
sezono *season (of year)*
si *oneself, etc.*; sia *(one's) own*
sidi *sit, be sitting*; sidiĝi *sit down (or up, if lying)*
signali, signalo *signal*
signifi *mean, signify*
silenti *be silent*; silento *silence*
silko *silk*
silueto *silhouette*
simfonio *symphony*
simila *like*; simili *resemble*
simpla *simple*
sincera *sincere*
sinjoro *Mr, sir, gentleman*; sinjorino *Mrs, madam, lady*
sitelo *bucket, pail*
situacio *situation, state of affairs*
situo *site, situation*; situi *be situated*
skatolo *box, can, tin*
skeĉo *sketch (theatrical)*
skio, skii *ski*
skolto *scout*; skoltino *girl-guide*
skoto *Scot*
skrapi *to scrape*; skrapgumo *eraser, rubber*
skribi *write*; priskribi *describe*; subskribi *to sign*
skui *shake* (tr.)
skulpti *sculpt, carve*
sociala *social*; socialisto *socialist*
societo *society*
socio *society, the community*
soifo *thirst*; soifa *thirsty*; soifi *be thirsty*
sola *alone, sole*; soleca *lonely*
soldato *soldier*
solena *solemn, ceremonious, formal*
solvi *solve, dissolve*; solvo *solution*
somero *summer*
sonĝi, sonĝo *dream*
soni, sono *sound*
sonori *ring* (intr.); sonorilo *bell*
sopiri *yearn, long for*
sorto *fate, destiny*
sovaĝa *wild*
soveto, soveta *soviet*; Sovetunio, Sovetio *U.S.S.R.*
spaco *space, room*
speciala *special*
specimeno *specimen*
speco *kind, sort*
spegulo *mirror*
spektaklo *spectacle, display*
sperti, sperto *experience*; sperta, spertulo *expert*
spico *spice*; spicisto *grocer*; spici *season*
spino *spine, backbone*
spinaco *spinach*
spiri *breathe*; spiro *breath*
spirito *spirit*
sporada *sporadic*
sporto *sport*
sprita *witty*; sprito *wit*

stacio *station*; stacidomo *railway station (building)*
standardo *standard, flag*
stango *rod, pole, spar*
stari *stand, be standing*; stariĝi *stand up*
stato *state, condition*
statuo *statue*
stelo *star*
stevardo *steward (on ship, plane)*; stevardino *stewardess, air-hostess*
stimuli *stimulate*; stimulo *stimulus*
stoko *stock*
stomako *stomach*
strando *beach*
stranga *odd, queer, strange*
strato *street*
streĉi *tighten, wind up*; malstreĉ(iĝ)i *relax*
strio *stripe, strip*
studento *(university) student*
studi *study*; studanto *student, learner*
stufi *stew, braise*
sub *under, beneath, below*
subita *sudden*
subtila *subtle*
suĉi *to suck*
sudo, suda *south(ern)*
Sudano *Sudan*
suferi *suffer*
sufiĉa *enough, sufficient*; sufiĉi *suffice*
sugesti *suggest*; sugesto *suggestion*
suko *juice*
sukcesi *succeed, manage (to)*
sukero *sugar*
sumo *sum (of money), total*
suno *sun*
super *over, above*; supera *superior*
supo *soup*
supozi *suppose, presume*
supre *above, upstairs*; supro *top*; supraĵo *surface*
sur *on, upon*; — la strato *in the street*
surda *deaf*
surprizi, surprizo *surprise*
suspekti *suspect*; suspekto *suspicion*
svedo *Swede*
svelta *slender, slim*
svingi *wave* (not *swing*)
svisa *Swiss*

ŝafo *sheep*
ŝajni *seem, appear*; ŝajnigi *pretend*
ŝako *chess*
ŝalti *switch on*; ŝaltilo *switch*; malŝalti *switch off*
ŝanco *chance (of success)*
ŝanĝi *change* (tr.); ŝanĝiĝi *change* (intr.)
ŝarĝi, ŝarĝo *load, burden*
ŝati *appreciate, think highly of*
ŝerci, ŝerco *joke*
ŝi *she, her*; ŝia *her(s)*
ŝinko *ham*
ŝipo *ship*
ŝiri *tear, rip*
ŝlosi *lock*; ŝlosilo *key*
ŝnuro *rope, cord, line*; ŝnureto *string*
ŝoseo *roadway, highway*; aŭtoŝoseo *motorway*
ŝpari *save, economise*
ŝranko *cupboard*
ŝtato *state (political)*; ŝtatparko *national park*
ŝteli *steal*; ŝtelisto *thief*
ŝtono *stone*
ŝtopi *stop up, to plug*; ŝtopilo *plug*
ŝtrumpo *stocking*; ŝtrumpeto *socks*; ŝtrumpkalsono *tights*
ŝtupo *step*; ŝtuparo *staircase*; ŝtupetaro *ladder*
ŝuo *shoe*
ŝuldi *owe*; ŝuldo *debt*
ŝultro *shoulder*

tabako *tobacco*
tabelo *table (list)*; hortabelo *timetable*
tablo *table (furniture)*
tabulo *board, plank*
tago *day*; tagmanĝo *lunch, dinner*
tajpi *to type*
taksio *taxi*
talento *talent*
talio *waist, waistline*
tamen *however, nevertheless*
Tamizo *Thames*
Tanzanio *Tanzania*
tapeto *tapestry, wallpaper*
tapiŝo *carpet*
taso *cup*; subtaso *saucer*
tasko *task, job*
taŭga *suitable*; taŭgi *be suitable*

teamo *team* (pron. teh-ah-mo, *not* teemo!)
teatro *theatre*; teatraĵo *play*
tegmento *roof*
tekniko *technique*
teksi *weave*; teksaĵo *textile*
teksto *text*
telefono, telefoni *telephone*
telero *plate*; telermeblo *sideboard*
televido *television*
temo *subject, theme, topic*
temperaturo *temperature*
tempo *time*
teni *hold, keep*
teniso *tennis*
teo *tea*; tekruĉo *teapot*
teorio *theory*; teoria *theoretical*
tero *earth, ground, land*; terpomo *potato*
teroro *reign of terror*; terorismo *terrorism*; teroristo *terrorist*
teruro *terror*; terura *terrible*
testudo *tortoise*
tia *such, that kind of*
tial *therefore, for that reason*
tiam *then, at that time*
tie *there, in that place*;—ĉi, ĉi—*here*
tiel *so, in that way*
ties *that one's*
tigro *tiger*
timi, timo *fear*; timigi *frighten*
tio *that, that thing*
tiom (da) *so much, so many*
tiri *pull, draw*; tirkesto *drawer*
titolo *title, heading*
tiu *that, that one*; — ĉi, ĉi — *this (one)*
toleri *tolerate*; — la elspezon de *afford*
tondi *shear, cut*; tondilo *scissors* (cf. tranĉi)
torĉo *torch*
tra *through*
tradicio *tradition*; tradicia *traditional*
traduki *translate*
trafi *hit (the mark), catch (train etc.)*
trafiko *traffic*
trajno *train (railway, military)*
trakti *treat, deal with*
tranĉi *cut (with knife, etc.)*; tranĉilo *knife*
trankvila *calm, tranquil*
tranokti *pass the night*
trans *across, at the other side of*
tre *very, very much*; treege *extremely*
trejni *train (for sport, etc.)*; trejnisto *trainer, coach*
tremi *tremble, quiver*
tri *three*
triki *knit*; trikilo *knitting needle*
trinki *to drink*
tro *too, too much*
trompi *deceive*
trotuaro *pavement*
trovi *to find*; troviĝi *be (in a place), be found*
trunko *trunk (of tree, body, etc.)*
truo *hole*
tuj *immediately, at once*
tuko *cloth (for particular purpose)*; kaptuko *headscarf*
turismo *tourism, travel*
turisto *tourist*
Turko *Turk*
turni *turn* (tr.)
turo *tower*
tusi, tuso *cough*
tuŝi *touch* (tr.)
tuta *whole, entire*; tute *quite*; tute ne *not at all*

-uj- *(see Appendix)*; ujo *container, receptacle*
-ul- *(see Appendix)*: ulo *fellow*
-um- *(see Appendix)*
ungo *nail, claw*
unika *unique*
universala *universal, world-wide*
universitato *university*
universo *universe*
unu *one*; unuiĝo *union*
urbo *town, city*; urba *urban, municipal*
urĝa *urgent*
Urugvajo *Uruguay*
Usono *U.S.A.*
utila *useful*; malutila *harmful*
uzi *use*

vagi *wander, roam*
vagono *railway carriage*; vagonaro *train*

valizo *suitcase, grip*
valo *valley*
valori *be worth*; valoro *value*
vango *cheek*
vaporo *steam*
varieteo *music-hall, variety*
varma *warm, hot*; malvarmumo *a cold*
varo *commodity*; varoj *wares*
vasta *spacious, vast*
vazo *vessel, vase*; la vazaro *the dishes, crockery*
ve! *alas! oh dear!*
veki *wake up, arouse* (tr.)
velo, veladi *sail*; velŝipo *sailing ship*
vendi *sell*
vendredo *Friday*
Venezuelo *Venezuela*
veni *come*; alveni *arrive*; kunveni *meet* (intr.)
venki *conquer, defeat*; venko *victory*
vento *wind*; ventumi *aerate, fan*
ventro *belly*
vera *true*; vere *truly, really*
verda *green*
verki *compose, write (original work)*
verŝi *pour (liquids)*
vertikala *vertical*
vespero *evening*
vesti *clothe, dress* (tr.); vesto *garment*
vestiblo *vestibule, entrance hall*
vetero *weather*
veti, veto *bet*; vetkurado *race*
veturi *go, travel (by or of a vehicle)*; veturilo *vehicle*
vi *you*; via *your, yours*
viando *meat*
vico *row, line, turn*; via — *your turn*
vidi *see*; vidbendo *video tape*
vigla *alert, wide-awake*
vilaĝo *village*
vino *wine*; vinbero *grape*
vintro *winter*
violono *violin*
viro *man*; virino *woman*; vir- *(as prefix) male*
virto *virtue*; malvirto *vice*
viŝi *wipe*; viŝtuko *duster*
vitro *glass*; okulvitroj *glasses, spectacles*
vivi *to live*; vivo *life*; vivu . . . ! *long live . . . !*
vizaĝo *face*
viziti, vizito *visit*
voĉo *voice, vote*; voĉdoni *vote*
vojaĝi *to travel*; vojaĝo *journey*
vojo *road, way, route*; vojeto *path*
voki *call, summon*
voli *want (to), be willing*; volo *will (power)*
volonte *willingly*; volontulo *volunteer*
volumo *volume*
volvi *wind, wrap round*
vorto *word*; vortaro *vocabulary, dictionary*
vosto *tail*
vundi *wound, injure*

zoologia ĝardeno *zoo*
zorgi *to care (for)*; prizorgi *take care of*

English–Esperanto Vocabulary

Notes to the student:
(*a*) When referring to this vocabulary (or to any dictionary) you may find more than one translation of the word you are looking up. Unless you are *quite sure* which is the appropriate translation, you are advised to look up each one in the Esperanto–English section of the vocabulary, to make sure which is the one you need.
(*b*) If the word you want does not appear, it may be that you will find its opposite listed, and will only need to add the prefix **mal-** to it.
(*c*) (tr.); *-iĝi* (intr.) indicates the verb is transitive (see Unit 15) and requires the ending *-iĝi* to make it intransitive. (intr.); *-igi* (tr.) indicates an intransitive verb requiring *-igi* to make it transitive.

abhor *abomeni*
able *kapabla, lerta*; to be able *povi*
about *ĉirkaŭ*; (concerning) *pri*
above *super, supre*
absolute *absoluta*
accelerate *akceli*, (tr.); *-iĝi* (intr.)
accept *akcepti*
accident *akcidento*
accompany *akompani*
according to *laŭ*
accuse (of) *akuzi (pri)*
acquire *akiri*
acrobat *akrobato*
across *trans*
act *ago, agi*; (on stage) *aktori*
activity *agado*
actor *aktoro*
actual *efektiva*; actually *efektive*
address *adreso*
admire *admiri*
admit *konfesi*
adore *adori*
adorn *ornami*
adult *plenkresk-a, adolt-a, -ulo*
advantage *avantaĝo*
adventure *aventuro*
advice *konsilo*; advise *konsili*
aerate *aerumi*
affable *afabla*
affair *afero*
afford *toleri la elspezon por*
afraid: be afraid *timi*
after *post, post kiam*;
afterwards *poste*
again *denove, re(foj)e*
against *kontraŭ*
age *aĝo, epoko*
agitate *agiti*
agree *konsenti*; agreement *konsento*
ah! *ha!*
aim *celi, celo*
air *aero, aerumi*
aircraft *aviadilo(j)*
airport *flughaveno*
alas! *ho, ve!*
alcohol *alkoholo*
alert *vigla*
algebra *algebro*
alive *vivanta*; be alive *vivi*
all *ĉio, ĉiuj, la tuta*; — the better *des pli bone*
allow *permesi*

almost *preskaŭ*
alone *sola, sole*
along *laŭ*
alphabet *alfabeto*
already *jam*
also *ankaŭ*
although *kvankam*
always *ĉiam*
amateur *amatoro, amatora*
amaze *mirigi*; be amazed *miri*
ambassador *ambasadoro*
ambulance *ambulanco*
America (continent) *Ameriko*; (U.S.A.) *Usono*
among(st) *inter*
amuse *amuzi*
ancestor *prapatro*
and *kaj*
anger *kolero, kolerigi*
angle *angulo*
angry *kolera*
animal *besto*
announce *anonci*; announcement *anonco*
annoy *ĉagreni*
another *alia*
answer *respondi, respondo*
Antarctic *Antarkto, antarkta*
any *ia, iu*
anybody, anyone *iu (ajn)*
anything *io (ajn)*
anywhere *ie (ajn), ien (ajn)*
apart from *krom*
apartment(s) *apartamento*
apocalypse *apokalipso*
apparatus *aparato*
appear *aperi, vidiĝi*; (seem) *ŝajni*
appearance *aspekto*
applaud *aplaŭdi*
apple *pomo*
appreciate *ŝati*
approve *aprobi*
approximate *proksimuma*
April *aprilo*
Arctic *Arkto, arkta*
arithmetic *aritmetiko*
arm *brako*; armchair *brakseĝo*; arms (weapons) *armiloj*
around *ĉirkaŭ, ĉirkaŭe*
arouse *veki*
arrange *aranĝi*
arrest *aresti*
arrival *alveno*; arrive *alveni*
arrow *sago*
art *arto*
artichoke *artiŝoko*
article (in magazine, etc.) *artikolo*; (thing) *objekto*
as *kiel*; — . . . — *tiel . . . kiel*; — if *kvazaŭ*
ashamed: be ashamed *honti*
Asia *Azio*; Asian *azia, aziano*
ask (question) *demandi*; (request) *peti*
asleep: be asleep *dormi*
ass *azeno*
assume *supozi*
at *ĉe, je*; (if it means 'in') *en*
atom *atomo*; atomic *atoma*
attack *ataki*
attain *atingi*
attempt *peni*
attend (be present) *ĉeesti*; (pay attention) *atenti*
attract *allogi*; attractive *alloga, ĉarma*
August *aŭgusto*
aunt *onklino*
Australia *Aŭstralio*; Australian *aŭstralia, aŭstraliano*
Austria *Aŭstrujo*; Austrian *aŭstra, aŭstro*
autumn *aŭtuno*
available *havebla*
aviation *aviado*
avoid *eviti*
await *atendi*
awake *veki* (tr.); *-iĝi* (intr.); wide-awake *vigla*
away *for*
axe *hakilo*

baby *infaneto, bebo*
back *dorso, malantaŭo*
backbone *spino*
bad *malbona*
badge *insigno*
bag *sako, saketo, valizo*
bake *baki* (tr.); *-iĝi* (intr.)

ball *pilko*; ballpoint pen *globkrajono*; (dance) *balo*
ballet *baleto*
bank (finance) *banko*; (of river, etc.) *bordo*
banquet *bankedo, festeno*
bar *bari, barilo*; *trinkejo*
bark *boji*
barrier *barilo*
base *bazo*; basic *baza*
basis *bazo*
basket *korbo*
bath *bano, bani*; (tub) *bankuvo*
bathe *bani sin* (intr.), *bani* (tr.)
battle *batalo*
be *esti*; (in a place) *troviĝi*; (in health) *farti*
beach *strando*
bead *bido*
bean (broad, etc.) *fabo*; (French, etc.) *fazeolo*
bear *porti*; (give birth) *naski*; (animal) *urso*
beat *bati*
beautiful *bela*; beauty *bel(ec)o*, (person) *belulino*
because *ĉar*; because of *pro*
become *iĝi, fariĝi*
bed *lito*; bedroom *dormoĉambro*
beer *biero*
before *antaŭ (ol), antaŭe*
begin *komenci* (tr.); *-iĝi* (intr.); beginner *komencanto*
behave *konduti, bone konduti*
behind *malantaŭ*
Belgian *belgo, belga*; Belgium *Belgujo*
believe *kredi*; belief *kredo*
bell *sonorilo*
belly *ventro*
belong *aparteni*
below *sub*
bench *benko*
beneath *sub*
beside *apud*; besides *krom*
best *plej bona, plej bone*
bet *veti, veto*
better *pli bona, pli bone*
between *inter*
beyond *preter*
Bible *Biblio*
bicycle *biciklo*
big *granda*
bill (hotel, etc.) *kalkulo*
bird *birdo* (pron. *beerr-do*)
birth *naskiĝo*; give birth *naski*
birthday *naskiĝtago*
biscuit *biskvito*
bit *peceto*
black *nigra*
blame *kulpo, kulpigi*
blank *blanka*
blanket *(lan)kovrilo, litkovrilo*
bleed *sangi*
bless *beni*
blind *blinda*
blood *sango*
blow *bato, frapo; blovi*
blue *blua*
blush *ruĝiĝi*
board *tabulo*
body *korpo*
boil *boli* (intr.); *-igi* (tr.)
Bolivia *Bolivio*; Bolivian *bolivia, boliviano*
bone *osto*
book *libro*; (= reserve) *mendi, rezervi*
boot *bot(et)o*
born *naskita*; be born *naskiĝi*
borrow *prunti, pruntepreni*
botch *fuŝi, fuŝaĵo*
both *ambaŭ*; — . . . and . . . *kaj . . . kaj . . .*
bottle *botelo*
bottom *malsupro, malsupra*
box *skatolo, kest(et)o*
boy *knabo*
brain *cerbo*; rack one's brains *cerbumi*
braise *stufi*
branch (of tree, etc.) *branĉo*; (of firm) *filio*
brave *kuraĝa*
bravo! *brave!*
Brazil *Brazilo*; Brazilian *brazila, brazilano*
bread *pano*
break *rompi* (tr.); *-iĝi* (intr.); *paŭzo*
breath *spiro*; breathe *spiri*
brick *briko*
bridge *ponto*; (game) *briĝo*
bright *hela*
brilliant *brila*

bring *alporti*; bring up (children) *eduki*
Britain *Britujo*; British *brita*; Briton *brito*
broad *larĝa*
broadcast *dissendi, disaŭdigi*
broccoli *brokolo*
broom *balailo*
brown *bruna*
brush *broso, brosi*
bucket *sitelo*
build *konstrui*; building *konstruaĵo*
Bulgaria *Bulgario*; Bulgarian *bulgara, bulgaro*
bull *virbovo*
bungle *fuŝi*
burden *ŝarĝo, ŝarĝi*
Burma *Birmo*; Burmese *birma, birmano*
burn *bruli* (intr.); *-igi* (tr.)
burst *krevi* (intr.); *-igi* (tr.)
bus *aŭtobuso*
business *afero(j), komerco*
busy *okupita*
but *sed*
butter *butero*
button *butono*
buy *aĉeti*
by *de, per, far, fare de*

cabaret *kabareto*
cabbage *brasiko*
cabin *kajuto*
café *kafejo*
cajole *kaĵoli*
cake *kuko*
calculate *kalkuli*
calendar *kalendaro*
call *voki, voko*; be called (named) *nomiĝi*
calm *trankvila*
camera *fot(ograf)ilo*
can *povas*; (container) *ujo, skatolo*
Canada *Kanado*; Canadian *kanada, kanadano*
candle *kandelo*
cannibal *kanibalo*
cap *ĉapo*
capable *kapabla*
capture *kapti*
car *aŭtomobilo, aŭto*
caravan *ruldomo*
card *karto*
care *zorgi, zorgo, prizorgo*; take care of *prizorgi*
career *kariero*
careful *zorga, atentema*; careless *senatenta*
carpet *tapiŝo*
carriage (rail) *vagono*
carrot *karoto*
carry *porti*
cart *ĉaro*
carve *skulpti*; (meat) *tranĉi*
case *kovrilo, ujo, valiz(et)o*
cash *mono*
cashier *kasisto*
cassette *kasedo*; cassette-recorder *magnetofono*
castle *kastelo*
cat *kato*
catch *kapti*
cathedral *katedralo*
catholic *katoliko, katolika*
cauliflower *florbrasiko*
cause *kaŭzo, kaŭzi*
cease *ĉesi* (intr.); *-igi* (tr.)
ceiling *plafono*
celebrate *festi*
central *centra*; central heating *centra hejtado*
centre *centro*
centrifugal *centrifuga*
century *jarcento*
certain *certa*; a — *iu*
chain *ĉeno*
chair *seĝo*; chairman *prezidanto*
chance *hazardo*; (of success) *ŝanco*
change *ŝanĝi* (tr.); *-iĝi* (intr.); (for a note) *moneroj*
charming *ĉarma*
chat *babili, babilado*
cheat *fripono, friponi*
check *kontroli*
cheek (face) *vango*
cheerful *gaja, bonhumora*
cheese *fromaĝo*
chess *ŝako*
chest *kesto, brusto*
chief *ĉefo, ĉefa, estro*
child *infano*
Chile *Ĉilio*; Chilean *ĉilia, ĉiliano*
chimpanzee *ĉimpanzo*

China *Cinujo*; Chinese *ĉina, ĉino*
chocolate *ĉokolado*
choice *elekto*
choir *ĥoro, koruso*
choose *elekti*
chop *haki*
Christ *Kristo*; Christian *Kristano*
church (building) *preĝejo*
cinema *kinejo*
circle *cirklo, rondo*
city *urb(eg)o*
clap *aplaŭdi*
class *klaso, kurso*
clay *argilo*
clean *pura*; cleanse *purigi*
clear *klara, hela*
clergyman *pastro*
clever *lerta, inteligenta*
climb *grimpi*
cloak *mantelo*; cloakroom *vestejo, vesto-deponejo*
clock *horloĝo*
close *fermi*
cloth (for a purpose) *tuko*
clothe *vesti*; clothes *vestoj*
cloud *nubo*
club (society) *klubo*
coach *aŭtobuso, vagono*
coal *karbo*
coast *marbordo*
coat *mantelo*
coax *kaĵoli*
cock (rooster) *koko*; male (bird) *vir-*
coffee *kafo*; —-pot *kafkruĉo*
coin *monero*
cold *malvarma*; (illness) *malvarmumo*
collar *kolumo*
collect *kolekti* (tr.); *-iĝi* (intr.)
college *kolegio*
colonel *kolonelo*
colour *koloro, kolori*
comb *kombi, kombilo*
come *veni*
comfort *komforto*; comfortable *komforta*
comic(al) *komika*
command *ordoni, ordono*
commence *komenci* (tr.); *-iĝi* (intr.)
comment *komenti, komento*
commerce *komerco*; commercial *komerca*
committee *komitato*
commodity *varo*
common *ofta, ordinara, komuna*; common sense *prudento*
community *komunumo, socio*
company *kompanio*
compare *kompari*
compartment *fako*
compel *devigi*; compulsory *deviga*
competition *konkurso*
complain *plendi*
complete *kompleta*
complicate *kompliki*; complicated *komplika*
comprise *ampleksi*
compute *kalkuli, komputori*
computer *komputoro*
concept *koncepto*
concert *koncerto*
condition *stato, kondiĉo*
confess *konfesi*; confession *konfeso*
congratulate *gratuli*
congress *kongreso*
conquer *venki*
consent *konsenti, konsento*
consequence *sekvo*
consist (of) *konsisti (el)*
constant *konstanta*
construct *konstrui*
consult *konsulti*
container *ujo*
content(ed) *kontenta*
contest *konkurso*
continue *daŭri* (intr.); *-igi* (tr.)
contrary *malo, mala, kontraŭa*; on the — *male*
contrast *kontrasto*
control *regi*
convenience *oportuno; necesejo*
convenient *oportuna*
conversation *konversacio, dialogo*
cook *kuiri* (tr.); *-iĝi* (intr.); *kuirist(in)o*; cooker *kuirforno*
copper *kupro, kupra*
copy *kopii, kopio; ekzemplero*
cord *ŝnuro*
cordial *kora*
corner *angulo*
correct *korekti; ĝusta, senerara*
correspond *korespondi*
correspondence *poŝtaĵo, korespondado*
corridor *koridoro*
cost *kosti, kosto*; costly *multekosta*

costume (for a special purpose) *kostumo*; (other) *vesto, kompleto*
cough *tusi, tuso*
count *nombri*
country *lando*; (not town) *kamparo*
couple *paro*
courage *kuraĝo*; courageous *kuraĝa*
course *kurso*; of — *kompreneble*
courteous *ĝentila*
cousin *kuz(in)o*
cover *kovri, kovrilo; ampleksi*
cow *bovino*
crafty *ruza*
crawl *rampi*
create *krei*; creation *kreaĵo*; creator *kreinto*
creep *rampi*
crime *krimo*; criminal *krimulo*
criticize *kritiki*
crook *fripono*
cross *kruco*
crowd *(hom)amaso*
crown *krono*
cruel *kruela*
cry *krio, krii; plori*
cuckoo *kukolo*
culture *kulturo*
cunning *ruza, ruzeco*
cup *taso*
cupboard *ŝranko*
curator *kuratoro*
cure *(re)sanigi*
curious *scivola*; (quaint) *kurioza*
curse *malbeni, malbeno*
curtain *kurteno*
custom *kutimo*
cut (with knife) *tranĉi*; (with scissors) *tondi*
Cyprus *Cipro*
Czech *ĉeĥa*; Czechoslovakia *Ĉeĥoslovakio*

Dad, Daddy *paĉjo*
dainty delikata
dam *bari, baraĵo*
damage *difekti, difekto*
dance *danci, danco, balo*
Dane *dano*; Danish *dana*
danger *danĝero*
dark *malluma, malhela*; darkness *mallumo*
darling *kara, karul(in)o*
dart *sageto*
date *dato*
daughter *filino*; daughter-in-law *bofilino*
day *tago*; daydream *revo*
dead *mortinta*
deaf *surda*
deal (with) *trakti (pri)*; a great — *multe*
dear *kara*; (expensive) *multekosta*
death *morto*
deceive *trompi*
December *decembro*
decide *decidi*
decorate *ornami*
dedicate *dediĉi*
deep *profunda*
defeat *venki*; a defeat *malvenko*
defend *defendi*
define *difini*
degree *grado*; (university) *licencio*
delicate *delikata*
delight *ravo, ravi*; delightful *rava*
deliver *liveri*
demand *postuli*
Denmark *Danlando*
dense *densa*
department *fako*
depend *dependi (de)*
deposit *deponi; antaŭpago*
depot *deponejo*
debt *ŝuldo*
describe *priskribi*
deserve *meriti*
design *desegni, desegnaĵo*
desire *deziri*
despair *malesperi, malespero*
despite *malgraŭ*
destiny *sorto*
destroy *detrui*
develop *evolui* (intr.); *-igi* (tr.)
devote *dediĉi*
dialect *dialekto*
dialogue *dialogo*
dictionary *vortaro*
die *morti*
differ *diferenci*
different *malsama, diversa(j)*

dig *fosi*
digit *cifero*
diligent *diligenta*
dine *(vesper)manĝi*
dinner *tagmanĝo, vespermanĝo*
direct *rekta*
direction *direkto*
disappear *malaperi*
disc *disko*
discuss *diskuti*
dish *plado*; the dishes *la manĝilaro, vazaro*
display *(el)montri, (el)montro, spektaklo*
dissolve *solvi*
distance *malproksimo*; (interval) *distanco*
distant *malproksima, fora*
distinguish *distingi*; distinguished *eminenta*
distract *distri*
distress *ĉagreno, ĉagreni*
distribute *disdoni*
district (region) *regiono*; (of city) *distrikto, kvartalo*
disturb *ĝeni*
dive *plonĝi*
divide *dividi* (tr.); *-iĝi* (intr.)
divine *dia*
divorce *eksedz(in)igi; -igo*
do *fari*
doctor *kuracisto*; (title) *doktoro*
document *dokumento*
dog *hundo*
doll *pupo*
dollar *dolaro*
donkey *azeno*
door *pordo*
dot *punkto*
doubt *dubi, dubo*
down *malsupre(n)*
downstairs *malsupre(n), sube(n)*
draw (pull) *tiri*; (picture) *desegni*
drawer *tirkesto*
drawing-room *salono*
dream *sonĝi, sonĝo*; day - — *revi, revo*
dress *vesti (sin)*; (woman's) *robo*
drink *trinki, trinko, trinkaĵo*
drive *peli*; (vehicle) *veturigi, konduki*
drop *fali, faligi; guto*
drown *droni* (intr.); *-igi* (tr.)
dry *seka, sekigi, sekiĝi*; dryer *sekigilo*
during *dum*
dust *polvo, senpolvigi*; duster *viŝtuko*
Dutch *nederlanda*; Dutchman *nederlandano*
dwell *loĝi*

each *ĉiu*; two eggs — *po du ovoj*
ear *orelo*
early *frua, frue*
earnest *serioza*
earth *tero, grundo*
ease *facileco*
east *oriento*; eastern *orienta*; eastwards *orienten*
Easter *Pasko*
easy *facila*
eat *manĝi*
ecology *ekologio*
economize *ŝpari*
edge *rando*
edit *redakti*; editor *redaktisto*
edition *eldono*
educate *eduki*; education *edukado*
egg *ovo*
eight *ok*
either *aŭ*; — . . . or *aŭ . . . aŭ*
elastic *elasta (fadeno)*
elect *elekti*
electric(al) *elektra*; electricity *elektro*
elegant *eleganta*
element *elemento*
elephant *elefanto*
else *alia, alie*
embrace *brakumi*
embroider *brodi*; embroidery *brodaĵo*
eminent *eminenta*
emperor *imperiestro*; empress *imperiestrino*
emphasis *emfazo*; emphasize *emfazi*
empire *imperio*
empty *malplena*
enamel *emajlo*
encounter *renkonti, renkont(iĝ)o*
end *fini* (tr.); *-iĝi* (intr.); *fino*
endeavour *peni, peno*
energy *energio*
engine *motoro, maŝino, lokomotivo*
England *Anglujo*; English *angla*; Englishman *anglo*

enigma *enigmo*
enjoy *ĝui*; enjoy oneself *amuziĝi*
enough *sufiĉa, sufiĉe(da)*
entertain *distri, amuzi*
enthusiasm *entuziasmo*; enthusiastic *entuziasma*
entire *tuta*; entirely *tute*
entrance *eniro, enirejo*
envelope *koverto*
epoch *epoko*
equal *egala*
erase *forskrapi, forviŝi*; eraser *skrapgumo*
error *eraro*
especial *aparta*
essence *esenco*; essential *esenca, nepra*
esteem *estimi, estimo*
Europe *Eŭropo*; European *eŭropa, eŭropano*
evade *eviti*
even *eĉ; ebena*
evening *vespero*
event *okazaĵo, evento*
ever *iam, ĉiam*
every *ĉiu*
everybody *ĉiu*
everyday *ĉiutaga, ĉiutage*
everyone *ĉiu*; —'s *ĉies*
everything *ĉio*
everywhere *ĉie*
evident *evidenta*
ex- *eks-*
exact *ĝusta, preciza*
examination *ekzameno*; examine *ekzameni*
example *ekzemplo*; for — *ekzemple*
exclaim *ekkrii*
excursion *ekskurso*
excuse *pardoni*; excuse me! *pardonu! pardonon!*
exercise *ekzerco, ekzerci (sin)*
exhibition *ekspozicio*
exist *ekzisti*
exit *eliri, eliro, elirejo*
expect *atendi, antaŭvidi*
expensive *multekosta*
experience *sperto*; experienced *sperta*
expert *sperta, spertulo*
explain *klarigi*; explanation *klarigo*
exploit *ekspluati; heroaĵo*
explore *esplori*
expression *esprimo*; (of face) *mieno*
extend *etendi* (tr.); *-iĝi* (intr.); extensive *ampleksa*
extinguish *estingi*
extreme *ekstrema*; extremely *(tre)ege*
eye *okulo*

face *vizaĝo*
fact *fakto*; in — *fakte, efektive*
factory *fabriko*
fail *malsukcesi*; without — *nepre*
fair *justa*
fall *fali, falo*
false *falsa, malvera*
family *familio*
famous *fama*
fan *ventumi, ventumilo*; (football, etc.) *fervorulo*
far *malproksima, malproksime(n)*
farm *farmbieno, farmi*; farmer *farmisto*
fashion *modo*; fashionable *laŭmoda*
fast *rapida, rapide*; (clock) *frua*
fat *dika, grasa, graso*
fate *sorto*
father *patro*; —-in-law *bopatro*
fault *neperfektaĵo*; my — *mia kulpo*
favour *komplezo*; favourite *preferata*
fear *timi, timo*
feast *festo*; (banquet) *festeno, bankedo*
feather *plumo*
February *februaro*
feed *manĝi* (intr.); *nutri* (tr.)
feel *senti*
female *ino, ina*
ferry *pramo, pramŝipo*
fever *febro*
few *malmultaj*; a — *kelkaj*
field *kampo*
fight *batali, batalo*
figure *cifero*; (form) *figuro*
fill *plenigi*
film *filmo*
final *fina*
find *trovi*
fine *bela, delikata*
finger *fingro*
finish *fini* (tr.); *-iĝi* (intr.)

Finland *Finnlando*; Finn *finno*; Finnish *finna*
fire *fajro*
firm *firma*; (commercial) *firmo, firmao*
fish *fiŝo*
five *kvin*
fit (suitable) *taŭga*; (healthy) *sana*
fix *fiksi*
flag *flago*; (military) *standardo*
flat (smooth) *plata*; (level) *ebena*
flatter *flati*; flattery *flatado*
flee *fuĝi*
float *flosi* (intr.); *-igi* (tr.)
flock *aro*; flock of sheep *ŝafaro*
floor *planko*; (storey) *etaĝo*
flow *flui*
flower *floro, flori*
fluent *flua*
flush (turn red) *ruĝiĝi*
fly (insect) *muŝo*; (in the air) *flugi*
fog *nebulo*
fold *faldi* (tr.); *-iĝi* (intr.)
follow *sekvi*; as —s *jene*
food *manĝaĵo, nutraĵo*
fool *stultulo, idioto*
foot *piedo*
football (ball) *piedpilko*, (game) *futbalo*
for *por*; (because of) *pro*
forecast *prognozo*
foreign *fremda, alilanda*
forest *arbar(eg)o*
forget *forgesi*
forgive *pardoni*
fork *forko*
form *formo*; (paper) *aliĝilo, mendilo*, etc.
formal *formala, solena*
fortunate *feliĉa*
found (establish) *fondi*
foundation *fundamento, fondiĝo, fondaĵo*
fountain *fontano*; — pen *fontplumo*
four *kvar*
fraction *frakcio, ono*
France *Francujo*
free *libera; senpaga*
freeze *frosti*; (food) *frostigi*; freezer *frostigilo*
French *franca*; Frenchman *franco*
frequent *ofta*
fresh *freŝa*
Friday *vendredo*; Good — *Sankta Vendredo*
fridge *fridujo*
friend *amiko*
frighten *timigi*
from *de, el*
front *antaŭo*; in — of *antaŭ*
fruit *frukto*
fry *friti*; frying pan *pato*
fulfil *plenumi*
full *plena*; (satiated) *sata*
fun *amuzo*
function *funkcio*
fund *kaso*
fundamental *fundamenta*
funny *amuza, komika*
furnace *forno*
furniture *mebloj, meblaro*
further *plu*

gain *gajni*; (clock) *frui*
gallery *galerio*
gallop *galopi, galopo*
game *ludo*
garage *remizo*; (for repairs) *garaĝo*
garden *ĝardeno*
garment *vesto*
gas *gaso*
gasoline *benzino*
gate *(ĝarden)pordo*; (of town) *pordego*
gather *kolekti* (tr.); *-iĝi* (intr.); *amasigi, amasiĝi*
general *ĝenerala*; in — *ĝenerale*
generous *malavara*
genius *genio, geniulo*
gentle *milda, dolĉa*
gentleman *sinjoro*
German *germana, germano*; Germany *Germanujo*
get *akiri, ricevi*; — up *ellitiĝi*
ghost *fantomo, spirito*
gift *donaco; talento*; gifted *talenta*
giraffe *ĝirafo*
girl *knabino*
give *doni*; (present) *donaci*
glad *ĝoja*; be — *ĝoji*
glance *ekrigardi, ekrigardo*
glass *vitro*; (drinking-) *glaso*; (looking-) *spegulo*; glasses (spectacles) *okulvitroj*

globe *globo*
glorious *glora, belega*; glory *gloro*
glove *ganto*
glue *gluo, glui*
go *iri*; (in or of a vehicle) *veturi*
god *dio*; goddess *diino*
gold *oro*; golden *ora*
good *bona*
good-bye *ĝis (la) revido; ĝis la; ĝis; adiaŭ*
govern *regi*; government *registaro*
gown *robo*
grade *grado*
grammar *gramatiko*; — school *gimnazio*
gramophone *gramofono*
grand *grandioza*
granddaughter *nepino*; grandfather *avo*; grandmother *avino*; grandparents *geavoj*; grandson *nepo*
granny *avinjo*
grape *vinbero*
grass *herbo*
grease *graso*; greasy *grasa*
great *granda*; — grandfather *praavo*
Greece *Grekujo*; Greek *greka, greko*
green *verda*
Greenland *Groenlando*
greet *saluti*; greeting *saluto*
grey *griza*
grocer *spicisto*
ground *tero*
group *grupo*
grow *kreski* (intr.); *-igi* (tr.); — up *plenkreskiĝi*
guarantee *garantii*
guard *gardi, gardisto*
guess *diveni, diveno*
guest *gasto*
guide *gvidi, gvidanto; gvidlibro; skoltino*
guilty *kulpa*
gun *pafilo*

habit *kutimo*
hail (weather) *hajlo;* hailstone *hajlero*
hair *haroj, hararo*; (single) *haro*
half *duono*; (as prefix) *duon-*
hallo *saluton*
halt *halti* (intr.); *-igi* (tr.)
ham *ŝinko*
hammer *martelo, marteli*
hand *mano*; handbag *mansaketo*
handkerchief *poŝtuko, naztuko*
hang *pendi* (intr.); *-igi* (tr.)
happen *okazi*
happy *feliĉa*
harbour *haveno*
hard *malmola*; *malfacila*; hardly *apenaŭ*
harm *malutili, malutilo*; harmful *malutila*
harvest *rikolto, rikolti*
hat *ĉapelo*
hatch *giĉeto*
have *havi;* — to *devi*
he *li*
head *kapo, ĉefo, estro*; heading *titolo*
heal *(re)sanigi* (tr.); *-iĝi* (intr.)
health *sano*; healthy *sana*
heap *amaso*
hear *aŭdi*
heart *koro*
hearth *kameno, fajrejo*
heat *varmo, varmigi, hejti*
heavy *peza*
heel (foot) *kalkano*; (shoe) *kalkanumo*
hello *saluton*
help *helpi, helpo*; helpless *senhelpa, senpova*
hen *kokino*
her *ŝi, ŝin, ŝia*; hers *ŝia*
here *ĉi tie(n)*; — is *jen*
hero *heroo*; heroine *heroino*; heroic *heroa*
hesitate *heziti*
hey! *he!*
hi! *saluton!*
hide *kaŝi* (tr.); *-iĝi* (intr.)
high *alta, alte*
highway *ĉefvojo, ŝoseo*
hill *monteto;* (slope) *deklivo*
him *li, lin*
hinder *malhelpi*
his *lia*
history *historio*
hit *frapi*; (not miss) *trafi*
hobby *ŝatokupo, flankokupo, hobio*
hold *teni*
hole *truo*

holiday *ferio(j)*
holy *sankta*
home *hejmo, hejmen*; at — *hejme*
honour *honoro, honori*
hook *hoko*
hope *esperi, espero*
horizontal *horizontala*
horse *ĉevalo*
hospital *malsanulejo*
hostel *gastejo*
hot *varma, varmega*
hotel *hotelo*
hour *horo*
house *domo*
how *kiel*; -- much, — many *kiom*
however *tamen*
hullo *saluton*
humble *humila*
humour (mood) *humoro*; (funny) *humuro*
humus *humo*
hundred *cent*
Hungarian *hungara, hungaro*; Hungary *Hungarujo*
hungry *malsata*
hunt *ĉasi, ĉaso*
hurry *rapidi*
hurt *dolori*
husband *edzo*

I *mi*
ice *glacio*; —-cream *glaciaĵo*
Iceland *Islando*
idea *ideo*
ideal *ideala, idealo*
idiot *idioto*
if *se*; (whether) *ĉu*
ignore *ignori*
ill *malsana*
illustrate *ilustri*; illustration *ilustraĵo*
imagination *imago(povo)*; imagine *imagi*
imitate *imiti*
immediate *tuja*; immediately *tuj*
immortal *senmorta*
important *grava*
impossible *neebla*
impress *imponi*; impressive *impona*
improve *plibonigi* (tr.) *-iĝi* (intr.)
in *en*
inclination *emo*; (slope) *kliniĝo*
incline *klini* (tr); *-iĝi* (intr.)
include *inkluzivi*; inclusive *inkluziva, -e*
indeed *ja*
India *Hindujo*; Indian *hinda, hindo*
indicate *indiki*; indication *indiko*
indifferent *indiferenta*
industrial *industria*; industry *industrio*
infant *infaneto, bebo*
inform *informi, sciigi*; information *informo(j)*
injure *vundi*; injury *vundo*
ink *inko*
insist *insisti*
instead of *anstataŭ*
instrument *instrumento*
insulate *izoli*
intelligent *inteligenta*
intend *intenci*; intention *intenco*
intense, intensive *intensa*
interest *interesi, intereso*; interesting *interesa*
internal *interna*
international *internacia*
interval *paŭzo*
introduce (thing) *enkonduki*; (person) *prezenti*
intuition *intuicio*
invent *inventi*
investigate *esplori*
invite *inviti*
Iran *Irano*; Iranian *irana, iranano*
Iraq *Irako*; Iraqi *iraka, irakano*
Ireland *Irlando*; Irish *irlanda*; Irishman *irlandano*
iron *fero, gladilo*; (clothes) *gladi*
island *insulo*
isolate *izoli*
Israel *Israelo*; Israeli *israela, israelano*
it *ĝi*; its *ĝia*
Italy *Italujo*; Italian *itala, italo*
item *ero*

jacket *jako*
January *januaro*
Japan *Japanujo*; Japanese *japana, japano*
Jesus *Jesuo*
jet (plane) *jeto*
Jew *judo*; Jewish *juda*

job *okupo, profesio, tasko*
joke *ŝerco, ŝerci*
journey *vojaĝo*
judge *juĝi, juĝisto*
jug *kruĉo*
juice *suko*
July *julio*
jump *salti, salto*
June *junio*
jungle *ĝangalo*
just (fair) *justa*; (a moment ago) *ĵus*

keep *teni, gardi, konservi*
kettle *boligilo*
key *ŝlosilo*
kill *mortigi*
kilogramme *kilogramo*
kilometre *kilometro*
kind *speco*; *bona, afabla*
kindness *afableco; komplezo*
king *reĝo*; kingdom *regno*
kiss *kisi, kiso*
kitchen *kuirejo*
knickers *kalsono*
knife *tranĉilo*
knit *triki*; knitting needle *trikilo*
know *scii*; (acquaintance) *koni*

label *etikedo*
lack *ne havi; manko*; be lacking *manki*
ladder *ŝtupetaro*
lady *sinjorino*
lake *lago*
lamp *lampo*
land (not sea) *tero*; (country) *lando*; (alight) *surteriĝi, alteriĝi*
landscape *pejzaĝo*
language *lingvo*
large *granda*
last *daŭri*; *lasta, fina*
late *malfrua, malfrue*
Latvia *Latvujo*; Latvian *latva, latvo*
laugh *ridi, rido*
lavatory *necesejo*
law *leĝo*; in-laws *boparencoj*
lawn *razeno*
lazy *mallaborema, maldiligenta*
lead *konduki, gvidi*
lead (metal) *plumbo*
leaf *folio*
learn *lerni*; learner *lernanto*
least *plej malgranda*; at — *almenaŭ*
leave *lasi, forlasi*
Lebanon *Libano*; Lebanese *libana, libanano*
leg *kruro*
legible *legebla*
lemon *citrono*
lend *pruntedoni*
less *malpli (da)*
lesson *leciono*
let *permesi, lasi*; let's *ni. . . u*
letter *letero*; (of alphabet) *litero*
level *nivelo; ebena*
library *biblioteko*
Libya *Libio*; Libyan *libia, libiano*
lick *leki*
lid *kovrilo*
lie *kuŝi*; (tell a —) *mensogi*
life *vivo*
light *lumo, lumigi*; (colour) *hela*; (not heavy) *malpeza*
lightning *fulmo*
like *simila (al)*; I — it *ĝi plaĉas al mi*
line *linio, vico; ŝnuro*
lion *leono*
liquid *likva, likvaĵo*
list *listo*
listen *aŭskulti*
literature *literaturo*
Lithuania *Litovujo*; Lithuanian *litova, litovo*
litre *litro*
little *malgranda, eta, malmulta*; a — *iomete*
live *vivi*; (dwell) *loĝi*
living-room *loĝĉambro, familia ĉambro*
load *ŝarĝi, ŝarĝo*
loan *prunto, prunti*
loathe *abomeni*
local *loka*
lock *ŝlosi; seruro*
lodge *loĝi*; lodgings *loĝejo*
London *Londono*; Londoner *londonano*
lone *sola*; lonely *soleca*
long *longa, longe*; — for *sopiri*
loo *necesejo*
look *rigardi, rigardo; aspekti, aspekto*; — for *serĉi*

lose *perdi*; (one's way) *vojerari*; (clock) *malfrui*
lot: a lot of *multaj, multe da*
loud *laŭta*
lounge *salono, sidĉambro*
love *ami*
lovely *bela, rava*
low *malalta, malalte*
lucky *bonŝanca, feliĉa*
lunch(eon) *tagmanĝi, tagmanĝo*
Luxemburg *Luksemburgo*
luxurious *luksa*; luxury *lukso*

machine *maŝino*
mackintosh *pluvmantelo*
macramé *makramo*
madam *sinjorino*
magazine *gazeto, revuo, magazino*
magnet *magneto*; magnetic *magneta*
magnificent *grandioza*
mail *poŝto*
main *ĉefa*
majesty *reĝ(in)a moŝto*
majority *plimulto*
make *fari, igi*
male *vir(seks)a*
man *viro*; (human being) *homo*; mankind *la homaro*
Man, Isle of *Manksinsulo*
manage (to do something) *sukcesi*
manner *maniero*; manners *ĝentileco*
manufacture *fabriki, fabrikado*
manuscript *manuskripto*
Manx *manksa*; Manxman *mankso*
many *multaj*
map *mapo*
marble *marmoro*
March *marto*
marry *edz(in)iĝi, geedziĝi*
mass *amaso*
Mass *meso*
master *mastro, estro, majstro, instruisto*
material *materialo*; (cloth) *ŝtofo*
mathematics *matematiko*
matter *afero; gravi*; it doesn't — *ne gravas*
mature *matura*
may *rajtas*
May *majo*
mayonnaise *majonezo*
mayor *urbestro*
me *mi, min*
meal *manĝo*
mean (miserly) *avara*; (signify) *signifi*
measure *mezuri* (tr.); *-iĝi* (intr.)
meat *viando*
medicine *medikamento*; (science) *medicino*
meet *renkonti* (tr.); *-iĝi, kunveni* (intr.)
meeting *kunveno, renkontiĝo*
melody *melodio*
member *membro, ano*
memory *memoro*
menace *minaci, minaco*
mend *ripari*
mention *mencii*
merely *nur*
merit *merito, meriti*
merry *gaja*
message *mesaĝo*
metal *metalo, metala*
method *metodo*
metre *metro*
Mexico *Meksikio*; Mexican *meksikia, meksikiano*
microphone *mikrofono*
microwave (adj.) *mikro-onda*
middle *mezo, meza*
migrate *migri*; migration *migrado*
mild *milda*
mile *mejlo*
milk *lakto*
millimetre *milimetro*
million *miliono (da)*
mind *menso*; never—! *ne gravas!*
mine *(la) mia; minejo*
minimum *minimumo, minimuma*
minister (church) *pastro*
minute *minuto*
miracle *miraklo*
mirror *spegulo*
miser *avarulo*; miserly *avara*
miss *fraŭlino; maltrafi*
mist *nebuleto*
mistake *eraro*; be mistaken *erari*
mistress *mastrino, instruistino*
mix *miksi* (tr.); *-iĝi* (intr.)
modern *moderna*
moment *momento*
Monday *lundo*

money *mono*
month *monato*
mood *humoro*
moon *luno*
moorhen *galinolo*
more *pli (da)*; — or less *pli-malpli*
moreover *cetere*
morning *mateno*
most *plej*; *la plimulto de*
mother *patrino*; —-in-law *bopatrino*
motor *motoro*; motorcycle *motorciklo*
motorist *aŭt(omobil)isto*
motorway *aŭtovojo, aŭtoŝoseo*
mountain *monto*
mouse *muso*
mouth *buŝo*
move *movi* (tr.); *-iĝi* (intr.); movement *movado*
Mr *s-ro*
Mrs *s-ino*
much *multe (da)*
mugging *rabatenc(ad)o*
Mum(my) *panjo*
municipal *urba*
museum *muzeo*
mushroom *fungo, agariko*
music *muziko*; —-hall *varieteo*
must *devas*
my *mia*
mystery *mistero*
nail (metal) *najlo*; (finger, toe) *ungo*
name *nomo*
nation *nacio*; national *nacia, ŝtata*
nature *naturo*
near *proksima, proksime*; nearly *preskaŭ*
necessary *necesa*
neck *kolo*; necklace *kolĉeno*
need *bezoni, bezono*
needle (sewing) *kudrilo*
neighbour *najbaro*
neither *nek*; — . . . nor *nek . . . nek*
nephew *nevo*
net *reto*
Netherlands *Nederlando*
never *neniam*
nevertheless *tamen*
new *nova*
New Zealand *Novzelando*; New Zealander *novzelandano*
news *novaĵoj*
newspaper *ĵurnalo*
next *venonta, proksima*
nice *bela, agrabla*
niece *nevino*
night *nokto, nokta*; spend the — *tranokti*
nine *naŭ*
no *ne; nenia, neniu*; no one *neniu*
nobody *neniu;* —'s *nenies*
noise *bruo*
none *neniu, neniom*
nonsense *sensencaĵo*
nor *nek*
Norman *normanda, normando*; Normandy *Normandio*
north *nordo*; northern *norda*
Norway *Norvegujo*; Norwegian *norvega, norvego*
nose *nazo*
not *ne*; — at all *tute ne*
note *noti, noto; bileto*
nothing *nenio*
notice *rimarki; anonco*
notify *informi, sciigi*
nought *nenio*; (figure) *nul*
nourish *nutri*
now *nun*; (interjection) *nu*
nowhere *nenie(n)*
number (amount) *nombro*; (figures) *numero*
nurse (hospital) *flegi; flegist(in)o*

obey *obei*
object (thing) *objekto*; (aim) *celo*
oblige: be obliged to *devi*
obstacle *baro, malhelpo, obstaklo*
obtain *akiri, ricevi*
obvious *evidenta, memevidenta*
occasion *okazo*
occupy *okupi*; occupied *okupita*
occur *okazi*
October *oktobro*
odd *stranga*
of *de*; (quantity) *da*
off *de (sur)*
offer *proponi*
office (function) *ofico*; (place) *oficejo, kontoro*
officer (forces) *oficiro*
official *oficiala; funkciulo, oficisto*

offspring *ido(j)*
often *ofte*
oh *ho*
oil *oleo*
old *malnova, maljuna;* ten years — *dekjar(aĝ)a*
on *sur*; (day) *je*
once (not twice) *unufoje*; (not now) *iam*
one *unu; oni*
oneself *si, sin, mem*
onion *cepo*
only *nur, sola, sole*
open *malfermi* (tr.); *-iĝi* (intr.); *malfermita*
opera *opero*
operate *funkcii* (intr.); *-igi* (tr.); *operacii*; operation *operacio*
opportune *oportuna*
opportunity *okazo, ŝanco*
oppose *kontraŭ(star)i*
opposite *kontraŭ, kontraŭa*; *malo*
or *aŭ*
orange *oranĝo, oranĝkolora*
orchestra *orkestro*
order *ordo*; (command) *ordoni*; (goods) *mendi*
ordinary *ordinara*
organization *organiz(aĵ)o*; organise *organizi*
original *origina*; (not a copy) *originala*
ornament *ornamaĵo*
other *alia*
ought *devus*
our *nia*; ours *la nia*
out *ekstere*; — of *el*
outside *ekster, ekstere(n)*
oven *bakujo*
over *super; pli ol*
owe *ŝuldi*
own *posedi; propra*
ox *bovo*

pace *paŝo*
pacifism *pacifismo*; pacifist *pacifisto*
pack *paki*
packet *pako*
page *paĝo*
pail *sitelo*
pain *doloro*; painful *dolor(ig)a*
paint *farbo; farbi*; (a picture) *pentri*
pair *paro*
Pakistan *Pakistano*; Pakistani *pakistana, pakistanano*
pale *pala, paliĝi*
pan *kaserolo*; frying — *pato*
panel *panelo*
panties *kalsono*
pants (trousers) *pantalono*; underpants *kalsono*
paper *papero*; (newspaper, etc.) *gazeto, ĵurnalo*
parachute *paraŝuto, paraŝuti*
parcel *pako*
pardon *pardono, pardoni*; —! *pardonu!*
parent *patr(in)o*
Paris *Parizo*
park *parko*
parsley *petroselo*
part *parto*; (theatr.) *rolo*
particular *aparta*
party *festo;* (polit.) *partio*
pass *pasi* (intr.); *-igi* (tr.)
past *pasinta, pasinteco; preter*
patent *patento, patentita*
path *vojeto*
patience *pacienco*; patient *pacienca*; (med.) *paciento*
pause *paŭzi, paŭzo*
pavement *trotuaro*
pay *pagi; salajro*
pea *pizo*
peace *paco; trankvilo*
peasant *kamparano*
pen *plumo*; (ball-point) *globkrajono*
pencil *krajono*
penny *penco*
people *homoj; popolo; oni*
pepper *pipro*
perfect *perfekta*
perfume *parfumo*
perhaps *eble*
period *periodo*
periodical *gazeto, periodaĵo*
permanent *konstanta, daŭra*
permission *permeso*; permit *permesi, permesilo*
Persia *Persujo*; Persian *persa, perso*
person *persono*
Peru *Peruo*; Peruvian *perua, peruano*
petrol *benzino*
phantom *fantomo*

pharmacy (science) *farmacio*; (place) *farmaciejo, apoteko*; pharmacist *farmaciisto, apotekisto*
phenomenon *fenomeno*
philatelist *filatelisto*; philately *filatelo*
philologist *filologo*; philology *filologio*
philosopher *filozofo*; philosophy *filozofio*
photograph *foto, fotografaĵo; foti, fotografi*
piano *piano*
pick *elekti*; — up *preni*
picture *bildo*
picturesque *pitoreska, pentrinda*
piece *peco*
pig *porko*
pile *amaso*
pin *pinglo*
pink *rozkolora*
pioneer *pioniro*
pipe *tubo*; (tobacco-) *pipo*
pity *kompati, kompato*; it's a —! *(estas) domaĝe!*
place *loko, ejo; meti*
plan *plano, plani*
plane *aviadilo*
plank *tabulo*
plant *planto, planti*
plastic *plasto, plasta*
plate *telero*
platform *podio*; (station) *kajo*
play *ludi*; *teatraĵo*
pleasant *agrabla*
please *plaĉi (al)*; *mi petas, bonvolu*
pleasure *plezuro*
plenty *multe (da)*
plug *ŝtopi, ŝtopilo*
plumber *plumbisto, tubisto*
plunge *plonĝi* (intr.); *-igi* (tr.)
pocket *poŝo*
podium *podio*
poem *poemo*
poet *poeto*
point *punkto*; (tip) *pinto*; (scoring) *poento*
Poland *Pollando*; Pole *polo*; Polish *pola*
pole *stango*; (geog.) *poluso*
police *polico*; policeman *policano*
policy *politiko*
polish *poluri*
polite *ĝentila*
politics *politiko*; political *politika*
poor *malriĉa; kompatinda*
pop *krevi* (intr.); *-igi* (tr.); *pop(ulara)muziko*
popular *populara*
population *loĝantaro*
pork *porkaĵo*
Portugal *Portugalujo*; Portuguese *portugala, portugalo*
possess *posedi*
possible *ebla*; possibly *eble*
post (mail) *poŝto*; *enpoŝtigi*
postcard *poŝtkarto*; picture — *bildkarto*
potato *terpomo*
pound (weight) *funto*; (£) *pundo*
pour *verŝi*
power *potenco*; powerful *potenca*
practice *praktiko, praktikado, ekzercado*
practise *praktiki, ekzerci (sin)*
praise *laŭdi, laŭdo*
pram *infanĉareto*
pray *preĝi*; prayer *preĝo*
precious *multvalora*
precise *preciza*
prefer *preferi*; preferably *prefere*
prepare *prepari (sin)*
present *ĉeestanta*; (present-day) *aktuala*; (gift) *donaco*; (to present) *prezenti, donaci*
preserve *gardi, konservi*
preside *prezidi*; president *prezidanto*
press *premi; presmaŝino; gazetaro*
presume *supozi*
pretend *ŝajnigi, preteksti*
prevent *malhelpi*
previous *antaŭa*
price *prezo*
prick *piki, piko*
priest *pastro*
principal *ĉefa, precipa; estro*
principle *principo*
print *presi*
prison *malliberejo*; prisoner *malliberulo*
prize *premio*
probable *verŝajna, kredebla*
problem *problemo*
proceed *procedi, antaŭeniri*

profession *profesio*;
 professional *profesia*
profound *profunda*
prognosis *prognozo*
programme *programo*
progress *progreso, progresi*
prohibit *malpermesi*
promise *promesi, promeso*
prompt *akurata*; *instigi*
pronounce *pronunci; elparoli*
proof *pruvo*
propel *peli*
propose *proponi*
protect *protekti*
protest *protesti*;
 protestant *protestanto*
proud *fiera*
prove *pruvi*
provide *provizi*; provided (that) *kondiĉe (ke)*
prudent *prudenta*
public *publika*; the — *la publiko*
publish *eldoni*
pull *tiri*
punish *puni*; punishment *puno, punado*
pupil *lernanto*
puppet *(gant)pupo*
pure *pura*
purpose *celo*
push *puŝi*
put *meti*; — on *surmeti*
puzzle *enigmo*

quaint *kurioza*
quality *kvalito*
quantity *kvanto*
quarrel *kvereli, kverelo*
quarter *kvarono*; (of city) *kvartalo*
quartet *kvaropo*
queen *reĝino*
queer *stranga*
quick *rapida*
quiet *mallaŭta, silenta*
quintet *kvinopo*
quite *tute*

race *raso; vetkuri, vetkurado*
radar *radaro*
radical *radikala*
radio *radio; radiofono, radioricevilo*
railway *fervojo, fervoja*
rain *pluvo*; it's raining *pluvas*
raincoat *pluvmantelo*
rapid *rapida*
rather *iom*
ray *radio*
razor *razilo*
reach *atingi*
read *legi*
ready *preta*
real *vera, efektiva*; really *vere, efektive*
realm *regno*
reap *rikolti*
rear *malantaŭo, malantaŭa*
reason *kialo*
reasonable *prudenta, racia*
receipt *kvitanco*; *ricevo*
receive *ricevi*
receptacle *ujo*
recipe *recepto*
reciprocal *reciproka*
recline *kliniĝi, kuŝi*
recognise *rekoni*
recommend *rekomendi*
record *registri, registro; disko*; (best performance) *rekordo*
recorder (tape, cassette) *magnetofono*
red *ruĝa*
refer *rilati*
refrigerator *fridujo*
refuse *rifuzi*; refusal *rifuzo*
regard *rigardi; rilato*;
 regarding *rilate al*
region *regiono*
register *registri*; *registrolibro*
regret *bedaŭri, bedaŭro*
regular *(laŭ)regula*
relate *rilati; rakonti*
relation *rilato*; (relative) *parenco*
relative *parenco; relativa, rilata*
relax *malstreĉi* (tr.); *-iĝi* (intr.)
religion *religio*
remain *resti*; remainder *resto, cetero*
remark *komenti, komento*
remember *memori*
repair *ripari, riparo*
repeat *ripeti, ripeto*
reply *respondi, respondo*
report *raporti, raporto*;
 reporter *raportisto*
repose *ripozi, ripozo*
represent *reprezenti*

reproach *riproĉi, riproĉo*
republic *respubliko*
request *peti, peto*
require *postuli, bezoni*
rescue *savi, savo*
research *esplori, esplor(ad)o*
resemble *simili*
reserve *rezervi*
resist *rezisti*
respect *respekti, respekto*
respond *respondi*; response *respondo*
rest *ripozi, ripozo*; (remainder) *restaĵo*
restaurant *restoracio*
result *rezulto, rezulti*
return *reveni, reiri, reveno, reiro*
revolution *turno*; (political) *revolucio*
revue *revuo*
rice *rizo*
rich *riĉa*
ride (horse, cycle) *rajdi*; (in vehicle) *veturi, veturo*
right *ĝusta, prava; dekstra; rajto*
rim *rando*
ring *ringo, rondo; sonori* (intr.); *-igi* (tr.)
rip *ŝiri* (tr.); *-iĝi* (intr.)
ripe *matura*; ripen *maturiĝi*
risk *risko, riski*
river *rivero*
road *vojo*; roadway *ŝoseo*
roam *vagi*
roast *rosti, rostaĵo, rostita*
rob *ŝteli, rabi*; robber *rabisto*
robe *robo*
robot *roboto*
rock *roko*; — garden *rokĝardeno*
rogue *fripono*
rôle *rolo*
roll *ruli* (tr.); *-iĝi* (intr.)
Romanche, Romansch *romanĉa*
Romania *Rumanujo*; Romanian *rumana, rumano*
roof *tegmento*
room *ĉambro, spaco*
rooster *(vir)koko*
root *radiko*
rope *ŝnuro*
rose *rozo*
rotten *aĉa*
round *rondo, ronda; ĉirkaŭ*
rouse *veki, instigi*
route *vojo*
row (line) *vico*
royal *reĝa*
rub *froti*
rubbish *rubo; sensencaĵo*
rubble *rubo*
rugby *rugbeo*
rule *regulo; regi, regado*
run *kuri, flui, funkcii*
Russia *Rusujo*; Russian *rusa, ruso*

sack *sako*
sacred *sankta*
sacrifice *oferi, oferaĵo*
sad *malgaja, malĝoja*
safe *sekura*; safety *sekureco*
sail *velo, veladi, ekvojaĝi*
saint *sanktulo*; St. Paul *Sankta Paŭlo*
salad *salato*
salary *salajro*
salon *salono*
salt *salo*
same *sama, samo*
sand *sablo*
satiated *sata*
satisfy *kontentigi;* satisfied *kontenta*
Saturday *sabato*
saucer *subtaso*
save (rescue) *savi*; (economise) *ŝpari*
say *diri*
scales *pesilo*
scarcely *apenaŭ*
scene *sceno, vidaĵo*
scenery *pejzaĝo*
school *lernejo*
science *scienco*; scientist *sciencisto*
scissors *tondilo*
scold *riproĉi*
Scotland *Skotlando*; Scot *skoto*; Scottish *skota*
scout *skolto*; scoutmaster *skoltestro*
scrape *skrapi*
screen *ekrano*
sculpt *skulpti*; sculptor *skulptisto*; sculpture *skulptaĵo*
sea *maro*; seashore *marbordo*
search *priserĉi*
season *sezono; spici*
seat *seĝo, benko, sidloko*

secret *sekreto, sekreta*
secretary *sekretari(in)o*
secure *sekura, sekurigi*; security *sekureco*
see *vidi*
seek *serĉi;* (try) *peni*
seem *ŝajni*
sell *vendi* (tr.); *-iĝi* (intr.)
send *sendi*
sense (meaning) *senco*; (common sense) *prudento*
sensible *prudenta, inteligenta*
sentence *frazo*
separate *aparta, apartigi*
September *septembro*
series *serio*
serious *serioza, grava*
serpent *serpento*
serve *servi*
service *servo, servado*; (religious) *Diservo*
set *aro, kompleto*; (radio, T. V.) *aparato*
seven *sep*
several *pluraj, kelkaj*
severe *severa*
sew *kudri*; sewing machine *kudromaŝino*
shade, shadow *ombro*
shake *skui*; — hands *manpremi*
shame *honto*; be ashamed *honti*
shape *formo*
share *dividi*
sharp *akra*
shave *razi (sin)*; shaver *razilo*
she *ŝi*
sheep *ŝafo(j)*
sheet *folio; littuko*
shelf *breto*
shine *brili*
ship *ŝipo*
shirt *ĉemizo*
shiver *(frosto)tremi*
shoe *ŝuo*
shoot *pafi*
shop *butiko, magazeno; butikumi*
shore *(mar)bordo*
short *mallonga*
should *-us, devus*
shoulder *ŝultro*
shout *krii, kriegi*
show *montri; spektaklo*
shut *fermi* (tr); *-iĝi* (intr.)
side *flanko, flanka*
sideboard *telermeblo*
sign *signo; subskribi*; signature *subskribo*
signal *signalo*
signify *signifi*
silence *silento*; be silent *silenti*
silhouette *silueto*
silk *silko, silka*
silver *arĝento, arĝenta*
simple *simpla*
sin *peko, peki*
since *de, ekde*; (because) *ĉar*
sincere *sincera*
sing *kanti*
sir *sinjoro*
sister *fratino*; — in-law *bofratino*
sit *sidi*; — down *sidiĝi, eksidi*; sitting-room *salono*
site *loko, situo*
situation *situacio*; (place) *situo*; be situated *situi*
six *ses*
size *grando, grandeco*
sketch (theatr.) *skeĉo*
ski *skii, skio*
skilful *lerta*
skirt *jupo*
sky *ĉielo*
slack *malstreĉita*
Slav *slava, slavo*
sleep *dormi*
slender *maldika, svelta*
slide *gliti* (intr.); *-igi* (tr.)
slim *svelta*
slip *gliti*
Slovak *slovaka, slovako*
slow *malrapida*; (clock) *malfrua*
smell *odoro, odori* (intr.); *flari* (tr.)
smile *rideti, rideto*
smoke *fumo, fumi*
smooth *glata; glatigi*
snake *serpento*
snow *neĝo, neĝi*; snowflake *neĝero*
so *tiel*; (therefore) *do*; — that *por ke*
soap *sapo*
soccer *futbalo*
social *socia, sociala; distra vespero*

socialism *socialismo*;
socialist *socialisto, socialisma*
society (general) *socio*;
(association) *societo*
sock *ŝtrumpeto*
socket *ingo*
soft *mola; mallaŭta*
soil *grundo*
soldier *soldato, militisto*
sole *sola*
solemn *solena, serioza*
solve *solvi*; solution *solvo*
some *iu(j), iom da, kelkaj*; — kind of *ia(j)*
somebody, someone *iu*; —'s *ies*
somehow *iel*
something *io*
sometimes *foje, kelkfoje*
somewhat *iom*
somewhere *ie(n)*
son *filo*; —-in-law *bofilo*
song *kanto*
soon *baldaŭ*; as — as *tuj kiam*
sorry: to be sorry *bedaŭri*
sort *speco*
soul *animo*
sound *sono; soni* (intr.); *-igi* (tr.)
soup *supo*
sour *acida*
source *fonto*
south *sudo*; southern *suda*
South Africa *Sudafriko*; South African *sudafrika, sudafrikano*
Soviet *soveto, soveta*; — Union *Sovetunio*
space *spaco*; spacious *vasta*
spade *fosilo*
Spain *Hispanujo*; Spaniard *hispano*; Spanish *hispana*
speak *paroli*
special *speciala*
specimen *specimeno*
spectacle *spektaklo*;
spectacles *okulvitroj*
speech *parolado*
speed *rapid(ec)o*
spend (money) *elspezi*; (time) *pasigi*; — the night *tranokti*
spice *spico, spici*
spin *(rapide) rotacii*; — drier *centrifuga sekigilo*
spinach *spinaco*
spine *spino*
spirit *spirito*
spite *malico*; in — of *malgraŭ*
splendid *grandioza; bonege!*
split *fendi* (tr.); *-iĝi* (intr.)
spoil *difekti* (tr.); *-iĝi* (intr.)
spoon *kulero*
sporadic *sporada*
sport *sporto*; sportsman *sportisto*
spot *makulo; loko, punkto*
spread *etendi* (tr.); *-iĝi* (intr.); *disvastigi, -iĝi*
spring (season) *printempo*;
(source) *fonto*
square *kvadrato*; (town) *placo*
stage *scenejo*
stain *makuli, makulo*
stair *ŝtupo*; staircase *ŝtuparo*
stamp *stampi, stampilo*;
(post) *poŝtmarko*
stand *stari*; — up *stariĝi, ekstari*
standard *nivelo, grado*;
(flag) *standardo*
star *stelo*
start *komenci* (tr.); *-iĝi* (intr.)
state (condition) *stato*; (polit.) *ŝtato*
station *stacio, stacidomo*
statue *statuo*
stay *resti*
steal *ŝteli*
steam *vaporo*
step *ŝtupo; paŝo, paŝi*
stew *stufi, stufaĵo*
steward (ship, etc.) *stevardo*;
stewardess *stevardino*
stick *bastono*; *glui* (tr.); *-iĝi* (intr.)
sticker *glumarko*
still *senmova; ankoraŭ*
stimulate *stimuli*; stimulus *stimulo*
sting *piki, piko*
stock *provizo, stoko, stoki*
stocking *ŝtrumpo*
stomach *stomako*
stone *ŝtono*
stop *halti* (intr.); *-igi* (tr.); *ĉesi* (intr.); *-igi* (tr.); *punkto*
store *magazeno*; (small) *butiko*
storey *etaĝo*
story *rakonto, historio*
stout *dika*

stove (*hejt-, kuir-*) *forno*
straight *rekta, rekte*
strange *fremda, nekonata*; (odd) *stranga*
street *strato*
strict *severa*
stride *paŝ(eg)o, paŝ(eg)i*
strike *frapi, bati*; (industrial) *striki*
string *ŝnureto*
strip *strio; senvestigi* (tr.); *-iĝi* (intr.)
stripe *strio*
strong *forta*
struggle *lukti, lukto*
student *studanto*; (university) *studento*
study *studi, studado*
subject *temo, subjekto*; (of study) *studobjekto*
subscribe (periodicals) *aboni*
substance *aĵo*
subtle *subtila*
succeed *sukcesi*; success *sukceso*
such *tia*
suck *suĉi*
Sudan *Sudano*; Sudanese *sudana, sudanano*
sudden *subita*
suffer *suferi*
suffice *sufiĉi*; sufficient *sufiĉa, sufiĉe da*
sugar *sukero*
suggest *sugesti*
suit *taŭgi (al)*; *kompleto*
suitable *taŭga*; be — *taŭgi*
sum *sumo*
summer *somero*
summit *pinto, supro*
summon *alvoki*
sun *suno*
Sunday *dimanĉo*
superior *supera*
supper *vespermanĝo*
supply *provizi*
suppose *supozi*
sure *certa*
surface *supraĵo*
surgeon *kirurgo*
surprise *surprizi, surprizo*
surround *ĉirkaŭi*; surroundings *ĉirkaŭaĵo*
suspect *suspekti*; suspicion *suspekto*
swallow *hirundo*
swan *cigno*
Sweden *Svedujo*; Swede *svedo*; Swedish *sveda*
sweep *balai*
sweet *dolĉa, dolĉaĵo*; sweets *bombonoj*
swim *naĝi*
switch (on) *ŝalti*; (off) *malŝalti*
Switzerland *Svislando*; Swiss *svisa, sviso*
sword *glavo*
symphony *simfonio*
Syria *Sirio*; Syrian *siria, siriano*

table *tablo*; (list) *tabelo*
tail *vosto*
take (pick up) *preni*; (carry) *porti*
talent *talento*; talented *talenta*
talk *paroli, parolado*
tall *alta, altkreska*
Tanzania *Tanzanio*; Tanzanian *tanzania, tanzaniano*
tape *bendo*; — recorder *magnetofono*
tapestry *tapeto*
task *tasko*
taste *gusto*; (have flavour) *gusti*; (with tongue) *gustumi*
taxi *taksio*
tea *teo*; (meal) *kolaziono*
teach *instrui*; teacher *instruist(in)o*
team *ludantaro, teamo*
tear *ŝiri* (tr.); *-iĝi* (intr.);
tear (-drop) *larmo*; tear gas *larmiga gaso*
technique *tekniko*; technology *teknologio*
telephone *telefono, telefoni (al)*
television *televido*; (set) *televidilo*
tell *diri al, informi*
temper *humoro; koleremo*
temperature *temperaturo*
ten *dek*
tennis *teniso*
terrible *terura*; terror *teruro*
terrorism *terorismo*; terrorist *teroristo*
testify *atesti*
text *teksto*
textile *teksaĵo*
Thames *Tamizo*

than *ol*
thank *danki*; thanks! *dankon!*
that *ke, tio, tiu*; (rel. pron.) *kiu*
the *la*; — more. . . — more *ju pli . . . des pli*
theatre *teatro*
their *ilia*
them *ili, ilin*
theme *temo*
then (at that time) *tiam*; (next) *poste*
theory *teorio*; theoretical *teoria*
there *tie(n)*; — is (nothing —) *estas (nenio tie)*
therefore *tial*
they *ili*
thick *dika, densa*
thief *ŝtelisto*
thin *maldika, maldensa*
thing *objekto, afero*
think *pensi, kredi, opinii*
thirst *soifo, soifi*; thirsty *soifa*
this *ĉi tiu, ĉi tio*
though *kvankam, tamen*; as — *kvazaŭ*
thought *penso*; thoughtful *pensema*
thousand *mil*
thread *fadeno*
threat *minaco*; threaten *minaci*
three *tri*
throat *gorĝo*
through *tra*; (because of) *pro*
throw *ĵeti*
thumb *dikfingro*
Thursday *ĵaŭdo*
ticket *bileto*
tiger *tigro*
tight *streĉita, strikta*; tights *ŝtrumpkalsono*
tighten *streĉi*
till *ĝis*; (shop) *kaso*
tilt *klini* (tr.); *-iĝi* (intr.)
timber *ligno*
time *tempo*; (of day) *horo*; (occasion) *fojo*
tin (box) *skatolo*
tiny *eta*
tip *pinto*; (gratuity) *trinkmono*
tired *laca*
title *titolo*
to *al, ĝis*; (in order to) *por*
toast *rostpano*; (drink) *tosti, tosto*
tobacco *tabako*
today *hodiaŭ*
toe *piedfingro*
together *kune*
toilet (W.C.) *necesejo*
tolerate *toleri*
tomorrow *morgaŭ*
tonight *hodiaŭ vespere, hodiaŭ nokte*
too (much) *tro*; (also) *ankaŭ* (*see* Unit 9)
tool *ilo, laborilo*
tooth *dento*
top *supro, pinto; supra, ĉefa*
topic *temo*; topical *aktuala*
torch *torĉo, poŝlampo*
tortoise *testudo*
total *sumo, tuto*
touch *tuŝi*
tour *rondvojaĝo, rondvojaĝi*
tourism *turismo;* tourist *turisto*
towards *al, en la direkto al*
towel *mantuko, bantuko*
tower *turo*
town *urbo*
toy *ludilo*
trade *komerci, komerco*
tradition *tradicio*; traditional *tradicia*
traffic *trafiko*
train *vagonaro, trajno*; (athlete) *trejni*; (animal) *dresi*
tranquil *trankvila*
translate *traduki*
travel *vojaĝi, vojaĝado*
tray *pleto*
treat *trakti*; (med.) *kuraci*
tree *arbo*
tremble *tremi*
trip *ekskurso*
trousers *pantalono*
true *vera*; truly *vere*
trunk (body, tree) *trunko*
trust *fido*; *fidi (al)*
try *peni*; — out *provi*
tub *kuvo*
Tuesday *mardo*
tumble *fali*; —-drier *agita sekigilo*
tune *melodio, ario*
Turkey *Turkujo*; Turk *turko*; Turkish *turka*
turkey *meleagro*

turn *turni* (tr.); *-iĝi* (intr.)
twin *ĝemelo, ĝemela*
two *du*
type *speco*; (with typewriter) *tajpi*
typewriter *skribmaŝino*

umbrella *ombrelo*
unanimous *unuanima*
uncle *onklo*
under *sub*; underneath *sub, sube*
understand *kompreni*
undertake *entrepreni*
underwear *subvestoj*
unfortunately *bedaŭrinde*
union *unuiĝo*
unique *unika*
unite *unuiĝi*; United States *Usono*
universal *universala*
universe *universo*
university *universitato*
until *ĝis*
up *supre(n)*; — to *ĝis*
upon *sur*
upstairs *supre(n)*
urban *urba*
urge *instigi*
urgent *urĝa*
Uruguay *Urugvajo*;
Uruguayan *urugvaja, urugvajano*
us *ni, nin*
use *uzi, uzo, utilo*
useful *utila*
usual *kutima*

vacation *ferioj*
vacuum-cleaner *polvosuĉilo*
vale *valo*
valiant *brava*
valley *valo*
value *valoro*; valuable *valora*
variety *diverseco*; (theatr.) *varieteo*
various *diversaj*
vase *vazo*
vast *vast(eg)a*
veal *bovidaĵo*
vegetable *legomo*
vehicle *veturilo*
Venezuela *Venezuelo*;
Venezuelan *venezuela, venezuelano*
vertical *vertikala*
very *tre*

vessel *ujo, vazo, ŝipo*
vestibule *vestiblo*
vex *ĉagreni*
vice *malvirto*;
—-president *vicprezidanto*
victory *venko*
video (recorder) *vidbendaparato*
village *vilaĝo*
violin *violono*
virtue *virto*
visible *videbla*
visit *viziti*; visitor *vizitanto*
vocabulary *vortlisto*
vogue *modo*
voice *voĉo*
volume (book) *volumo*
vote *voĉdoni, voĉ (don)o*
voyage *vojaĝo*

wage(s) *salajro*
wager *veti, veto*
waist, waistline *talio*
wait *atendi*
wake(n) *veki* (tr.); *-iĝi* (intr.)
Wales *Kimrujo*; Welsh *kimra*;
Welshman *kimro*
walk *piediri, marŝi*
wall *muro*; wallpaper *tapeto*
wallet *biletujo*
wander *vagi*
want *deziri, voli*
war *milito*
wares *varoj*
warm *varma*
warn *averti*; warning *averto*
wash *lavi*
waste *malŝpari, malŝparo*
watch *rigardi; brakhorloĝo*
water *akvo; akvumi*
wave *ondo; svingi* (tr.) *(la manon)*;
-iĝi (intr.)
way *vojo, maniero*
W.C. *necesejo*
we *ni*
weapon *armilo*
wear *porti, esti vestita per*
weather *vetero*
weave *teksi*
wedding *edz(in)iĝo, geedziĝo*
Wednesday *merkredo*
week *semajno*; weekend *semajnfino*

weep *plori*
weigh (have weight) *pezi*; (find weight of) *pesi*
weight *pezo*; weighty *peza*
welcome *bonvena, bonvenigi*; —! *bonvenon!*
well *bone; sana; nu*; — done! *brave!*
Welsh (*see* Wales)
west *okcidento, okcidenta*
wet *malseka*
what *kio, kiu; tio kio*; — kind of *kia*
whatever *(kio) ajn, (kiu) ajn*
wheel *rado*
when *kiam*
where *kie(n)*
whether *ĉu*
which *kiu*; whichever *kiu ajn*
while, whilst *dum*
whisper *flustri*
whistle *fajfi, fajfilo*
white *blanka*
who *kiu*
whole *tuta, tuto*
whose *kies*
why *kial*
wide *larĝa*; width *larĝo, larĝeco*
wife *edzino*
wild *sovaĝa*
will *volo*; (fut.) *-os*
willing *volonta*; willingly *volonte*
win *gajni, venki*
wind *vento*; (watch, etc.) *streĉi*
window *fenestro*
wine *vino*
wing *flugilo*
winter *vintro*
wipe *viŝi*
wisdom *saĝo*; wise *saĝa*
wish *deziri, deziro*
wit *sprito, spritulo*
with *kun*; (by means of) *per*
without *sen*
witness *atesti, atestanto*
witty *sprita*
woman *virino*
wonder (marvel) *miri*; (ask oneself) *scivoli*
wonderful *mirinda*
wood (material) *ligno*; (trees) *arbaro*
wool *lano*; woollen *lana*
word *vorto*
work *labori, laboro; verko; funkcii* (intr.); *-igi* (tr.)
worker, workman *laboristo*
world *mondo*; —-wide *tutmonda, universala*
worry *ĝeni, ĉagreni* (tr.); *-iĝi* (intr.)
worse *pli malbona*
worship *adori, adoro*
worst *plej malbona*
worth *valoro*; be — *valori*
worthy *inda*
wound *vundi, vundo*
wrap *(en)volvi*
wrestle *lukti*
write *skribi*; (original work) *verki*; writer *verkisto*

year *jaro*; yearly *(ĉiu)jara, (ĉiu)jare*
yearn *sopiri*
yellow *flava*
yes *jes*
yesterday *hieraŭ*
yet (already) *jam*; (still) *ankoraŭ*; not — *ankoraŭ ne*
you *vi*
young *juna*
your *via*; yours *la via*
yourself, yourselves *vi, vin*
youth *junulo, junularo, juneco*
Yugoslavia *Jugoslavio*; Yugoslav *jugoslava, jugoslavo*

zero *nul, nulo*
zoo *bestĝardeno, zoologia ĝardeno*

Index

ESPERANTO DICTIONARY

J. C. WELLS

A comprehensive two-way dictionary designed for beginners and more advanced students of Esperanto.

John Wells has drawn on a wide variety of sources in compiling a dictionary which reflects the extensive developments in both English and Esperanto this century. A useful summary of the grammar and pronunciation of Esperanto makes this a valuable reference book for all students.

TEACH YOURSELF BOOKS